Making the grade for primary humanities

Making the grade for primary humanities

ALAN BLYTH

OPEN UNIVERSITY PRESS
Milton Keynes · Philadelphia

Open University Press
Celtic Court
22 Ballmoor
Buckingham MK18 1XW

and

1900 Frost Road, Suite 101
Bristol, PA 19007, USA

First Published 1990

British Library Cataloguing in Publication Data

Blyth, W.A.L. (William Alan Lansdell), *1921–*
   Making the grade for primary humanities.
   1. England. Schools. Curriculum subjects: Humanities.
   curriculum Development
   I. Title
   001.3'07'1042

   ISBN 0 335 09365 5
   ISBN 0 335 09364 7 (pbk.)

Library of Congress Cataloging-in-Publication Data

Blyth, W.A.L. (William Alan Lansdell)
   Making the grade for primary humanities / by Alan Blyth.
      p. cm.
   Includes bibliographical references
   ISBN 0-335-09364-7   ISBN 0-335-09365-5
   1. Education, Elementary—Great Britain—Curricula.
2. Humanities—Study and teaching (Elementary)—Great Britain—
—Evaluation.   I. Title.
LB1564.G7B62   1990
372.19'0941—dc20   89-48153   CIP

Typeset by Vision Typesetting, Manchester
Printed in Great Britain by Biddles Limited, Guildford and Kings Lynn

To my
colleagues and students
past and present

Contents

List of figures

Preface: Acknowledgements

The preparation of this book could not have been completed without grants from the Schools Council and from the University of Liverpool, mentioned in Chapter 2. I take this opportunity of warmly acknowledging my gratitude and indebtedness to them both.

I am also very conscious of the help generously given to me by so many people who have helped shape my ideas and have criticized my suggestions. I could not possibly list them all, but some deserve my special gratitude.

First, I must mention the head teachers, staffs and children in the schools where I did most of my learning. I visited some frequently, and others once each, but they all figure somewhere in this alphabetical list:

Brinscall St John CE/Methodist Primary School, near Chorley, Lancs.
Euxton CE Primary School, near Chorley, Lancs.
Great Sankey County High School, Warrington, Cheshire.
Heygarth County Junior School, Eastham, Wirral, Merseyside.
Mosspits Lane County Junior School, Wavertree, Liverpool.
Redbrook Middle School, Rochdale, Greater Manchester.
St Michael's CE High School, Chorley, Lancs.

I also gained much from discussions with colleagues and higher-degree and PGCE students in the Department of Education at Liverpool University. I could not name all of them, but must at least mention Ray Derricott, Geoff Hall, Wynne Harlen, Bill Marsden, Ron Stewart and former members of the *Place, Time and Society 8–13* team – Keith Cooper, Gordon Elliott, Hazel Sumner, Fred Thompson and Allan Waplington.

In addition, I have had the privilege of discussing assessment in primary humanities over the years with many other sympathetic, enthusiastic and, I believe, like-minded head teachers and other teachers, advisers, inspectors, and people, some of them widely known, who have been involved in educational studies and in teacher education in many parts of England and beyond. Some of them may not know just how helpful they have been. I find it easiest simply to list them in alphabetical order, hoping that I have not made too many omissions. In this list I have also included a very few members of staff from the schools already listed, since their observations have been particularly valuable:

David Alexander; Robin Alexander; Mike Ashton; Frank Baldock; Alan Bateson; Stephen Bateson; Neville Bennett; Colin Biott; Tony Boddington; Laurie Bolwell; Richard Bramwell; Jim Campbell; Brian Chaplin; Elizabeth Engel Clough; Olga Collier; Hilary Cooper; Chris Cowell; Stephanie Denovan; Keith Dickson; Frank Earle; Nancy Elliott; Jean Evans; Bryan Ewing; Gordon Ewing; Jane Field; Alan Forster; David Franklin; Stella and Dennis Gunning; Steven Hales; Roger Hennessey; John Heywood; Mavis Hilton; Tony Holland; Mike Hughes; the late Colin Humphreys; Maggie Jackson; Mary Jefferson; Trevor Kerry; Peter Knight; Ian Lawrence; Vivienne Little; Tom Marjoram; Connie Marsh; Alan Matthews; Roy Moore; Leslie Mullins; Steve Munby; Roger Murphy; Brian Odgers; Anne Osborne; Ow Suek Yin; Maggie Perryman; Richard Pring; Marian Rawnsley; Colin Richards; Alistair Ross; Colin Selby; Duncan Smith; J.R. Spalding; J. Stead; Nigel Stewart; Peter Stopp; Norman Thomas; Gloria Varley; Patrick Waite; Chris Warn; Bruce Weston; Alan Wilkins; Jack Wilson; and the other members of the Schools/Industry (5–13) Research Group.

Finally, it is a great pleasure to me to thank my wife Joan Blyth for the tolerant yet constructively critical support that she has given me during the long gestation of this book without, apparently, any interference with her own extensive publications and activities. I only wish I could be as well organized as she is.

Alan Blyth
Chester

Part One
Introductory

1 The nature and purposes of the book

I think we all need to understand more about assessment in primary humanities. This book is one attempt to extend that understanding. I hope that it will soon be followed by others; but here is a start.

The way I want to approach assessment in primary humanities is in the light of three statements, all of which I think important to anyone and everyone concerned about primary education. The first step must be to consider in turn those three statements, starting with what I consider to be the most important. Later, I shall have considerably more to say about each of them but, like themes in a classical composition, they should be enunciated at the outset.

1 Humanities is an essential, but also a problematic, part of any primary curriculum

Few elements in the primary curriculum are as difficult to consider as Humanities. The very name gives rise to problems, expecially now that everything in our national curriculum has to be spelled out more precisely than in the past. Before going any further, I should state what I mean by Humanities. I shall use the term to refer to that part of the primary curriculum that is concerned with individual human beings living and working in particular places and linked together with groups and societies, past and present. In my view, this is an essential part of every child's curricular 'entitlement', as we now have to say, and one that is significantly distinct from all the others, even from moral or religious education. It takes into account the historical, geographical, social and economic aspects of what children encounter as curriculum.

Not everyone would agree either with my definition, or with my emphasis on the importance of the part of the curriculum to which it refers. That is one reason why humanities is problematic. There are many others, and they will be encountered in due course; but I want to make clear now what my standpoint is.

2 Although much is now known about assessment in general, too little attention has hitherto been paid to assessment in primary humanities

Consider, for a moment, the amount of guidance that is available on the subject of assessment in English, in mathematics, and now in science too, for Key Stages 1 and 2. Now think of how little, in comparison, has been done to develop a coherent and effective means of assessing children's response to what they learn as humanities. This contrast became increasingly apparent to me a few years ago, following my experiences as Director of the Schools Council Project *History, Geography and Social Science 8–13*, or *Place, Time and Society 8–13* as it was often called (W.A.L. Blyth *et al.* 1976). At that time, the Project's evaluator, Keith Cooper, prepared a pioneering booklet entitled *Evaluation, Assessment and Record Keeping in History, Geography and Social Science* (Cooper 1976). Subsequently, after a further venture which included an aspect of assessment of children's learning in primary humanities (Derricott and Blyth 1979), I was fortunate in obtaining further small-scale financial support from the Schools Council, and also from the University of Liverpool and from what is now the School Curriculum Industry Project, to pursue further activities among which assessment in primary humanities figured prominently.

One part of these activities consisted of exploratory work with children, mostly at the age of 10–11, and with their teachers. For the rest, I tried to find out what interesting practice and investigation were going on elsewhere in the country. The names of the schools and individuals who have helped me in these ways are listed in the Preface, and the outcome is embodied in the rest of the book, though without further detailed acknowledgement. I did not conduct rigorous experimental research, though at first I had hoped to do something of the sort. Instead, my ideas gradually took shape through encounters with children and adults, emerging in a process more akin to the fashioning of a piece of sculpture than to the preparation of a research report. This 'sculpture' has itself been scrutinized by critics on in-service courses and in academic discussions, and must still be considered rough-hewn, but I am sufficiently encouraged by its initial reception to be able to write about it now, especially since teachers are calling out for help in the situation indicated in the third and last statement.

3 Humanities is now officially represented at the primary stages of the national curriculum

By placing this statement last, I am signalling that I am not basing my mandate for writing on any legal requirement. I believe, not that humanities is important because it is represented in the national curriculum, but rather, that it is represented in the national curriculum because it is important. All the same, the legal requirement is of considerable, if subsidiary, significance. History and geography are now foundation subjects, while the historical, geographical, social and economic perspectives are all necessary to the many cross-curricular considerations emphasized in the new structure. So teachers, who have in the past been free to include only some, if any, aspects of humanities in their programmes will henceforth have to guarantee to pursue Attainment Targets and follow Programmes of Study in history and geography. This obligation will be explored in later chapters, but it is necessary to emphasize from the outset that it exists, and that this will imply some kind of assessment. In one sense, that is good news, because what must be assessed is sure to be taught.

To return to the very first point: the introduction of the national curriculum has made it all the more necessary that we should now increase our understanding of assessment in primary humanities. Previously books on this subject would have been interesting, even useful. Now, they are essential.

So here is mine. It is divided into three parts. The first includes this chapter and also another in which I set out three models, of learning, development and curriculum, which underlie all that follows. The second part considers, in turn, the three issues raised by the three statements with which this chapter began: the place of humanities in the primary curriculum; the development of means of assessment in primary humanities; and the consequences of the introduction of the new national framework.

In Part Three, the longest, attention is focused on how assessment could be conducted in practice. First, I consider how a school might develop a coherent and relevant strategy of assessment. This is followed by an examination of how teachers may form their judgments. I go on to make some suggestions about everyday appraisal, and assessment of children's 'products', and then about testing. The compilation and use of records are given special consideration, and finally some possibilities are indicated for further development and research in assessment of primary humanities.

I have written with teachers in mind, and also student teachers, advisers, lecturers, and others engaged in the business of primary education. This is intended to be much more than a do-it-yourself handbook or apprentice's manual, since I believe that teachers are more than craftsmen and that their professional task is more than something that can be learned by rote. Every teacher eventually evolves a personal style of assessment, just as every teacher eventually develops a personal style of teaching. Nobody can use a universally applicable recipe with parade-ground precision. For that matter, nobody can offer a universally applicable list of suggestions about how other people might set about developing their personal style of assessment. I have tried to base what I have written on other people's experience and expertise as well as my own rejuvenating encounters with children and teachers, but the ideas that have emerged are my own. To emphasize my awareness that they are not eternal or even consensual truths, but only the opinions of one person who has made a study of the subject, I have written quite substantially in the first person singular.

A word is needed about the title. 'Assessment' does not actually appear among its six component words. Instead, it is implied by the first three of those words, 'Making the grade'. They have been used in a title before. A well-known American sociologist of education, Becker, once coined it for his study of college students in his own country (Becker *et al.* 1968). The actual phrase is, of course, familiar, particularly in the United States, because it denotes the process by which every child and every student has to make progress from one stage to the next. Becker however showed that, among the freshmen in his study, this process was not as simple as it seemed. For the college teachers (instructors) had to find out where to pitch their grade-levels and how to match those to students' learning. In that sense the teachers, too, had to 'make the grade'. More than that: they could decide on their standards for assessment only after thorough knowledge and understanding of the students as well as of the course content. For their part, the students were able to learn not only the material required for satisfactory grades, but ways of presenting themselves to advantage. Thus, for students and teachers alike, the process of 'making the grade' involved more than the acquisition and recognition of knowledge. It also required a process of interaction between the two groups.

It may appear to be a far cry from an American college in the sixties to British primary schools in the nineties; and so it is. There are differences in decade, in age-level, in culture, and in content, and anyone familiar with Becker's study will recognize that there are also differences in the nature and purpose of assessment. Yet there is one similarity between Becker's field of study and our situation that seems to me to warrant the respectful adoption of his title. For any thoroughgoing assessment of primary humanities must also involve a kind of interaction. It may sound easier to impose external tests, or on the other hand to depend on broad, warm-hearted, subjective judgments casually arrived at. The point of view to be taken throughout this book is that teachers cannot decide on the standards that they can expect except through interaction with other teachers, and that they cannot decide what standards have actually been reached except through interaction with children over a long period of time. That is why I have completed the title as 'Making the grade for primary humanities', and not 'Making the grade in primary humanities'. When teachers have made the grade for humanities, children can make meaningful grades in humanities.

For there is no such thing as an absolute standard of assessment. There can only be agreement about making the grade, among the people with most experience of making the grade. That is a long way from mere subjectivity. It can be recognized by children and others as valid. It can be made reliable through shared professional competence, experience and integrity. The achievement of that level of competence, experience and integrity can be one of the most interesting and stimulating aspects of a primary teacher's role. I hope to show that it is also something that can be managed practicably within the tight compass of a teacher's professional life. Once achieved, it is the key to the best and most productive kind of assessment and, as the main Task Group on Assessment and Testing (TGAT) *Report* recognized (TGAT 1988a), it must be a central element in any national framework.

I have to emphasize that one important issue has not been specifically treated at all. It concerns the assessment of humanities for children with special needs of various kinds. This omission indicates nothing more than my incapacity to do it justice, but it remains for others to consider, especially since it is still uncertain how, and how far, exemptions from the national curriculum will be agreed for children with special needs.

The book is meant for use in initial training, in staff development, in local school or community groups, in day conferences, and in longer and more coherent courses of further professional study. Not all of it is equally suitable for all these purposes. For some it would be possible to concentrate on just one or two chapters. For the benefit of anyone who is quite unfamiliar with the language in which these matters are habitually discussed, I have followed the example of the TGAT *Report* and have added, as Appendix 1, a glossary of terms.

I hope that what I have written will help not only in the assessment of children's progress but, more importantly, in the firm and convincing establishment of humanities in the primary curriculum. For unless this aim is achieved, there will be nothing to assess. All that follows will be based on this double meaning of *Making the Grade for Primary Humanities.*

2 Three models: learning, development and curriculum

Before any programme of curriculum or assessment can be suggested, it is necessary to find some basis on which that programme can be established. The basis suggested in this chapter comprises three models; one of learning, one of children's development, and one of curriculum. A model in this sense is a simplified pattern intended to approximate to a complex process in such a way as to make it easier to grasp. Each of the three is presented in a simple form, but one that is relevant to assessment in primary humanities. All three are open to major objections as well as to detailed criticism, but none of them is without a substantial theoretical basis.

A model of learning

The first model is based on the simplest of notions, that of the acquisition of a physical skill such as learning to swim or to ride a horse. At first the learner is quite hapless, able to make only one or two spasmodic movements before touching bottom or falling off. The next step is when the stroke or the response to the horse 'works' occasionally, but unpredictably and erratically. Then the point is reached when it usually works, and quite soon, with increasing confidence, it always does, though this fourth level of learning may not be attained in a triumphant, straight-line progression but more waywardly, with occasional despondent slips back to a previous level: there is a parallel here with learning to drive a car. So when the fourth level is firmly attained, that might seem to be the final step. It is not. The last stage is when the new skill becomes so much a part of the learner that it can be deployed almost unconsciously in pursuit of something further, such as water polo or dressage.

The sequence of learning indicated in this model can be summarized in an acronym that will be quoted many times in the following chapters. That acronym is NOFAN. It is built from the five stages thus:

Never
Occasionally

Frequently
Always
Naturally

The final step denotes a kind of *mastery* learning, and so it might seem preferable to use the slightly different acronym NOFAM, which would have the added advantage of avoiding using one letter of the alphabet twice. However, the emphasis on 'doing it naturally' conveys more exactly the idea of internalizing a skill, making it part of oneself.

This sequence was derived, as I have indicated, from the processes of skill acquisition. However, it can be applied just as effectively to the learning of concepts and, at least in some situations, of attitudes, and also to the understanding and memorizing of particular pieces of knowledge. It could, of course, be criticized, refined and extended in accordance with the classification of types of learning as proposed by Gagné (1965), with Stones' strategies of psychopedagogy (Stones 1979), with the stages in complex learning adopted and elaborated by Bennett *et al.* (1984), and with some of the insights reviewed by Entwistle (1985). Yet, even in this crude and simple form, it can act as a useful reminder that learning in any aspect of curriculum is far from automatic, but proceeds at first in a wayward and tentative fashion and then more confidently until, perhaps after a snakes-and-ladders approach, the goal is reached and the learning internalized. Mathematics, music and physical education perhaps show this NOFAN sequence at its clearest, but the rest of this book is based on the belief that it applies also in other parts of the primary curriculum, including humanities.

The learning process as a whole is, of course, much more complex than this. For any individual it consists of myriads of NOFAN sequences, overlapping and intertwined. Sometimes children falter, especially when several simple ideas at the 'always' level are brought together, because then the bringing together is itself only at the 'occasionally' stage. At other times, when ideas converge, learning may proceed by leaps and bounds. With young children, these NOFAN sequences often coalesce into learning episodes, interspersed with 'fallow' periods, so that it is impossible to plan learning for even one child on the assumption that it will proceed in neat, linear steps, while, for a whole class, the complexity of the learning process defies imagination. For in one sense children are in command of their own learning and cannot be compelled to conform to a synchronized programme, while in another sense they are not yet in control of their cognitive processes and so are unable to conform to such a programme.

A model of development

Cognitive Thus, over the years, children go through thousands of such episodes, some brief, some prolonged, some successful and some less successful, and often overlapping one another in a complex flow. Again, internalization of one skill becomes the basis for starting to acquire another. Formation of some concepts makes it possible to proceed to the establishment of others. So it is important to envisage a second model, one that fits with the first but takes account of changes over the years. That second model is one of development and, in particular, development of <u>thinking skills.</u> For one thing, as children grow, they form a capacity to see themselves more specifically as learners and to criticize their own learning; as cognitive psychologists say, they develop a capacity for metacognition. As will be suggested in Chapter 4, one of the major justifications for assessment is that it helps children to assess themselves, and clearly the achievement of a modicum of metacognition is of considerable significance for that purpose as well as others. Alongside that development there is another, particularly true of the upper junior years, namely the advent of a capacity to qualify statements with 'perhaps' or 'unless', or 'sometimes', and then to proceed to formulate hypotheses. This development, deliberately encouraged in primary science, is equally important, though in a slightly different mode, in primary humanities. It gives rise in turn to readiness to put forward generalizations, sweeping at first but then more tentative, built on the understandings that have become 'natural'. In these ways the complex flow of learning becomes more organized and effective.

It does not proceed at the same pace, or even in the same order, for all children. Nor does it necessarily fall into neat stages, as some of Piaget's more literalistic followers used to believe. Just as individual learning episodes can be wayward, so can the process as a whole, with halts on plateaux of learning, or even backward slips, which are baffling even to the children themselves, and exasperating to their teachers. Despite the smooth intentions of Education Reform Acts, nothing ever goes entirely to plan. Yet when children are observed in large numbers, there emerges a pattern of cognitive development which is quite central to any procedure for assessment, and which must be taken into account. The essential point to remember is that individual variations from the pattern are as important as the pattern itself.

One aspect of development in learning is important because of its particular relevance to humanities. Although most primary-age children can go further in understanding than many people realize, they are not usually able to think far enough outside their experience to envisage whole economic or social systems. When they appear capable of systems thinking, they may well be manipulating words and symbols rather than understanding realities. Where their understanding is genuine, it is usually particularized and focused. Even at the secondary level, systems thinking in humanities is often uncertain, but it can be progressively encouraged, and this indicates one kind of differentiation that may be possible between primary and secondary approaches, though of course there should be progression from the one towards the other.

Physical, emotional and social   A model of development must also take account of these other aspects. In fact, it is difficult to distinguish meaningfully between any one form of development and others. However, there are some recognizable trends in development that teachers confidently trace from 'reception class' (R) – which now often means four-year-olds – to 'top juniors' (Y6). From common knowledge, study and experience it may be suggested that importance should be attached to:

- curves of growth in stature, strength and co-ordination
- increasing capacity to form, understand, and work in social groups
- changing patterns of moral understanding as traced by Kohlberg and others
- growing capacity of children to see themselves as people.

This is only a very bare outline of the sort of non-cognitive considerations that should figure in a model of development. It scarcely deserves the title of model, for it is little more than a listing of categories of what must be borne in mind. It would be possible to draw on the work of developmental psychologists and others and to develop a large-scale model of considerable complexity and diversity, showing for example the significance of steady physical growth during the primary-school years in relation to more subtle variations in the nature and extent of social relations. That is outside the scope of what is necessary or practicable for present purposes. The important point is to remember to think developmentally in relation to learning and growth and to be in the habit of looking upon each piece of learning and each piece of curriculum as part of an ongoing process. Also, here again, as with the cognitive aspects, it must be stressed that individual children, and groups of children, may legitimately differ from whatever 'average' patterns are drawn up. Yet irrespective of such differences, these categories of development are always important, and nowhere more so than when considering development in humanities.

A model of curriculum

These models of learning and development have been presented before the model of curriculum in order to emphasize that they must be taken into account before any curriculum, however desirable, can be proposed. In the end children and young people engage, to a greater or less extent, with whatever curriculum is presented to them. In that sense they construct their own curriculum. If that engagement is to be genuine and significant, then any practicable model of curriculum must be designed with those other models in mind.

At the same time, I believe, it must direct children's potential for learning and development in such a way as to enable them to realize that potential more fully. As they grow, children undergo a continuous interaction between their own genetically controlled development and the experiences that they meet in life and in school. As I have defined it elsewhere (W.A.L. Blyth 1984), the curriculum should be viewed as *planned intervention in the interaction between development and experience.* Curriculum is not something that can be externally imposed on the grounds that is intrinsically so embedded in tradition, or so important in its own right, or so much to be desired that children ought to receive it irrespective of any other considerations. On the other hand, it is not something that can arise solely through cultural extension of children's individual or collective experience and motivation. In that respect it differs from the impressively and consistently well-reasoned empiricist curriculum proposed by Blenkin and Kelly (1987a).

My proposal is essentially for an *enabling curriculum*, depending on a measure of positive intervention. I see this approach as offering children growing familiarity with different ways of understanding and endeavour. In a sense, these resemble Hirst's 'forms of knowledge' (Hirst 1965) and involve some element of 'initiation' as suggested by Dearden (1968), following Peters' terminology. Without that kind of intervention, children's education is impoverished. However, what I have in mind is much more than a cognitive diet, let alone mere subject study. It consists of broad groupings of activities and viewpoints that represent major types of human achievement that have something to say to all children, and not only to the ablest or to those 'sponsored' for the fast lane in a competitive society. Nor is it intended to belittle the validity of children's own interests or experiences, or to suggest that some ways of understanding and endeavour are necessarily superior to others. It is just that collective human understanding has evolved over time, and continues to evolve, in particular, distinguishable ways, and that all children should encounter all of them as a means of nourishing their potential. It is no kindness to children to expect them to reinvent the wheel.

With these considerations in mind, it is possible to be more explicit about the heavenly twins of contemporary curriculum debates, that is, *aims* and *objectives*.

Any work collectively undertaken with children has to have aims. Those who deny that aims are necessary or desirable usually demonstrate, sooner rather than later, that they themselves have in mind something very like aims, even if they prefer a different term. Nobody should embark, and few do embark, on what is a part of a school's official programme without some idea of what is supposed to happen. It may, of course, be true in practice that, after years of routine experience, a teacher can go into a classroom, perhaps a colleague's classroom, with little more than a well-tried story or number game or stimulus in art or music or physical education (PE) with which to keep children busy and amused. Most primary teachers can recall occasions when they have had to dredge up from experience some such pieces of 'craft knowledge' to act as a lifeline. (Perhaps some teachers can recall, even more poignantly, occasions when they could not even manage the dredging act.) Yet no teacher would seriously defend such survival tactics as a basis for curriculum planning. There must be purposive, long-term planning, even when there is plenty of scope for flexibility of response to children's interests and urges. Indeed, a teacher who considers it important to allow flexibility of response to play an important or even a paramount part in curriculum planning already has an aim.

It is important to emphasize that point because it is sometimes assumed that any curricular aim must be something arbitrarily imposed on children who deserve better. In that view some aims may appear superficially more humane and developmental than others, but because they are aims, they are also constraints and, in the extreme view constraints imposed in the interests of a ruling class or an educational establishment or whatever. This view is usually advanced by those who regard themselves as champions of children, especially working-class children, and who claim to be in the business of liberating children from the restrictions of a curriculum divided into subjects, or indeed divided at all, and to be defending the paramount importance of children's autonomy. Historically there has been some justification for being a freedom fighter of this kind, but I believe that it is not an adequate stance today. Informality in primary education still has a part to play (W.A.L. Blyth 1988b), but it is compatible with the element of initiation involved in an enabling curriculum. Irrespective of social or political context, too, children expect teachers to decide, at least initially, what goes on in school: that is seen as their job. It may of course be argued that this is because children everywhere have been indoctrinated into that expectation; but in the real world it exists and is not negligible. So children expect teachers to have aims, though they may respond with more enthusiasm to some aims than to others. In addition, once they are in the artificial setting of school, children have to learn to formulate aims for themselves: they do not have that capacity to start with. It is necessary for teachers to set the stage in the early years. Yet from the start, in an enabling curriculum, there is every reason why a teacher should have the aim of involving children progressively in the collective design of a scheme of work and in the management of their own learning, and of encouraging children to become more autonomous as they grow older, all the more so because their vision and capacities have been broadened through their encounter with a range of ways of understanding and endeavour.

If aims are inescapable, that does not apply in quite the same way to *objectives*, the term applied to what it is actually hoped to achieve within a scheme of work. In an enabling curriculum, it is much less legitimate to lay down precise objectives in advance. In this kind of curriculum, objectives have to be seen as, in Taba's phrase, 'roads to travel' (Taba 1962; see W.A.L. Blyth *et al.* 1976). They are not, in the traditional sense, 'behavioural objectives' but rather 'emergent objectives'. For, as the scheme of work develops through interaction between teacher and children, it becomes more possible to define what the outcome is likely to be. Indeed it becomes essential to do so. A lively piece of work in primary education inevitably rings with something of a sense of drama, and children work out for themselves roles which are quite precise, such as making up a poem or doing one particular job on a collective model, while a teacher, who has come to think that a particular experience such as a planned visit is desirable, will and should be able to define sharply what benefit the children, individually and collectively, are expected to derive from that experience. There is therefore no harm in objectives of this kind; indeed they become increasingly necessary as a scheme of work develops. They are a joint product of teachers' planning and children's activity. That is a very different matter from objectives believed to be laid up in heaven, or spelled out in somebody's manual of instruction.

With this view of aims and objectives, as well as the models of learning and development, in mind, I shall try to present a 'map' of an enabling curriculum as it can develop over the span of primary and secondary education. Within it countless acts of intervention in the interaction between development and experience and countless episodes of individual learning take place, with the acts of learning having some, but not a predictable one-to-one, relationship with the acts of intervention. For children do not all engage with the curriculum with equal enthusiasm or capacity and, as was emphasized in discussing the model of learning, teaching cannot be an automatically effective process, thank God. As children grow older, the nature of the curriculum becomes more differentiated. It branches out like a tree. Therefore I have used the adjective 'dendritic', from the Greek for

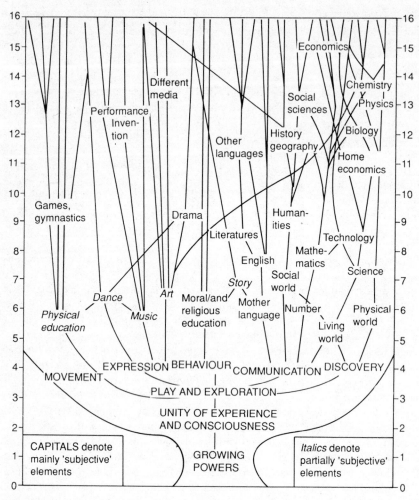

Figure 2.1 A 'dendritic' model of curriculum in action

'tree', to describe it. (Others such as geographers have used the same term for different purposes, and psychologists speak similarly of concept trees.)

This dendritic diagram is quite condensed and calls for careful and critical study. Underlying it there is an important assumption, sometimes glossed over in studies of curriculum, to the effect that we can make a transition from *subjective* modes of behaviour in early childhood, such as movement and expression, to much more *objective* activities with which those subjective modes come to engage. (The term 'objective' is, of course, used here in a different sense from the one discussed two paragraphs ago; it is a tiresome confusion that is bound to arise in any discussions of curriculum, now that this terminology has been established.) The distinction between the subjective and objective elements is indicated by the difference in lettering. Thus from the early years of compulsory schooling, objective terms such as language, mathematics, art and PE begin to appear, with the first two, comprising the 'Three Rs', taking formal shape first. These terms are so regularly employed, as forms of activity with which the subjective modes will engage, that the transition from subjective to objective is scarcely noticed. Indeed, some of the objective activities, particularly those substantially concerned with the learning of content, are more directly concerned with the external world than are others such as physical education. All branches of the dendritic curriculum are, however, pitched somewhere between the totally subjective and the totally objective. The learner and the learned are always both represented.

There is however one wholly subjective mode, that of play, that does persist a little longer in its own right, thanks to its hallowed status in infant education. Play has no label that attaches it to particular areas of experience. In due course it, too, gives way to the more or less objective categories which in turn yield, especially within secondary education, to what are now frankly subjects, and then to subdivisions of subjects. I believe that this kind of differentiation is in accordance with children's own development. They themselves like to become mini-specialists in matters such as sports records and pop music and find parts of themselves also through aspects of curriculum that become more precise as they grow older. 'Compartmentalization' is often a bogey in the minds of teachers and, it must be admitted, of curriculum theorists, rather than of children. They may groan at the mention of particular subjects, but not at the idea of subjects as such. They grow into subjects.

Here is yet another focus for individual differences. For some grow into subjects faster than others. Some do so with such ease and readiness that they lose sight almost completely of the wholeness of knowledge. Others never do. In the end, of course, the unity-in-diversity of knowledge and experience should be every young person's entitlement, irrespective of his or her personal preference for the parts or the whole of the curriculum. So I believe that at the upper end of secondary education there should be a stage at which the branches are bound together in something like a tree-house of combined understanding and endeavour, a finale to secondary education in which the advantages of separate kinds of experience are capitalized as a prelude to citizenship. The Technical and Vocational Education Initiative (TVEI) did achieve something of that sort. I believe that it should be part of the agenda of all secondary education, and it is mentioned here only as an indication that there need be no ultimate conflict between a dendritic pattern of curriculum, that is, a differentiation into subject areas, and an eventual re-integration dignifying every young person before he or she leaves compulsory education. Meanwhile, what concerns primary education is that the whole curricular process should be conceived not only as a unity but also as a continuity through which each individual child makes his or her own personal way, never quite smoothly, never on quite the same path as anybody else, sometimes protesting, sometimes dreaming, sometimes preoccupied with anything rather than the curriculum, but nevertheless moving generally and consistently towards further enablement.

That is the curriculum model that will be used, along with the models of learning and development, in the chapters that follow. In that model, as will already have been noticed, humanities appears as a developmental extension from children's exploration of the physical and social environment, but also with some relationship both to the nurture of their imaginative world and to the encouragement of their moral and spiritual development, all within the totality of early school experience. From these origins, humanities develops toward the separate and more systematic study of history, geography and the social sciences, though without becoming separated from the other modes of understanding and endeavour that constitute the whole curriculum. The following chapter considers more thoroughly the purpose and nature of humanities in an enabling primary curriculum, within the framework of the three models of learning, development and curriculum that have been outlined.

Part Two
Basic concerns

3 Primary humanities in an enabling curriculum

In Part Two, each of the statements made at the beginning of Chapter 1 will give rise to a whole chapter, spelling out one of the basic concerns that must be borne in mind when the assessment of primary humanities is considered. The first of these chapters, a long one, will consider how primary humanities should figure in an enabling curriculum; the second, how primary humanities can be assessed, and the third, how the context of assessment has been altered through the introduction of the new national framework of curriculum and assessment. We begin, then, with the place of humanities in an enabling curriculum.

What is primary humanities?

This is a question that will be explored in detail by Campbell and Little (1989), following the lead given by Ross (1987). As I indicated in Chapter 1, I mean by 'humanities' the part of the primary curriculum that is concerned with real people, individuals and groups, living in societies past and present all over the world, and with their survival, doings, feelings and thoughts. That is a huge field, and obviously incapable of treatment in any depth, so that the principle of selection of material is of paramount importance both to what is taught and to how it is assessed. Yet there is little evidence that such matters are systematically considered. Even the title used to designate this part of the curriculum is uncertain. Some refer to it as 'History and Geography'. Some, perhaps sensitive about sociological criticisms of subjects as socially constructed systems, speak of 'Social Studies' or 'Environmental Studies'. Many use the term most fashionable until recently: 'Topic', or 'Topic Work' – not always with the clarity intended by writers such as Rance (1968). Occasionally the title 'Social Subjects' has been imported from Scotland and adapted in the process; it is a useful umbrella term for this part of the curriculum and my colleagues and I used it in *Place, Time and Society 8–13*, (W.A.L. Blyth *et al.* 1976), but I now consider that it is not quite suitable to designate a part of the primary curriculum. At the secondary level, since the time of the Schools Council, the terms 'Integrated Studies' and 'Humanities' have gained currency, and now, I think increasingly, primary schools are also using the title 'Humanities'. But the diversity of usage remains.

These various terms are not, of course, quite synonymous or interchangeable, even though they are sometimes used as though they were. Where the subject terms 'History' and 'Geography' are used, it is likely that the work undertaken will be more systematic but perhaps also more restricted in scope. (If 'Social Subjects' are referred to, the scope might be greater but the approach just as systematic.) If 'Social Studies' is the label, then there may be some representation of the social sciences as well as of history and geography, but much depends on how the work is approached; at its worst it may do little more than relay children's unstructured experience back to them under a series of headings, an approach to curriculum which does achieve something positive, but much less than an enabling curriculum requires. 'Environmental Studies' implies something rather different, quite probably involving at least some aspects of primary science as well as the material which I am discussing. 'Topic' is the least predictable title of all, ranging over almost anything left over after the basic skills, Alexander's 'Curriculum I' (Alexander 1984), have been taken out for systematic attention usually in the morning, and provision has been made for activities such as physical education and music which make particular demands on space. In 'Topic', representation of humanities depends on the goodwill of teachers rather than on any logical imperative, though in practice this goodwill is usually present, and something patchy but quite thorough in the historical and geographical fields usually appears somewhere in the programme. Such, at any rate, was the situation before the coming of the national curriculum to be considered in Chapter 5.

If that is how humanities has figured hitherto in the practice of primary education, it has not been treated with much more consistency by those who have written about it. The book edited by Campbell and Little (1989) is one of the very few to consider the whole field since the work sponsored by the Schools Council in the 1970s (e.g. Lawton, Campbell and Burkitt 1971; W.A.L. Blyth *et al* 1976). The Schools Council Environmental Studies 5–13 Project (Harris 1972) and the World Studies 8–13 Project (Fisher and Hicks 1985) gave substantial attention for particular purposes to a large part of the field, but not to all of it. Environmental studies also received extensive treatment in the years 1960–80, and more recently by some, but not many, specific studies (e.g. Raven *et al.* 1985; Ross 1988; Pluckrose 1989; see also the *Bulletin of Environmental Education*). Most recent work on social studies has been conducted at the secondary level. Humanities as such has been thoughtfully considered by a number of LEAs and one adviser involved in work of this kind has also produced a comprehensive text, confined however to the middle and secondary years (Driscoll 1986). Primary history and geography as separate subjects have fared rather better (e.g. Bale 1987; Mills 1988; Joan Blyth 1988, 1989), perhaps reflecting changing climates of attitudes toward subjects in the primary curriculum. Meanwhile topic work has benefited from purposive criticism through attempts to tighten up its rather prevalent lack of structure and progression by writers such as the team at Trent Polytechnic (Gunning, Gunning and Wilson 1981), another at Oxford Polytechnic (Tann 1988), by Wray's lively introduction (Wray 1988), by a Schools Council project on children's thinking skills (Kerry and Eggleston 1988), and by a recent orientation of topic work towards equal opportunities (Antonouris and Wilson 1989).

Why have primary humanities at all?

Partly owing to this lack of coherence and consistency, this area of the primary curriculum has been regularly criticized by Her Majesty's Inspectors (HMI) in their surveys of primary and middle-years education (HMI 1978; 1982; 1983; 1985a) and it has been clear for some time from official policy statements, culminating in the Education Reform Act, 1988, that some stiffening and structure were expected. In addition, HMIs' own innovatory contribution on *History in the Primary and Secondary years* (HMI 1985b) and their volumes on geography, history and environmental studies (HMI 1986; 1988; 1989) and others in the *Curriculum 5–16* series bear out that expectation.

Much the same was said about primary science. Yet the response to the two areas of concern could hardly have been more contrasted. In the case of science, the establishment of concern was followed by a concentration of resources of material and manpower, quite justifiably, on the elimination of the problem in what is now one of the core subjects. In the case of humanities, however, the main effort has been restricted to a mixture of exhortation and criticism, combined with occasional hints that perhaps the way to handle such a disaster area in the curriculum might be to omit it altogether. Some people might even incline to believe that human affairs are inappropriate to an enabling curriculum for young children and that it is better to stick to primary science: 'Keep the child dependent on things only', as Rousseau said about Emile, though he would have excluded literature, morality and religion too. Few have actually taken that extreme position. More usually, if faced with a blunt question whether past and present human societies and their environments should figure specifically in primary education, those responsible for policy have replied, after a pause, in the affirmative: 'Why . . . yes . . . of course!' Why should that affirmative answer be given?

First, society and its works surround children all the time. If they explore their environment, they find not only languages, mathematics, science and art, but society and the palimpsest of its past. What is more, they are part of society. They are also part of science and art and mathematics and the rest, but it could be maintained that the part of them that is part of society – their *humanity* – is the most significant part, and in any case they have an impulse to be curious about what they see and about the people among whom they live.

In addition, in an enabling curriculum, they *ought* to learn about society. As individuals, they need to understand, progressively, through and after the primary years, the interdependence of lands, of peoples, of economies, of cultures and of generations, within a global ecosystem. Every child has an indelible stake, if not an equal one, in the human story. There is a sense in which everyone has a heritage to be known as well as an environment in which to live. The mixture of identification with that heritage and alienation from it varies from child to child and from one subculture to another, though nobody can by totally identified or totally alienated.

For these purposes the habits and methods of the scientist, the artist, the writer, the philosopher and the theologian are relevant; but they are not the totality of what is needed. One tenet of an enabling curriculum, set out in the curriculum model in Chapter 2, is that there are different ways of understanding and endeavour that have developed over the ages. In order to make the terminology simpler, I shall write henceforth of *perspectives* rather than of ways of understanding and endeavour, for perspectives are the outcome of those ways. Three of those, the perspectives of the historian, the geographer and the social scientist, are meaningfully distinct from those of other thinkers about humankind and the world, and children build themselves a distorted picture of the world if they are deprived of those three. That does not imply that they exist in complete isolation from other perspectives, any more than that those other perspectives are entirely distinct from each other. Nor, incidentally, does it imply that those three ways of understanding and endeavour necessarily make children good. It does, however, suggest that they become better educated if they experience all three, and that each of them contributes uniquely to that education. Now that this claim has been made, it must be rendered more explicit.

Three perspectives in primary humanities

The historical perspective

The first of these perspectives on social affairs is that of the historian. Controversy has raged around this perspective almost since written history itself began. Yet on one or two points there is general agreement. One is that historians have to be concerned with the nature, evaluation and significance of evidence, including the rather special kinds of evidence derived from archaeology and palaeo-anthropology. In view of current controversies about secondary history, I must make it clear that questions of evidence are not the end-point of history in the curriculum, but they are a very necessary component of historical study in an enabling curriculum because they make it possible for children to engage with history in a meaningful way. This is one reason why local history or family history is particularly valuable, because here children themselves can look for the raw material of history, instead of doing exercises on secondary material provided by somebody else. A second issue on which there is a broad consensus is that historians must be concerned with accurate reconstruction and interpretation of the past in its own right, of its time relationships, and of real people who really lived, though when this approach is styled as empathy, in practice the consensus breaks down (Knight 1989).

Beyond these two areas of agreement there are matters of great importance over which disputes continue, such as the sort of trends, events and people who merit consideration, and how to round off understanding where evidence fails. For example, is a prince about whom documentary evidence is plentiful more important than a peasant of whom nothing is known except his and his wife's baptisms, marriage, and burials and his one unfortunate recorded appearance before the Court Leet? Is an Egyptian scribe, who wrote something, more significant than an Aztec warrior who could write nothing? For although historians know mostly about the history of literate peoples, and especially about the recent history of the most literate people among literate peoples, that does not mean that history, in the sense of the whole of the past doings of humankind, can be identified with that literate record. Yet even the history of literate peoples can never be fully known. In order to round off the story of a literate people, or an episode or aspect of that study, historians have to cultivate the skill of making informed and logical conjectures. How much more necessary such skill cultivation becomes when written records are scarce or non-existent! Even if new evidence should come to light, as occasionally and excitingly happens, it can do no more than somewhat reduce the degree of uncertainty and lead to new interpretations of the unknown. For historians can never know as much about the past as did the people who lived in their own age.

Yet, in another sense, historians know more about the past than did the people who lived at the time. Even the imperfect records on which they work are usually much fuller than anything that was then at the disposal of individuals. They behold the entire scene, from a distant vantage-point. They know what came after as well as what happened before. As they watch Alexander the Great or Charlemagne take imperial power, historians cannot forget what fate befell their empires in the years that followed, and that memory impels them to look with some scepticism on any claims to finality that are made today.

This sense of superior perspective can however easily give rise to a false historicism, a belief in the existence within historical processes themselves of patterns, progressions and purposes which are really constructs, however brilliant, within the historians' own minds, forged in the realms of philosophy or metaphysics. That kind of historicism may underlie the assumptions, sometimes heard, that history can and should teach patriotism or morality or a reverence for cultural tradition and heritage, or the inevitability of a Long March to a Marxist millenium. These are intentionally high-minded if controversial goals, worthy of close scrutiny; but history cannot teach them. At most, history as written by historians is a neutral source-book from which patriotic or moral or cautionary tales can be selected, and aspects of heritage specified for admiration and affection; but the grounds in which the stories and the aspects of heritage are chosen lie outside history. The nearest thing to moral insight or political sagacity that the historical perspective can provide, in an enabling curriculum, is a reminder that society's slate cannot be wiped clean in this world. All human affairs have origins that stretch far back into time. The present is our scene, but it is inextricably bound up with the past, and in particular with some aspects of the past, which was neither a Golden Age nor a subhuman zoo nor an imperfect version of the present or the future. This is a fundamental lesson that, in an enabling curriculum, ought to be learned.

Related to this is the other lesson that, in an enabling curriculum, should be gleaned from history, namely that people in any age differed among themselves in their understanding of, and attitudes to, their own societies. This was not only because the evidence available to any one person or group was incomplete, but also because they were inclined, by virtue of their individual or group values, to adopt one interpretation rather than another. In a sense, the same is true of historians and others trying to interpret past, and present, societies. Their evidence, too, is imperfect, and they also tend to adopt one stance rather than another, thus showing that there is no one 'right' or perfect way of understanding and evaluating what happened in the past – or in the present.

The geographical perspective

In Hirst's initial analysis of curriculum, geography did not have the accolade of a distinctive form of understanding, but was designated as a field of study to which forms of understanding, notably those of the historian and the natural and social scientist, should be applied. There is, of course, a logical basis for that viewpoint, but it barely does justice to the ways of understanding and endeavour that have come to be associated with the academic and secondary-school study of geography, carefully constructed over the years (Goodson 1983). For the habitual perspectives of the geographer are those according to which everything is perceived in terms of places (Daugherty 1989) and of the spatial relationships of different kinds of phenomena. To put it more simply, geographers think of places, how they have developed, and how they relate to each other. They also think of movement in rivers and aircraft and diseases and ideas and armies around and above the earth and on and under the seas in patterns which are interrupted and modified by the physical and social world as it is. They talk of location, distribution, rate of flow and volume of trade, centre and periphery, and they are often particularly interested in, and concerned about, inequalities and inefficiencies within and between societies in different parts of the world, and with how people and peoples respond to those inequalities and inefficiencies. Geographers also have their own modes of research and of representing information: maps and other aspects of graphicacy (Boardman 1983) are their special tools.

Some of the phenomena that they study are non-human and relatively permanent, such as continents and oceans and the earth's envelope: St Patrick's 'stable earth'. Even these are in fact in long-term geophysical flux; without that flux the conditions for human life would not exist, and eventually that flux could bring human life on earth to an end. Other phenomena considered by geographers are also non-human but less permanent, such as glaciation, permafrost, soil leaching and erosion, volcanoes, short-term crustal instability leading to earthquakes, changes in weather patterns, and migrations of locusts and diseases. More variable still, but central to the concerns of geographers, are the dynamic patterns of human response to natural phenomena and to other kinds of human activity. In particular, geographers try to understand the ways in which people and peoples interact with the planetary ecosystem and the apparent equilibrium of 'Nature', and to predict the effects on the world's resources and food supply and on their distribution of the policies of some governments, and the lack of policies of others, and of the activities of groups and individuals. In some of this activity, geographers act not unlike economists or sociologists or ecologists, but their perspective is quite distinctive and indispensable.

In recent years the geographical perspective has acquired a further dimension. Attention has been focused not only on how geographers see the world from their own perspective, but also on how individual children and adults construct geographical perspectives of their own. Studies have been made of what parts of the world children think important to themselves, and why (see Bale 1987, chapter 1), and of how these 'personal maps', which are also of interest to psychologists, can be reconciled in due course with the shared knowledge and experience of geographers.

Within this range of activities and interests there is as much room for controversy as among those of historians; but here again there is a measure of shared agreement about matters such as the importance and the difficulty of accurate mapping of phenomena; the need to study the interrelation of different kinds of physical and human data on a small as well as a large scale; and the importance of the global village as one interdependent and finite habitat, the 'face of the earth' upon which everything else has to be enacted. Yet the limitations of the geographical perspective are similar to those of the historical perspective. Geographers have long forsworn the kind of determinism that suggests that, for example, Islam is to be 'explained' by hot-desert conditions, or that irrigation can of itself make people better or even better nourished, or, for that matter, that learning about other people's droughts or irrigation projects can make children more generous. Moral stories can be derived from geography, as they can from history, but the grounds for their choice must be derived from elsewhere. But again, as with history, there is one moral lesson that the geography of the geographers can teach directly, namely that the real physical and human world is there; that we are existentially in it, and that human life is both diverse and indivisible.

The social-science perspective

The social-scientific form of knowledge was admitted by Hirst, at least sometimes, as something distinctive. However, it is questionable whether one should simply think of *the* perspective held by social scientists, for there are several. To some extent there are separate perspectives for economists, sociologists, social psychologists, anthropologists, and political scientists. Within each of these fields, too, there are differences as sharp as those within history and geography, and the position is further complicated because some geographers, and even some historians, would themselves claim to be social scientists. However, there are ways in which their activities show a family resemblance. Somewhere among their activities they all find a place for methods of collecting data such as questionnaires and interviews, sampling within populations, controlled observation and documentary searches. They all make some use of theoretical models of human behaviour to be matched against what they find out by empirical means. Some, notably psychologists, also conduct experiments. All of them make some use of statistical analysis and of computer-based predictions. The activities of all of them show some similarity to the activities of natural scientists, but all of them are at pains to point out that their methods and findings are quite different from those of natural scientists, and especially of physicists. For they set out to observe patterns and regularities in human behaviour that do not aspire to the status of 'laws', while their predictions indicate what *may* happen if certain conditions are fulfilled, and not what *will* happen because those conditions are virtually certain to be fulfilled.

At first sight it may appear that this kind of perspective has little if anything to do with primary education. Lawton, Campbell and Burkitt (1971) showed convincingly that the social sciences have quite a lot to say to primary-age children, and there is a growing body of evidence to support their view. Through this perspective children can become enabled to look at themselves and each other and society with heightened interest. They can begin to use the tools of social science for themselves, when observing life or enquiring about behaviour. They have shown themselves substantially capable of looking at economic activities with the rudiments of economic understanding (Smith 1988), of probing issues of planning and development in communities, and of thinking about homes and families and schools and cultures in a purposive way, learning to set up their own hypotheses and try them out.

Of course, such learning can give rise to alarm among those who consider that young children should not be encouraged to think about such matters – the Emile argument again – or that the historical and geographical perspectives will give them quite enough in the way of critical thinking without invoking this third and still more suspect mode. Others have seen a social-science approach, as, for example, in Bruner's scheme of work, *Man: A Course of Study* (Bruner 1966), as making assumptions both of a humanist belief system and of the redundancy of separate historical or geographical perspectives, once social science is established. In some instances traditional, nationalistic history has been enlisted by the political Right to combat social science advanced in its place by the political Left, as happened once in Iceland (Edelstein 1987), with geography left in an equivocal suspense. In such cases social imperatives are given more weight than enablement. In addition, there have been some whose own commitment to the social-science perspective has encouraged them to believe that children are capable of much more grasp and enthusiasm than is the case. Their assumption could even give to some children a rather precocious idea of their own understanding of society, and too ready a tendency to be dismissive of other interpretations: a negation of what the social-science perspective should imply. None of these outcomes really has a place in an enabling curriculum.

Nor is this perspective, any more than the historical or the geographical, able to teach moral lessons without falling into the historicist or determinist positions previously indicated. What it can and should do is to induce caution in attributing beliefs or motives to people without first using the methods of social science to check the accuracy of one's assumptions. It can and should also indicate something about the ways in which people do behave, and the moral necessity of taking them as they are, without implying that this is what they should be like or making the determinist assumption that they could not be otherwise. It cannot and should not attempt to usurp the historical or geographical perspective, or suggest to children that they can derive from social science alone a set of principles to live by.

Unity in diversity

I believe that all three of these perspectives are necessary to primary humanities in an enabling curriculum, for each represents a particular form of understanding and endeavour. The question then arises: why should not each of them constitute a separate subject in the primary curriculum? Two of them do often figure in that guise, suiting some schools and teachers and the preferences of some parents; and now the national curriculum will provide added impetus towards that kind of curricular structure. It is possible to take this argument further. Might it not be maintained that history really has more in common with literature, morals and religion, geography with the subject-matter of the natural sciences, and social science with their methodology? What is more, relations even between history and geography have not always been harmonious (Proctor 1987), while, as I have already indicated, both have sometimes been on terms of mutual suspicion with the social sciences. So is it not a piece of false curriculum theory to try to combine these three perspectives in a spurious trinity?

If the alternative were to see them all three excluded from any positive place in the curriculum, I would accept that as a second-best arrangement; but very reluctantly. For the understanding of people living and working in actual human societies, past and present, in their earthly context, constitutes for children a powerful unity within which the trinity of perspectives blends logically. Other perspectives may enrich that unity, but, if they disrupt it, then an enabling curriculum loses one of its principal bulwarks. Moreover, in practice, topics with an emphasis on one of the three perspectives are greatly enriched if the others are also borne in mind. To take one well-worn example: an imaginative reconstruction of a village at the time when its school was founded can be brought more vividly alive if its map is used, and its space-relationships and the patterns of people's life and work in families and the community remembered.

That example also illustrates another important point. Representation of all three perspectives certainly does not mean that they should all be equally present in every topic that is considered. Such artificial constraints, in the apparent interests of proportional representation of subjects in the curriculum, are absurd. Occasionally, in an enabling curriculum, an individual topic may happen to draw equally on two or three perspectives, but not usually. The important consideration is that they should figure in a balanced way in primary humanities as a whole, and not in each episode within it. In the same way the important consideration is that primary humanities with its three perspectives should figure in a genuinely balanced way in the curriculum as a whole.

The boundaries of humanities

If humanities as a curricular entity is to be firmly established, it is necessary also to consider what lies outside its boundaries, and how those other ways of understanding and endeavour relate to primary humanities. In each case the answer is slightly different.

Moral and religious education constitutes one aspect of curriculum which, I believe, is distinct from humanities. The boundary here is a subtle, but a very important, one. For humanities is concerned with what other people think and believe as well as with what they do; the omission of values and beliefs would lead to a desiccated and distorted view of human society. Moral and religious education for their part challenge children to encounter their own reality, behaviour, attitudes and beliefs. It is one thing to learn about Afrikaners or Rastafarians, and another to face what my life is like, and what I believe, and why. Of course, in some primary and middle schools, these matters are included under the label 'Humanities,' which is, as with humanities itself, preferable to giving them no consideration at all; but the conceptual distinction between what happens 'out there' and what I am remains fundamental, even though I have to engage creatively with what is 'out there'. Attempts to combine humanities with moral and religious education may in any event result in some distortion of what goes on, leaving on some children the impression that the whole field is rather distant and unimportant, inhabited by people who do quaint things at festival times, rather than by adult faith communities that speak to the human condition, and to them as growing people.

Again, humanities cannot in itself convey fully the ways of understanding and endeavour displayed in the literatures, poetry, art, crafts, music or dance of peoples. For children Arthur Ransome's *Swallows and Amazons* (Ransome 1970) is more than a study of middle-class holiday experience in Lakeland in the inter-war years; it is an adventure tale in its own right. Steel-band music tells something about Afro-Caribbean culture, but it is also fun to perform.

The relation of humanities to science and technology is rather different. Both aspects of curriculum are concerned with observation, exploration and manipulation, with an overlapping interest in the human body and in human use of the environment. Science is at least as much concerned as humanities with noting regularities and patterns, but in addition it lays more emphasis on experimentation and aspires to greater precision, although the basic habits of scientific thinking are shared to a considerable extent with geography and with the social sciences. Technology is more concerned with design and with problem-solving and decision-making, so that it abuts on humanities and especially on economic concerns in a distinctive way. So there is overlap of content and interest, but there remain fundamental differences between the perspectives associated with science and technology and the three linked in humanities.

There are evident and important relationships between humanities and the rest of the curriculum. Every culture has its own forms of physical recreation and sport. It also has its own concern for, and contribution to, mathematics: it is interesting to note that when HMI spoke of the relation of history to the rest of the curriculum (HMI 1985b), mathematics was the area selected as an exemplar. Language, as well as literature, is central to cultural concerns of many kinds, including the issues raised in linguistics and the special considerations that arise when a people has more than one language, or when one of them is not written. All of these ways of understanding and endeavour figure as aspects of human societies considered in humanities, but considered as parts of other people's lives rather than as part of the apparatus of personal growth and development. Humanities has the unique function of relating what children do to what the world does, and thus of enabling them to adjust within the world without necessarily conforming to it.

Figure 3.1 is an attempt to summarize what has been said hitherto about the place of humanities in the primary curriculum.

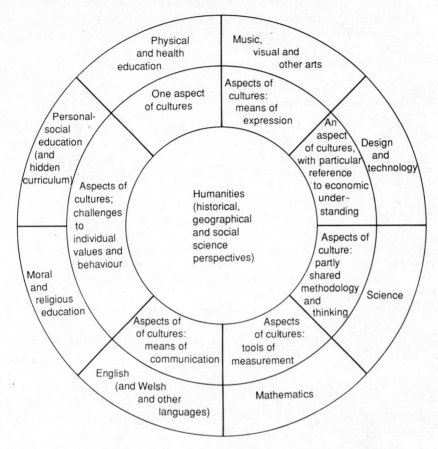

Figure 3.1 Humanities in relation to other elements in the primary curriculum

All of this argument applies essentially to the *primary* curriculum. According to the 'enabling' model, the primary years are those in which the three perspectives of humanities are first encountered. By seeing the value of each, children can learn to value them all. Then the distinctive characteristics and also the major frameworks of history and geography, and perhaps also of economics, business studies or sociology, can and should be separately considered within secondary education, either from the outset or after one year of combined humanities. The 'dendritic' pattern of curriculum shown in Figure 2.1 allows for, and indeed encourages, curriculum division or differentiation on those lines. It is important for primary teachers to look ahead on behalf of children to subject studies and to regard these as an extension and fulfilment of their own work, rather than the compartmentalized prison house that they are often thought, with occasional justification, to be. At the same time, secondary teachers should expect that children coming up from primary into secondary education already have some appreciation of the three perspectives and of their importance.

What they evidently cannot and should not expect is an encyclopaedic knowledge of history, geography and the social sciences. They could not provide that within secondary education either. There must be selection, on the basis of what is important at the primary stage.

Process strands in primary humanities

In all that has been said hitherto, the emphasis has been on the three perspectives, or ways of understanding and endeavour. If these perspectives in an enabling curriculum are looked at in the light of the models of learning and development set out in Chapter 2, it becomes clear that particular importance attaches to the *processes* by which learning in humanities proceeds. Much is made nowadays of the relationship between process and content in curriculum discussions. That issue will be considered subsequently, but the processes should be examined first.

There is a slight element of ambiguity here, since 'process' is sometimes used to connote aspects of children's developing powers, and sometimes also to indicate how they acquire and develop those powers: the *learning of process*, but also the *process of learning*. These two uses are in practice related, and both will be implied when the term 'process' is used in the rest of the book.

A further definition is required. I shall henceforth use the term *process strands* to refer to the skills, concepts and attitudes which comprise the 'process' aspects of primary humanities. It may be a clumsy term, but it does refer to those continuous, intertwined threads that make up the evolving apparatus of understanding. As children move towards understanding, they also develop a capacity to mobilize skills and concepts 'naturally' as part of what will be described as task procedures, means of setting about problem-solving and similar activities, and 'task attitudes' that accompany those task procedures. Each of these process strands requires further consideration.

Skills

It is impossible nowadays to talk about curriculum without referring to skills. A map of important skills could be constructed, with some stretching across the curriculum (e.g. Wray 1985; Morrison 1988), others common to humanities, and still others peculiar to each of the three perspectives. Many schools and others have worked out lists of skills such as those set out in Figure 3.2.

The next step is a fairly obvious one. These skills have to develop. Therefore children grow in respect of each of them, by a series of NOFAN steps, from a simple to a more complex use. For example, one of the most familiar representational skills, that of mapping, as traced by Catling (1979; 1980; 1988) and others, begins from quite crude spatial representations and proceeds by steps to the mapping of different kinds of data including three-dimensional relief, and of more abstract ideas such as density of population or spending power. A parallel instance in historical understanding is that of time-represention as explored by investigators such as West (1981; 1982; see also Lally and West 1981) and Joan Blyth (1989, pp. 106–9), starting from simple sequencing (which of these three events

Representational	Map and globe skills Time skills Other graphicacy skills, etc.
Investigational	Purposive observation e.g. in fieldwork Reference (retrieval): library Reference (retrieval): other databases Enquiry: questionnaire and interview Enquiry: data collection
Thinking	Classification Analysis and evaluation Hypothesis-formation Generalization Toleration of ambiguity: 'we can't be sure'
Manipulative	Use of equipment, including photographic and recording Organization of working space Making of models and artefacts
Social	Role-taking (→empathy?) Co-operation

Expressive	Written presentation
	       artwork
	Presentation in: other media
	       artefacts

Figure 3.2   Skills in primary humanities: a classification

came first?) and leading to the use of time-lines of increasing complexity showing how events interact in time within longer episodes, themselves located firmly within major historical epochs. The social-science component of skill acquisition proceeds similarly, from pie- and bar-graph representations learned in mathematics to the idea of clustering (which features ought to be grouped together?) to the graphing of one variable against another as in the relation of sales to demand, and eventually to the notion of probability: in our traffic count, was there one day when the traffic pattern was so different from all the others that it could have happened by chance once in fifty times? And if so, what seems to us to have made that day so different?

Of course, not all children learn these skills at the same rate, and not all teachers would want to foster their development in the same way. Yet there is a case for designing, over the primary and middle years, a sequence that should be broadly followed; not every day or uniformly, but consistently in each child's curriculum over the primary years.

The other skills are more complex. Investigation involves purposive observation, calculation, library and database resources (retrieval skills). Here developmental considerations are essential as a guide. Simple observation and right/wrong answers lead on to the formulation of hypotheses (perhaps the houses are up there because the river floods sometimes: let's see where we could find if there are any records of floods) and generalizations (these three countries all had kings and queens, so perhaps at that time all countries had kings and queens). Perhaps the most difficult step, emotionally as well as cognitively, in the developmental sequence is what is sometimes described as 'toleration of ambiguity', the acceptance of uncertainty by children who are inclined to yearn for certainty (maybe the firm went bankrupt because their products went out of fashion, or because somebody else made them more cheaply, or because they couldn't afford to buy new machinery, or maybe it was for a mixture of reasons, but we can never really be sure). For the weighing of incomplete evidence and of alternative accounts of events and changes near and for in place and time is something with which children have to come, progressively, to terms. In this way they become habitually, but constructively, sceptical about what any one book, or teacher, or TV programme or other medium of communication says.

So much for the cognitive skills. Manipulative and social skills are also important in humanities learning. These, too, develop as children grow. The social skills are particularly significant because children learn to relate to each other and to compete and co-operate with each other at the same time that they are learning about people in different ages and places and cultures relating and competing and co-operating. Finally, expressive skills must be mentioned, since they figure as the means by which learning can be communicated. Meanwhile, for this whole range of skills, we still know relatively too little about how they are actually acquired.

Concepts

Despite the attention accorded to concepts in discussions about curriculum, they are rarely given the rigorous attention paid to them by philosophers such as Bolton (1977) and Langford (1987), or by psychologists following the lead of Bruner and his colleagues (Bruner *et al.* 1956), emphasizing the distinction between concept formation and concept attainment, and Stones (1979) with his concern for pedagogic procedures. Various fruitful schemes of classification of concepts have been proposed; the one to be used in this book is avowedly more eclectic and pragmatic than most, and leaves ajar the wide-ranging question of whether all children can, or should, acquire the same sets of concepts.

In humanities, the work of Taba (1962) paved the way for much that has followed. Elliott (1976) made a series of practical suggestions about how teachers might foster concepts in humanities in the middle years of schooling in England and Wales. One recent and interesting review of research in concept learning that is particularly relevant to primary humanities is provided by Stanley and Mathews (1985). In practice, concepts are quite loosely described, lists are drawn up almost arbitrarily, and their relationship to skills is often left unresolved. The list presented in Figure 3.3 is itself no more sophisticated, though it is based on those

Type of concept	Main category	Elaboration	Related skills
Categorical	Space Time	Location Distribution Sequence Change	Map skills Time skills
Methodological	Similarity/ difference Continuity change Concomitance	Coarse contrasts→ fine distinctions One change→multiple changes Explanation→alternative or partial explanation	Classification and analysis Higher thinking skills
Substantive (general)	Communication Power Values and beliefs Conflict/ consensus Interdependence	Physical and social Political, military and social control of people and resources Religious, traditional, political, intellectual and social Political, military, legal and organizational; conflict management Economic, political, social, ecological and technological	
Substantive (more specific)	'Open' 'Closed'	To be developed progressively in the curriculum 5–11 (and beyond), e.g. choice, law, trade Particular to one theme or topic, but significant in their own right	

Figure 3·3 A classification of concepts to be developed in primary humanities

originally established in *Place, Time and Society 8–13* (W.A.L. Blyth *et al.* 1976) and subsequently modified.

The first two kinds of concept are necessary if children's work in humanities is to mean anything to them. The categories of space and time, as Kant long ago emphasized, are necessary if events are to be placed in any meaningful relationship to one another. The 'methodological' ideas of similarity and difference, continuity and change, causes and concomitance are also necessary if the doings of humankind are to be sorted out and interpreted. (By *concomitance* I mean the tendency for things to happen together, such as starvation and revolution, without implying that either causes the other.) All of these general concepts are built up, progressively, over the primary years. They are learned through large-scale NOFAN sequences.

They are also closely linked with skill acquisition, for the representational skills assist the notions of space and time, and the thinking skills help the development of the methodological concepts. The skills of classification and discrimination help to indicate similarities and differences; when those skills are applied to a sequence of events, they can be used to unravel continuity and change; and when children begin to formulate hypotheses and generalizations, they are in a better position to consider causes and concomitance and to distinguish, for example, situations where it is possible to attribute causes from those where only concomitance can be claimed. This discussion may sound remote from classroom realities, but in fact it is quite central to what teachers do. It is the way in which children learn how to look at what goes on in the world, and how far it is possible to explain what happens without falling into the trap of thinking that everything that happens has a simple cause and might therefore have a simple cure, and that everybody would want to apply that cure, and that everybody would know when the cure had worked. If that were the case, we should be living in a mechanistic world. Children need to learn to understand the world we have, and to realize that, although it has its patterns, it also offers possibilities of choosing among its patterns. The future is not a clean sheet, but it is more than a genetic code.

The key substantive concepts are quite a different matter. They are major organizing ideas that run right through any understanding of human societies. Probably any learning helps their eventual development, but where teachers take them positively into account in their selection and organization of material, they can be built up more rapidly and consistently. They are shared with ways of understanding and endeavour outside humanities, but each has a particular importance within humanities. Communication refers to how people and peoples relate to each other. Power here means not physical sources of energy but the power that people exercise over one another. Values and beliefs, conflict and consensus are basic to any understanding of political and social organization. The fifth in the series, interdependence, emphasizes the links between past and present, across the world, and also across the various disciplines that contribute to primary humanities and to the rest of the curriculum; the recent escalation of interest in ecological matters underlines the importance of this as one of the key substantive concepts.

Specific concepts are different again. Some belong to one perspective; some to another, or to more than one. Some such as *choice, law*, or *location*, are so central to one of the perspectives that they need consistent sequential development over the whole span of primary education. Others, such as *castle* or *prairie*, are essential within particular topics, but have less significance elsewhere. It would be possible to distinguish here between *open concepts* of the ongoing kind, and *closed concepts* which relate only to those particular areas of subject-matter. Both kinds do, however, depend on acts of judgement by teachers. Only a few open ones and relatively few closed ones can be included. It is a necessary, but not an easy, task to decide which ones a particular group of children ought to have at any price, and which others are desirable. The new framework outlined in Chapter 5 is intended to give guidance on such matters.

It is also important to remember that concepts, like skills, are acquired through some kind of NOFAN sequence. Stones (1979) suggests ways in which teachers can assist concept formation. It is obvious that some concepts depend on the prior learning of others. It is impossible to conceive (same word-family as 'concept') of the deforestation of Amazonia or of the encroachment of the Sahara without first having some idea of what an equatorial forest or a hot desert is like. A few attempts have been made to chronicle concept formation, for example in historical thinking related to time (Smith and Tomlinson 1977), to change (Crowther 1982) and to empathy (Knight 1989); in economic understanding (Schug and Birkey 1985; Furnham 1986; Waite and Ross in Smith 1988); or more widely in social awareness (Gabarino *et al.* 1978; Furth 1980). In the article already mentioned, Stanley and Mathews (1985) suggest some of the implications of social concept formation for teachers. A team already referred to, at Trent Polytechnic, has pursued the possibility that teachers can devise 'concept ladders', marking the steps which they think children should take on their way to forming social concepts (e.g. Gunning *et al.* 1984) and this has now been further elaborated (Antonouris and Wilson 1989).

Despite these initiatives, it is clear that we know far less than we need to know about children's formation of concepts in humanities. A glance at the literature on the parallel processes in language, mathematics and science only serves to emphasize the deficiency. At present primary humanities has to proceed with such guidance as we have. It is a moot point as to which, in primary humanities, is the area of greater relative ignorance: acquisition of skills or formation of concepts.

Task procedures

As children grow older, they become more capable of organizing their growing repertoire of skills and concepts to decide how to set about a task. Most teachers are well aware of this. A collective project with six-year-olds takes so much organizing, partly because at that age children have as yet so little capacity to organize themselves. Nine-year-olds can do much more on their own, and older children in primary and middle schools can do more still. It is important to bear in mind this evolution of the capacity to deploy task procedures. For in this way children do more than acquire skills and concepts. They become aware of their potential use; and this is an important part of their developing self-awareness, their own metacognitive growth.

Attitudes

The developmental model that I outlined in Chapter 2 includes references to social and emotional as well as to physical and cognitive growth. So it is important to include some reference to attitude formation within the scope of humanities in an enabling curriculum. Indeed, one of the reasons often given for including humanities in the primary curriculum at all is that it encourages positive attitudes. So it may, and that is worth trying. The consistent presentation of attitudes that are agreed as desirable should figure in any teacher's repertoire, even though the lists of desirable attitudes drawn up by a group of teachers would probably not coincide entirely. However, much of the build-up of general attitudes is unpredictable and powerfully influenced by what goes on outside school. Humanities is more likely to bring about change in particular, focused ways.

One of these is that familiarity breeds understanding, so that fear of the unknown, which so often brings about stereotyped reactions to stranger groups, can be reduced by some measure of acquaintance. This does not happen easily, for learning about particular strangers does not in itself eradicate prejudice; but something can be achieved. Other kinds of prejudice, for example against industry as 'dirty' or the countryside as 'dull', or fear of mixing with handicapped people, can be more realistically reduced through particular kinds of study, and the outcome actually appraised (e.g. Smith 1988).

Also, very important in their own way, are the *task attitudes* already referred to. They develop hand in hand with task procedures. It is in fact no mean achievement to bring children to realize, genuinely and without heavy-handed reminders, the importance of bringing to bear, on their interests at hand, skills and concepts from the three perspectives and beyond; to realize that they are relevant to matters such as philately or the Olympic Games that are of current interest to them; and thus to make humanities more 'naturally' part of themselves. Indeed there could be a NOFAN sequence here, though its nature is less well known than in the case of skill and concept formation.

What should never be lost to view is that all attitudes develop over the years. They may not develop as one would like, and when they do, it is rather like the Parable of the Sower: some thirty, some sixty, and some an hundredfold. They never develop predictably, puppetlike, partly because the attitudes of the teachers and others who are concerned with children themselves differ. Yet they do not differ totally. A school can usually establish some sort of consensus about some values, in humanities and more generally.

The importance of knowledge

It is sometimes believed that an enabling curriculum that stresses processes and understanding in primary humanities must therefore play down the importance of knowledge. That is not so. Knowledge matters, in three ways.

First, any topic followed by children involves learning, and therefore the acquisition of knowledge. Indeed, skills and concepts cannot be acquired except in the context of knowledge. A group of children that has studied 'the Victorians' will have extended their range of process strands; but they will have learned something about the Victorians too. The debate hinges on what they have learned, and not on whether they should learn anything. Evidently it is impossible to learn everything about an age, or even a few things. There must always be rigorous selection. Even a 'fact' such as the Golden Jubilee of 1887 turns out to be a complex series of events whose significance is difficult to convey, and soon becomes something 'out there' to be memorized. Again, it is difficult to stipulate 'facts' about Australia if a class is 'doing' that Commonwealth. It is much more productive to convey the flavour of the Victorian age or of Australia through different kinds of experiences in such a way as to make a distinctive impression that endures. Yet, if the relevant process strands are adequately borne in mind, that impression would certainly include a realization that the Victorian era was not a flat-wash, uniform age, as Chinese dynasties are sometimes represented, nor is Australia all Sydney and outback.

A sequence of topics would each have knowledge-content of this kind. Suppose that, in addition to the Victorians and Australia, the children's diet in humanities had included 'The Leather Factory' (there was one half a mile away) and 'Our Families' (a theme previously explored at the infant stage). This would be a classic instance of the lack of sequence and progression that HMI deplored. Each of the four topics could generate knowledge, but it could soon degenerate into unstructured and unrelated knowledge, a patchwork quilt of information. So a second kind of knowledge is also needed. That sort begins from the mapwork and time-scale skills already mentioned and should be sustained by constant reference to globe, atlas, local maps and time-lines, so that, among the questions asked in each scheme of work, there should be not only a 'How?' but also a 'Where?', a 'When?' and a 'How does it fit in?' In this way it is possible not only to build up a repertoire of experiences of places and events accurately located and warmly remembered, but also to become increasingly aware of the general distribution of time epochs, and of continents and oceans and place-relations, without which the historical and geographical perspectives lack significance. As for the social-science perspective, it has a different framework, that of the actual local, regional, national and international economy and society within which children live. There is, in fact, a whole backcloth of knowledge that children should eventually attain at the 'naturally' level, so that the broad sweeps of history and geography and of the economic and social world emerge, so to speak, from the mists of childhood encounters with humanities and gradually take a majestic shape in the broad light of maturity.

That is only half of what needs to be said about this kind of background knowledge. The other part is that here, too, some selection is essential. For several reasons, there is a case for extending the metaphor of the backcloth and claiming that the firmest knowledge should be in the foreground of experience, the locality, where in any case the three perspectives blend most readily and the possibility of relative completeness of knowledge is greatest. There is indeed also a case for claiming that local knowledge is particularly meaningful to children and is a useful base of experience to be carried forward from primary into secondary education and pooled with others' local knowledge as a starting-point there. While they are still in primary schools, there is also a case for extending from that foreground and for taking their own country as an arena for at least some topics, especially those with a historical emphasis. Beyond that it is important to open up a world horizon too, so that once ideas such as Middle Ages and West Africa have become established, they can be further refined through realizations that Mali is not Nigeria, and that 'our' Middle Ages look very different from the standpoint of the more enlightened Caliphates of Islam and mean nothing at all to, let us say, the traditional inhabitants of Fiji. The intention of this 'concentric' approach to knowledge is not to reinforce parochialism or to assert the necessary superiority of one's own country, but simply for developmental reasons to build on growing experience. It does, however, intentionally imply that a chronological treatment is not in place in primary education.

Of course, there are bound to be difficulties. What is the locality? What is their own country? The United Kingdom and England tend too often to be regarded as synonymous. Which other countries are looked at, and why? But these are issues to be faced rather than reasons for abandoning the attempt. In any case, this concentric pattern would be followed by a still more systematic treatment in secondary education where, for example, a chronological account of British and European history, with a world dimension, and a filling out of geographical knowledge would be in place.

Of course, some children sketch in the backcloth sooner than others. Some paint much of it for themselves. Some, defying received educational wisdom, do eagerly absorb factual knowledge in humanities of the Mastermind nature, much as others absorb the *Guinness Book of Records* or Trivial Pursuits, and nobody should stop them unless they become insufferably conceited about their knowledge. But they are not the majority, and nobody could seriously base the curriculum for the majority on the interests and capabilities of that minority.

There is still one other kind of knowledge that must be mentioned. For a case is frequently made that children ought to know certain kinds of material, not because it helps their intellectual, social, emotional and spiritual growth, but because society requires it. To a large extent, the knowledge expected for such purposes blends well with the process strands and the kinds of knowledge that have been discussed. Sometimes, however, there can be conflicts. If, for example, children are expected to learn more about their own community and its history, or other communities and theirs, than is practicable in the primary years, then this is regrettable, whether the expectation is based on economic or political grounds or in the interests of antiracist, antisexist or any other aims. This is not meant as a criticism of those aims, but of the overpressured approach to which they can give rise. An enabling curriculum cannot proceed by disabling children through premature socialization of any kind.

The sensitivity of humanities and the teacher's task

Throughout this long discussion, the sensitivity of the issues raised through primary humanities has been apparent. Even that last point about social requirements serves as an illustration. Writers about secondary humanities have frequently discussed the implications of that sensitivity, but at the primary level it has been treated more often in the context of the whole official and hidden curriculum than specifically in respect of humanities. There have been assiduous efforts to eliminate racism and sexism from texts, and courses to make teachers aware of such matters, but that is not quite the same thing as facing up to the inherent delicacy of the very issues that are central to the three perspectives. It is even possible that in some cases the concentration on process strands on the one hand, or on traditional knowledge on the other, may be symptomatic of an attempt to evade the controversies with which humanities is shot through. For there is scarcely a locality or a topic that does not present problems that could affect a teacher's or a school's relations with children, parents, governors and the community. The fact that the community itself may be split into two or more parts only serves to emphasize the point. Of course, much the same is true of moral and religious education, and of English, and to some extent of almost every aspect of the primary curriculum; yet it acquires a special kind of prominence in humanities which could arouse controversy in any situation, but more acute controversy in some than in others.

Therefore, in concluding this survey of primary humanities in an enabling curriculum, I have to emphasize how important it is for teachers to be able to detect and to anticipate controversies that may arise, to think out their own position (neither too dogmatic nor too pliable) and to learn the skills of managing discussion among immature and growing minds without either concealing what they themselves believe in, or abdicating the kind of jocund authority that primary teaching requires. That is a tall order. It is understandable if some teachers, sometimes, take the view that, after all, humanities is too tall an order, and that it would be simpler just to try to get by without the extra effort that humanities in its full development seems to demand. With that view I can only sympathize, but also repeat the arguments for humanities that were given at the beginning of the chapter. What has to be recognized is that the maturity and courage and sheer knowledge that humanities really calls for does demand a level of professional capability which teachers cannot have at the start of their careers, but towards which teachers themselves grow, as the children do. There is as much need for an enabling curriculum for teachers as there is for them to provide an enabling curriculum for children. Teachers believe that they need every support, and not a condescending or hectoring approach, if they are to sustain humanities in the primary curriculum. They are right.

4 Approaches to assessment in primary humanities

In this chapter the emphasis moves to a general consideration of assessment. The first step will be to consider why we should assess primary humanities at all. This will be followed by a survey of the principal considerations that any assessment policy devised nowadays should take into account; here a fourth model, of assessment, will be introduced, to be set alongside the three outlined in Chapter 2.

Why assess primary humanities?

The reasons to be considered are derived from an enabling curriculum, not from an Act of Parliament. I believe them to be valid, whatever the legal position was or is or will be. There are three main reasons.

The first is that, as was emphasized in Chapter 2, all teaching must have aims, and that therefore it must be the concern of all teachers to see how far those aims have been implemented; how far the children have benefited in ways considered desirable. Even in those unfortunate instances referred to in that chapter, where improvisation has to be the order of the day, some benefit is expected and indeed often demonstrably achieved, maybe through the sheer novelty of a change of teacher and the informality of the occasion.

If that applies to such incidental intervals in the curriculum, it should be much more true of its carefully planned heartland. To think otherwise would indeed be irresponsible. That is not only because, in the current phraseology, taxpayers' money is at stake. It is also, and just as importantly, a matter of professional ethics, an obligation that teachers owe themselves and each other, and it is taken for granted in parallel situations in medical and social work. Of course, it raises all sorts of questions about who else may be interested in the outcomes of assessment, and what for, as well as how feasible assessment may actually be. Such matters have been ably discussed by philosophers (e.g. Dearden 1979) and by general writers on assessment, mainly basing their work on the secondary stage (e.g. Satterly 1981; Black and Dockrell 1980; 1984; Black and Broadfoot 1982; Broadfoot 1984; Frith and Macintosh 1985; Lloyd-Jones and Bray et al. 1986; Murphy and Torrance

1988; Desforges 1989b). Others have concentrated more specifically on the primary years (Shipman 1983; Harlen 1983; Duncan and Dunn 1988; Conner forthcoming). Within their writings there is a considerable variation in emphasis, particularly on the forms and the social implications of assessment, but they are all agreed that some form of assessment is important as a means of estimating what learning has taken place. The collective significance of those published before 1988 was taken into account in the foundation document of the national framework of assessment, the main *Report* of the Task Group on Assessment and Testing (TGAT 1988a), and some of these studies will be referred to later, in particular contexts.

In an enabling curriculum, assessment also has another important function which receives some attention in most of the major studies of assessment. It relates directly to the model of development. Children become able, as they grow, to envisage a longer future as well as a clearer past, and they perceive themselves as getting ready for that future, however unrealistically they may at first imagine it. Their perception of school is that it is 'a place where you go to learn', and learning is something that will be useful later. So there is some point in knowing whether you know something. If teachers were to appear indifferent as to whether children had learned or no, then this would appear not only discouraging, but even a betrayal of a school's obligation to the children themselves. This expectation is sometimes combined with another, namely that one child's progress should be compared with that of the class as a whole; and that expectation may be welcomed by at least some of those who would expect to profit from the comparison. The claim that this competitive approach is welcomed by children is sometimes reinforced by another argument, that it promotes the attitudes needed in an enterprise culture. That argument remains open to dispute, to say the least. In any event, a league-table status need not be important to any individual, since it is his or her own growing competence that really matters and motivates.

A third reason for assessment, one which also appears in most of the relevant literature, is that it constitutes an important part of personal/social education. Children may want to know how they are progressing, but in addition they should want to know, and they should be helped to want to know. One part of the process of intervention in the interaction between development and experience that is central to an enabling curriculum is that children should be *enabled* to gain a clearer understanding of themselves and their relationships and their capacities (Blanchard 1988). During the primary years most children develop very markedly both in the capacity to 'see themselves as others see them' and also to look on their peers with a more discerning and objective eye. As their personalities become more distinctive, they respond differently, some with too exalted an idea of what they can do, and many – especially girls, I fear – too modest a view of their potential. As realism gains ground on fantasy or romanticism in their thinking, they become both more capable of seeing themselves objectively and more anxious to do so. They want to find what they can do as well as what they palpably cannot do, and thus they become interested in a 'profile' approach to assessment, to which they themselves learn to contribute. Then they should be enabled to aim strenuously high.

For this is yet a further important feature of assessment. Children need not only to be told how they are doing, when they ask. They need also to be guided into deciding for themselves. An increasing number of schools now encourage children to identify their own skills, concepts, knowledge and even attitudes and to indicate how they think they have developed during a piece of work, or a term, or a year. They then compare their own self-assessments with those given by others. Parents, peers, perhaps clergy, and other adults can all play a constructive part in this process, but their views do not always coincide. For the children, it becomes a case of 'Who am I?'; and in this procedure of self-identification the teacher's opinion carries particular weight. This is for two reasons. First, it is school business that is under consideration, and not what happens in the home or the church or the street or the park. Second, teachers are perceived as being more professionally capable of making assessments and, usually, also as being more impartial than some of the others who pronounce verdicts. It is a part, and not an easy part, of a teacher's role, one that any national system of assessment must recognize as important.

Of course, all these arguments apply to the primary curriculum as a whole. It should therefore follow that they apply to humanities. If they did not, there would be an immediate devaluation of the currency of humanities. For, if only the core aspects of primary education were to be assessed, then, irrespective of the rhetoric, everyone would assume that those were all that really mattered. The educational history of many countries confirms this impression. If any subject area stakes a claim to assessment, on the legitimate basis of the preceding arguments, then all the other subject areas must do the same in order to survive and flourish. Therefore assessment cannot be bypassed by any subject area on the grounds that it is more difficult to do than in other areas; that, for example, humanities is less susceptible to assessment than mathematics. As will be seen later, there are specific difficulties in assessing primary humanities, but they must be overcome, and help given in overcoming them. In Chapter 5 it will be seen that some pressures do exist which might lead to a call for keeping assessment of humanities and of some other aspects of the primary curriculum at a humbler level than in the case of the core subjects. That might have the immediate appeal of reducing the very heavy demands on teachers, but it would be at the expense of curriculum and children alike. The reduction of pressure must be sought through the means by which assessment of humanities is conducted, and not by calling into question the need for assessing humanities at all. It is therefore necessary to consider next how an assessment programme that is both user-friendly and humanities-friendly can be devised, and that in turn requires a prior survey of the procedures available.

A structure of assessment for primary education

Until recently, there was no agreed body of knowledge and experience on which assessment in primary education could be based. There was not even a general recognition that assessment was an issue. There were procedures, whose necessity was taken as self-evident, for checking on progress in language and mathematics. To some extent these were linked with 'schemes' and were used quite imaginatively to locate difficulties and blockages and suggest how these might be overcome, as well as to mark achievement. For the rest, assessment was regarded with suspicion, as something restricting both for children and for teachers, and even as the sort of prison chains that had been left behind with the pre-1939 elementary school. Recently there has been a marked change in emphasis, not only because of the formation of the new national framework, but also for reasons emerging from the curriculum itself. The books already mentioned (e.g. Shipman 1983; Harlen 1983; Duncan and Dunn 1988), and indeed the references to the primary years in the main Task Group on Assessment and Testing (TGAT) *Report* itself (TGAT 1988a) indicate how this new emphasis has come to be established in primary education. So it is now possible to look systematically at approaches to assessment across the curriculum, with some basis in study and experience.

Clients

The first question about assessment asks: Who is it for? Who are, so to speak, the clients of assessment? The prime answer must be that assessment is for the benefit of children. It must not only provide data on which other people can comment on their progress, it must also assist them in learning how to mark their own progress, drawing on its terminology, and to formulate their own aims. Once this prime purpose is established, then assessment is also for teachers, since it provides a running guide to their own effectiveness as well as the data they need in their pastoral capacity. Moreover, head teachers have a special stake in assessment, for it helps to indicate how children develop through their school life. Some head teachers have been known to devise elaborate or even idiosyncratic procedures of their own for this purpose, but for the most part there are sensible schemes of record-keeping, a topic which will be further discussed in Chapter 11.

Assessment also provides information for parents, though in two senses it may not be quite the information that they want. The first of those senses is obvious enough. Assessment informs parents, eager for news of success, that the child's performance is just what a young Jones or Montmorency should be doing, or else that it is unsatisfactory, leading to a painful domestic confrontation. The second reason is closely related to the first, because assessment may provide a profile of a child's strong and weaker points without giving the clear-cut picture of 'getting on' to which parents think they are entitled, so that they are unable to mete out praise or even blame, either to the child or to the teacher, in the way that they might think appropriate.

There are other clients too, whose interest in assessment tends to arouse more suspicion. Local Education Authorities (LEAs) may be seen as interfering if they require specific information from assessment, especially if it leads to decisions about children, or teachers, or schools. (The role of assessment in relation to special needs and statementing is a separate though related issue.) Central government, in the shape of the Department of Education and Science (DES), is more suspect, since the possibility exists that the outcomes of assessment might be used for administrative, political, organizational or social purposes on a much wider plane than is open to an LEA. These suspicions are entertained almost irrespective of the party-political opinions of individual teachers or of the political character of the central or local authority, though the situation can be particularly uncomfortable if these two masters are of different colours.

Purposes

Assessment is usually thought of by all its clients as a means of finding out how successful a piece of learning or teaching or experiencing has been. The usual term for this is *summative* assessment, for it sums up what has been achieved.

But there is also a place in contemporary practice for *formative* procedures which pick out the motivations and potentialities that an individual child, or a class, has, and how these can shape their participation in present and future activities. Formative procedures indicate, in short, what kind of work a child or a class is ready to undertake next. In any actual planning, the decision about a collective aim must to some extent require that assessment at the beginning of a scheme of work should be used for formative purposes. Then those girls or boys who, in this formative exercise, have shown particular capacities or promise could be encouraged to extend one part of the scheme beyond what has originally been intended. For example, two seven-year-olds who had been expected to contribute to a collage on 'Bridges' might show sharp recent improvement in writing skills, together with a deeper interest in bridges than the teacher had expected; so they might be encouraged to do some writing about a particular bridge that they know, or about one in a favourite story or poem.

There is a third aspect of assessment, usually referred to as *diagnostic*, whose main purpose is to locate particular difficulties or deficiencies in children's understanding, but also particular long-term interests and capacities. This kind of assessment has long been used in relation to the basic skills, and less formally in physical education and music, but it also has more general application. A useful example of diagnostic assessment in humanities, though in this case in Scottish secondary geography, has been provided by Black and Dockrell (1980). In primary humanities the diagnosis of particular blockages in understanding has not been extensively explored, but there are instances in some of the studies of skill and concept formation mentioned in Chapter 3, and there is plenty of scope for more.

It will be noticed that I have not actually used the customary expression *formative assessment*. This is because I believe that the actual approach is similar, whether assessment is for formative or for diagnostic purposes. The adjective 'formative' has come to be applied to assessment by analogy with its use in relation to evaluation, where it is clearly appropriate. But it seems to me that, although assessment data are used formatively in the planning of schemes of work, the assessment is not itself formative. This remains strictly the case, even when diagnostic assessment shows that children are particularly well suited to take part in formative planning. However, this is a minor point and does not affect the major distinction between diagnostic and formative considerations on the one hand, and summative assessment on the other.

The significance of these three purposes of assessment has been discussed in the books already mentioned and also in the TGAT *Report*, though there are slight differences of definition between one author and another. I shall use the three terms in the way that I have defined. There may in fact be some overlap in procedures, even when purposes remain distinct. For example, at the end of a piece of work, there is a necessary place for summative assessment, but, if it is sensitively designed, this may also yield formative and diagnostic information which helps in the planning of the next piece of work, and so on. A comprehensive programme of assessment would include all three purposes.

Referencing

If summative assessment is to have any meaning, it must involve measuring children's performance against something. Some element of comparison can also apply to formative procedures, but it is in relation to summative assessment that measuring is most evidently important.

The most obvious comparison, often taken to be the only one, is with the performance of other children. In its simplest form this approach assumes that there is an average performance, a norm, and that everybody above that has done well, or even very well, while everybody below that line has done badly, or even very badly. This is what most people really have had in mind when they speak of 'making the grade'. Because it depends on the use of a norm, this kind of procedure is usually referred to as *norm-referenced* assessment. Superficially it seems likely to foster healthy competition, as everybody tries to get above the norm, which, of course, then has itself to be redrawn at a higher level, thus denoting general improvement. It is not quite so simple in practice. Norm-referencing can convey a false picture of success, or lack of success, by defining success in terms of relative performance. Standardization of norms across a larger population, as for example in the case of A-level grades, can produce a much greater measure of objectivity than norm-referencing within one school or one class, but it still provides a self-contained system of assessment, one in which the notion of the norm takes precedence over the nature of the capacities to be assessed. What is more, the very terminology of norm-referencing soon almost shades into implicit moral judgement. To be 'bright' is good; to be 'thick' is bad. The 'bright' (and therefore good) children may enjoy their status, but it labels them 'bright' rather than defining what they are bright at, and it may also encourage them to rest on their laurels. Conversely, those who become labelled 'thick' (and therefore bad), as a result of much exposure to norm-referenced assessment, may react in such a way as to confirm their label. According to the theory of the enterprise culture, their dunce label should stimulate each of them to make greater efforts to escape, as it were, from the relegation zone. In practice, it is just as likely that, when they find that such effort as they do makes fails to alter their rank order or to remove their label, they will metaphorically shrug their shoulders and opt out by way of apathy or disruption or 'getting by', instead of concentrating on their stronger points until they gain sufficient confidence to work at the weaker ones too.

In addition, as experts in educational measurement and evaluation have long been aware, arbitrary manipulation of the distribution of scores around the norm, by skewing the curve, can soon distort the outcome of norm-referenced assessment, while the scores themselves are open to question through reliability errors, so that one child's rank position may be different on one occasion from what it is on another a fortnight later. Such problems are not likely to distort the rank position of the ablest or of the least able children in any particular trait that is being measured, but they are much more prone to upset the neat distribution at the mid-point, the norm itself, where the majority of children are bunched. So norm-referenced assessment is neither as simple as it appears, or as sure to produce the outcomes expected from it. Yet there is always public pressure to resort to it, because its efficacy appears initially so self-evident.

It could, however, be the case that assessment might be more effective if other kinds of comparison were used. The most obvious is the use of *criterion-referencing*. Here, an individual's performance is measured against a relatively objective standard. If a pole is 1.15 metres from the ground, then a jumper either can clear it or cannot. In one respect the outcome may be uncertain, for the jumper may clear the pole twice and fail the third time. The same can apply in a parallel situation in music, where the aspiring violinist may play a scale with beautiful intonation twice and end up slightly flat the third time. For such contingencies it is possible to plan effective strategies as to what counts as success. The important point is that the decision has nothing to do with any other individual's performance, except in the most general sense that the position of the pole and the demands of the musical performance test are themselves determined by general knowledge of what children of a particular age are likely to be able to do. The outcome of criterion-referenced testing may be built into some competitive aggregate, such as a total of points in an athletic or musical competition, but the criterion-referenced tests are not themselves competitive.

Difficulties with criterion-referencing begin to arise when there is inherent disagreement as to the criterion itself. It is possible to measure 1.15 metres in such a way that any number of judges would agree with the measurement. It is possible to establish, in a number of ways, if a violin is being played in tune, and the same is true of getting sums right or giving Mastermind answers such as the regnal years of George II or the name of the capital of Zimbabwe. But as soon as assessment is concentrated on something more intangible, problems arise. In the case of the violin test, there is likely to be less agreement about the child's interpretation of a piece than about his/her capacity to play in tune. As I found in my own work with children, the capacity to use concepts and to engage in higher thinking skills gives rise to more disagreement among assessors than arises over factual answers. Yet in spite of its limitations, criterion-referencing is more desirable than norm-referencing, because it places emphasis on the capacities that are being assessed and not on the competitive status of the individual children involved.

A further extension of criterion-referencing that is particularly important for the learning of self-assessment is *self-referencing*. This involves bringing children to compare what they have recently done with what they had achieved previously. It enables them to think in terms of progress, as they do in physical achievement, and thus more in terms of bettering their own performance than of competing against other people's achievements or even against one single objective measure. It encourages them to see their own development as an ongoing process, in terms of learning (metacognition) and also of striving and feeling and loving. In humanities it involves a complex, but also a particularly deep and intimate kind of self-knowledge. In fact, it goes to the heart of the educative process. Yet it shares the limitations, as well as the strengths, of criterion-referencing.

There could be a dilemma in any strategy of assessment. On the one hand, norm-referencing seems fatally flawed; but, on the other, criterion-referencing and self-referencing are open to the charge of unreliability as soon as they are applied to what is really interesting and important. In addition, some people retain a suspicion that in criterion- and self-referencing it might be too restrictive even to take note of children's average behaviour in the very general sense previously mentioned, that of establishing criteria in the first place. They might claim that it would have helped nobody if Paganini had been required to show how well he could play a scale. The point is taken; but the broad pattern of children's development must still influence in general terms what all except the genius or the severely handicapped may be expected to do. That does imply some general use of norms of development, both because that is part of what teachers know about children, and also because it is a way of convincing the public that assessment is not purely subjective and fanciful. The difference between this kind of norm and the use of norm-referencing is that it does not carry the moral overtones previously discussed, or the implication that what matters is beating the norm; being above par. Nor does it substitute grades for potentialities. Pious though it may sound, the aim has to be that of maximizing everybody's range of potential and thus motivating everybody, rather than of encouraging complacency above the norm and disengagement from the curriculum below it.

Therefore assessment should be criterion referenced and, when possible, self referenced, coupled with an awareness of the limitations of these approaches. If this is to be the strategy, then one further step is necessary.

Baselining

Before any piece of work can be undertaken, some kind of formative and diagnostic assessment is important. Of its nature, that leads towards a recognition that children all start work from different points of origin. Some are at once almost irritatingly anxious to show what they already know and can do, while to others the piece of work is new, and to a few it still appears bewildering even after the work has begun. This is evident to any teacher without having to resort to specific diagnostic tests in the tradition of Burt or Schonell. The next step in the process is to set individual goals (formative) and to locate specific individual powers or problems (diagnostic), while avoiding the dangers of labelling and stereotyping to which Desforges (1989a) calls attention. For it is never to be expected that each child will start or finish at quite the same point in their development as is the case for any of the other children. Each will gain, during a piece of work, some nourishment for their own developmental features, while also acquiring some common knowledge from the common theme. Each should, too, make full and strenuous progress in his/her own self-referenced way towards more complete self-assessment and self-awareness.

This process of baselining is particularly important in humanities, because of the

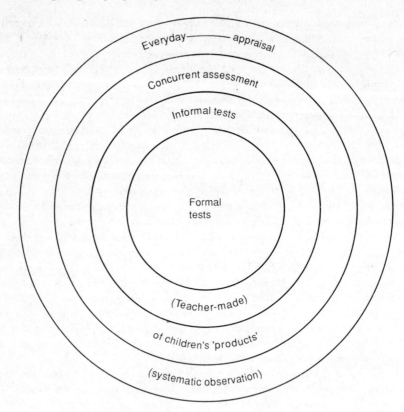

Figure 4.1 Focusing assessment

wide spread of process strands, of general understanding, and of specific
knowledge with which even the youngest children encounter any new topic.
Particular attention will be paid to baselining in later chapters.

Focusing

The remaining considerations are not so usually treated in discussions about
assessment. The first is concerned with the social contexts of assessment. Figure
4.1 presents four of these contexts.

    To start with the outer ring, the first context is that of *appraisal*. The term is
adapted from Tough's usage in connection with the development of communication skills (Tough 1979). It includes the sort of general observations that all
teachers use, but it concentrates systematically on particular, selected features of
children's understanding and activity. It represents the first stage in focusing
purposefully on what children do.

    The second stage, as the focus moves towards the centre of Figure 4.1, is
referred to as *concurrent assessment*. This term is similar to continuous assessment as

used in secondary and higher education, but this is not continuous. It is confined to the particular 'products' or pieces of work undertaken by individual children, the sort that they keep in their folders or shelves or exhibit on the walls of their classroom. It need not be confined to written work, for it includes artwork, especially for younger children, photographs, models and even print-outs and oral data preserved on audio-tape. It can, at a teacher's discretion, be referred back for editing or improvement if, for example, it is disfigured by a splodge of paint or by a careless and particularly glaring error in spelling; but there must come a stage, also at a teacher's discretion, when it is declared complete. What distinguishes concurrent assessment clearly from appraisal is that the material on which it operates exists independently of the children. They do not need to be present in person when this aspect of their work is scrutinized.

It is also desirable, if not essential, that concurrent assessment should involve some kind of personal feedback, probably orally or in writing, which goes beyond a peremptory tick or expression of approval or disapproval, and has a formative element in it. An example might be:

> This is much better than your last piece of work, Cheryl. But don't forget that it is cold at night as well as hot in the daytime. What difference do you think that would make when they were planning their journey?

Further towards the centre of Figure 4.1, there is a place for actual *testing*. This is now a battleground issue. Some people view any sort of testing with extreme aversion. One good reason for this is that all published, standardized, tests, however technically sophisticated they may be, inevitably display some kind of bias: against girls, against ethnic minorities, against the working class, against children with rural backgrounds, or simply against those who are wayward in their learning (their NOFAN sequences are untidy), or terrified by the fearful ritual of tests, or on the contrary careless and indifferent (or with the defensive air of indifference) when testing occurs. These arguments against testing apply with greater force in some situations than in others. To telescope a whole series of arguments into a single sentence, it might be claimed that testing is most acceptable (or least unacceptable) when it is regular, perhaps frequent, incorporated in the regular teaching programme, sensitively designed for a particular purpose with particular children, ingenious, good and even hilarious fun, and known not to be in itself decisive. It may also be useful for children to take part in designing tests for one another, within reason, since the aim is to encourage and confirm learning and a good way of doing so is by finding whether children ask suitable questions, even more than whether they give suitable answers.

The objections to testing and the kind of testing devised to meet those objections are both likely to be dismissed by others who vociferously claim that formal testing is the only way of ensuring efficient assessment of any kind, and therefore of guaranteeing cost-effective teaching. From that point of view it is often maintained that testing should involve exactly the kind of formality against which objectors to testing are most opposed, whereby children should sit, pencil poised, in suitably awed silence, to answer sets of searching, no-nonsense questions designed to ensure that Education is more than mere play. To some who hold this view the consensus of professional experience against testing of that kind is proof not of the shortcomings of testing, but of the deficiencies of professional opinion which is regarded as little more than a charade pursued in emperor's clothes for ends which range from occupational empire-building to downright in-doctrination.

The TGAT *Report* (TGAT 1988a) was written by a group well aware of these conflicting points of view about testing and came to a statesmanlike conclusion. That conclusion occupies the central, bull's-eye part of Figure 4.1. My own view is that, in primary humanities, there is also a place for the kind of frequent, non-threatening testing already discussed, testing that depends on individual teachers' initiatives and that is virtually indistinguishable from teaching. In any case it should figure shortly after learning, to maximize reinforcement, and to ensure (as concurrent assessment also should) that every child is brought under scrutiny. Absentees present an inevitable problem but, for all but the persistent truants and those with long absence for illness, some sensible arrangement can be made, while for the long-term absentees there are other and more insistent problems to be met. I believe too that there is a place for more substantial, though still carefully designed, summative testing at the end of a year. Clearly there is a still stronger case for summative testing at the end of a phase of schooling, more particularly at the end of the junior than at the end of the infant years, though here too it is important that the weight attached to a particular occasion should not be great, and the nature of the testing as varied and stimulating as possible. This procedure will fall within the national framework outlined in Chapter 5, and will also be further discussed in Chapter 9.

Ranging

The final consideration to be encountered is that of the range of assessment that is needed. I use the term 'range' here to describe a procedure familiar in, for example, the assessment of mathematics. Suppose that children are learning a new process, such as place value. They are introduced to it, as individuals or as a class, by dint of one or two examples. The first step in understanding is that they are able to reproduce those examples, to show that they have understood what has been going on. This I would describe as *recall*. But that would not count as real understanding until they could begin to do the same kind of thing with other digits. In order to pursue their NOFAN sequence they would need to realize not only that a 2 in a column stands for 20, but also that a 5 in the same column stands for 50. In other words, they would need to be able to *transfer* the concept that they have learned. To complete the sequence entirely, they would need to go beyond that again and to form the general notion of place value, in fact, to reach the stage of *generalization*. Assessment needs to take in all three stages. This sequence is not itself quite the same as a NOFAN sequence, for it is concerned with extension rather than consolidation of understanding; but neither kind of sequence is complete until the other is also complete.

It is much the same, though again more complex, in humanities. The first step here too is often concerned with simple recall. For example, a study of patterns of

Week 0 — 1 — 2 — 3 — 4 — 5 — 6

Aspects	Content (Week 0 → 6)
Aims	General, based on teacher's and school's interpretation of national curriculum → Increasing participation of children in formulation of aims
Process strands — Skills	Specification of one or two for emphasis: others continue. → Combination into task procedures
Process strands — Concepts	Exercise of categorical and methodological concepts and some general substantive ones / Well-chosen specific 'open' concepts developed and 'closed' ones introduced
Process strands — Attitudes	Emphasis on particular attitudes in accordance with aims / Development of task attitudes
Knowledge and understanding	Probing of initial knowledge and experience → Promotion of specific new knowledge → Relating to 'backcloth' knowledge / Link, through process strands with general understanding
'Delivery'	Topic introduced by teacher: 'brainstorming' → Joint planning; Baseline procedures; → First 'products'; Fieldwork? Visit? ; Children work in groups; Work arranged for newcomers/absentees; Second 'products': topic books, worksheets, artwork, etc. / Some additional individual work; Children and teacher plan final phase; Third 'products', final phase of ground and individual work; Preparation of display, exhibition of other 'finale'; Perhaps suitable testing
Assessment — Clients	Children (feedback: self-assessment) : Parents / Governors : (Reporting) : Teachers (records)
Assessment — Purposes	Diagnostic/formative → Summative
Assessment — Referencing	Mainly self-referenced but with some use of criterion-referencing
Assessment — Baselining	Use of school records: encounters with class; questioning; first 'products' → Baselining of newcomers/absentees → Final assessment forms part of next baseline
Assessment — Focus	1st concurrent assessment — Everyday appraisal — 2nd concurrent assessment — { Third concurrent assessment (and testing?) }
Assessment — Range	Mainly recall → Development of transfer — generalization → Recall combined with transfer/generalization
Relation to national curriculum	Drawing on core/foundations / Records and programmes → Relation of chosen topic to attainment targets (combined into profile components) and programmes of study

Week 0 — 1 — 2 — 3 — 4 — 5 — 6

Figure 4.2 A general model of topic development and assessment in primary humanities

housing in a school's locality could first require the learning and remembering of what the patterns are and where they are; then trying to identify the same or similar patterns in nearby districts, noting similarities and differences; and finally, a general approach to the concept of housing patterns and their significance, involving the formulation of hypotheses and generalizations. I have indicated elsewhere how this process of ranging could be applied to the particular case of primary industry education (W.A.L. Blyth 1988a).

Each of these steps – recall, transfer and generalization – should involve assessment by one means or other; but the process would not be complete until the final stage has been covered. Indeed it would not be complete even then, for once the 'naturally' level has been reached, generalizations should be challenged (Are you sure that all the houses there fit into this pattern? . . . Why do you think so?), and the way thus opened for the next episode of learning and assessment.

Putting assessment together

In this general outline of considerations relevant to assessment, including assessment of primary humanities, six aspects have been considered: clients, purposes, referencing, baselining, focus and range. I have devised the last two of those terms, but the rest will be found in the general literature on assessment. It is relatively easy to discuss each of them at some length. The really demanding task is that of fitting them all together in such a way as to give some idea of how the whole process might work. Figure 4.2 constitutes an attempt to show this in relation to one topic followed by one class. This is not a record of an actual class's story, but a composite account intended to convey the process fairly clearly.

This model of assessment will constitute the basis of Part Three. An application of Figure 4.2 to an actual instance will be found in Chapter 10. The next step now will be to consider the third of the basic concerns, the new national framework, within which this model of assessment must be applied to an enabling approach to primary humanities.

5 Assessment and primary humanities in the new national framework

In order to understand the framework which is now taking shape, it is necessary to apply the historical perspective to curriculum and assessment themselves.

The origins of national assessment policy for the primary curriculum in England and Wales

In the years between 1870 and 1939, assessment began from a very rigid concentration on performance in the three Rs under the Revised Code of 1862, but was subsequently extended to cover most of what eventually became quite a broad, if subdivided, elementary curriculum. However, within that curriculum the assessment of language and number, Alexander's Curriculum I (Alexander 1984), retained pride of place. This was true not only of the care and sophistication with which it was conducted, but also the weight accorded to it, especially after 1907, in the procedures devised for selection for secondary education which culminated in 'the eleven-plus'. Ironically, as that care and sophistication developed and it was increasingly found that learning across the curriculum was prone to social bias, it became the practice to restrict public assessment to language and number, and eventually also to 'intelligence' which almost became a part of Curriculum I in its own right. Since the main purpose of assessment came to be that of ensuring accuracy in selection, then this trinity of language, number and 'intelligence' probably served as well as any set of assessment data could have done, though it never eliminated agonies along the borderline. That purpose is, of course, not one of the three specified in Chapter 4 as important in an enabling curriculum.

For many primary teachers, there were two consequences of this historical phase, both of which were regrettable from the standpoint of primary humanities. The first was that the focus of attention was diverted away from anything outside the selection trinity. Science, where it existed, was just as badly affected as humanities, while, as it happened, contemporary changes in other aspects of the primary curriculum such as art and physical education tended to work against the notion of assessment. The other outcome of the eleven-plus culture was that assessment itself came to be identified with selection for secondary education so that, when selection was widely abolished, it was often assumed that assessment would also disappear. The talk was all about freeing the primary school from the restrictions of the eleven-plus and thus from formal assessment of any kind. The arguments for assessment appropriate to an enabling curriculum, namely that it is desirable on grounds of professional conscience, of children's expectations and of personal/social development, probably belonged to the future. At any rate, they were rarely heard.

It was not until the next turn of the wheel, the post-Plowden reaction against informal primary education (Cunningham 1988; W.A.L. Blyth 1988b) that assessment in the primary curriculum as a whole again became an issue. A change in the political climate in education, associated with the William Tyndale affair, the first Black Papers, Bennett's first study of teacher effectiveness (Bennett 1976), and Callaghan's weighty launch of the 'Great Debate' on education was soon by HMIs' first primary survey (HMI 1978) and by a growing demand, on all sides, for greater accountability in teaching. This development gave renewed impetus to the work of the Assessment of Performance Unit (APU), established in the Department of Education and Science since 1973 but organized by HMI. It was hoped that the APU would lead to a halt in the decline in standards that was widely believed to be taking place, and then to some improvement.

The work of the APU has been adequately chronicled and criticized by a number of writers (e.g. Gipps and Goldstein 1983; Gipps 1985). In common with many other official and semi-official contributions to curricular thinking in the 1970s, the APU espoused areas of development rather than subjects as elements in curriculum, and was thus congruent with an enabling approach. Six aspects of development were chosen: linguistic, mathematical, scientific, aesthetic, physical and personal/social. In all of them, it was intended that there should be some kind of 'light sampling', and the inception of procedures which should render possible the monitoring of children's performance across the country without bearing hardly on individual children or schools. The intentions were good, and the strategy ingenious.

In three of the 'areas', rapid progress was made. The first two areas built on the unbroken tradition of assessment in language and mathematics and on the recommendations of the Bullock and Cockcroft Reports which were being widely discussed. The third took account of the current work of Harlen and others in primary science. Imaginative forms of testing were devised in all three of those areas and will be referred to in subsequent chapters. The move away from the traditional emphasis on grammar and comprehension in English towards a search for more global qualities was particularly constructive.

Unfortunately, the sixfold developmental model became distorted (W.A.L. Blyth 1987). To begin with, the remaining three areas were never fully worked out. They produced admirable guidelines, but reasons were advanced why the evolution of a systematic testing programme would not be practicable. Indeed in one case, that of personal/social development, considerable controversy was encountered. Meanwhile the agenda of the APU itself was expanded to include modern languages (supposedly different from 'language') and technology (an addition to a sixfold framework that had been put forward as comprehensive). In fact, the APU came to appear more like an agency for testing subjects: English, mathematics, science, modern languages and technology, an array that looked uncannily like the core curriculum that was coming to be discussed by officialdom (e.g. DES/WO 1980). It was hardly surprising that this change gave rise to apprehension among those concerned with other aspects of the curriculum, including the arts and physical education, who felt that the 'cover' provided by the APU and its areas of development was being withdrawn. It gave rise to still greater unease in humanities which had not been directly represented even among the areas of development, as Figure 5.1 shows.

It is also fairly evident that the APU's thinking had been based on secondary education, from which it undertook an incursion into primary education, rather than the reverse procedure. No doubt this was seen as something of a corrective to the 'Plowden' approach, but in spite of the rhetoric of the time about primary education, influenced as it was by the William Tyndale case and the Black Papers, APU tended to leave primary issues to be tidied up after the main subject areas in secondary education had been delineated.

Thus, from the standpoint of primary humanities, two unfortunate though unintended consequences arose from the activities of the APU; first, the comparative marginalizing of humanities and then again the slightly subordinate status accorded to primary education as a whole. It is admittedly true that representatives of humanities held watching briefs on the APU's committees and that they did bring about a recognition of the relevance of humanities to the different areas of development; but, as was emphasized in Chapter 4, the exercise, for example, of mathematical skills in an historical context is still mathematics, and not adequate as an exemplification of the perspective of the historian. Thus, although the APU has sanctioned some imaginative innovations in assessment, with a measure of professional approval that continues, its contribution to assessment of primary humanities has been at best indirectly beneficial and, at worst, through comparative neglect, detrimental.

Meanwhile, however, HMI had maintained a parallel and rather more liberal approach to curriculum, also based on areas of experience, but with a more inclusive list set out in a number of documents published during the early 1980s. This stance by HMI sustained the hope that humanities would receive a measure of influential support in any impending official curriculum.

More recently assessment has become more than a means of systematic monitoring of children's attainments. It has become more overtly what it had for some time appeared likely to be, namely a central feature of government policy. The rest of this chapter will be concerned with the implementation of that policy and its impact on primary humanities.

Establishment of the national framework

By the time of the General Election of 1987, it was evident that a broad cross-party consensus had emerged in favour of the introduction of a national curriculum. Not everybody favoured the neat kind of curriculum envisaged by the Government

Elements in the primary curriculum	Aspects of development selected for assessment by the Assessment of Performance Unit					
	Linguistic	Mathematical	Scientific	Aesthetic	Physical	Personal/social
English	////					
Mathematics		////				
Science			////			
Technology			////			
Craft				////		
Art				////		
Music				////		
Other arts				////		
PE					////	
RE						////
Moral education						////
History						
Geography						
Other social subjects						

//// 'Best fit' elements

Figure 5.1 Assessment of Performance Unit areas of development seen in relation to elements in the primary curriculum

and its civil-service agents. On the other hand, few people felt that primary education should remain sacrosanct and immune from the impending reform. For, between these two positions, one rejectionist and one lustily in favour, there was room for a wide variety of opinion.

One such body of opinion was in broad agreement with the principle of an imposed curriculum, but differed about who should do the imposing, and why. Another, rather differently, felt obliged to cavil at the very notion of an imposed curriculum as such, irrespective of who imposed it, though those who were in that camp did favour a national framework based on co-operation and consent. This second point of view espoused something like an enabling curriculum, in which, where humanities was concerned, it would be the process strands, the fostering of skills and concepts and attitudes, perhaps linked to a broad outline of knowledge, rather than any detailed prescription of content, that should constitute the common element. In this version of a national curriculum, the process strands would ensure some framework within which children moving from school to school or from region to region would feel at home in their new surroundings, and parents would be reassured that progression in learning was being maintained.

Very soon after the General Election, a Consultation Document (DES/WO 1987) was issued. From this document, it became apparent that there was to be a new national framework and that it would be very much on the lines advocated by the Government. The 'consultation' took the form of substantial representations submitted within a short time-scale. These were duly noted and in some cases gave rise to marginal modifications of the original suggestions; but, when the Education Reform Bill was published early in 1988, its proposals for curriculum and assessment followed very closely what had been adumbrated in the Consultation Document. Nor, as the Bill passed through Parliament, were those proposals substantially amended either in the House of Commons or even in the House of Lords, where other aspects of the Bill were criticized quite substantially and even referred back to the Commons before being endorsed a second time in much their original form.

Meanwhile, since 1986, HMI had themselves played a significant part in shaping thought about curriculum. Through their influential *Curriculum Matters* series (e.g. HMI 1986; 1988) and especially the basic document entitled *The Curriculum from 5 to 16* (HMI 1985c), they continued the broad 'areas of experience' approach already established. At the same time they also cultivated in the public mind the assumption that the spelling out of curricular aims should include the specification of competences listed for children at particular age-levels, usually 11 and 16, often also 7, and sometimes 14. These age-levels, three of which corresponded to ages of transfer in most of England and almost all of Wales, were concurrently coming to be identified in official parlance with what the Task Group on Assessment and Testing (TGAT) *Report* (TGAT 1988a) was to designate as 'reporting ages'. So the idea took root that all children ought to be assessed on what HMI considered appropriate for them to know or do at those ages. Thus HMI contributed another component to the emerging framework, in parallel to what was being designed through legislation. It was a component that chimed in with much popular perception of what is supposed to happen in schools, but it should be noted that it is also one which begs most of the questions with which curriculum study is designed to grapple.

Thus the new national framework came to be established by a series of processes culminating in the Education Reform Act, 1988. By that Act, the Secretary of State for Education and Science and the Secretary of State for Wales were accorded a wide range of new powers. Through one of those powers, the national curriculum came technically into force almost immediately, though its details were to be developed through a series of Working Groups, some of which, including the Task Group on Assessment and Testing (TGAT), were already in existence. It would be monitored by the new National Curriculum Council (NCC), the Curriculum Council for Wales (CCW) and the School Examinations and Assessment Council (SEAC), nominated by the Secretaries of State through the array of new powers which they now wielded. To further these processes, the Department of Education and Science set about the preparation of Statutory Orders and Instruments and Circulars, directing schools and Local Education Authorities as to how they should implement details of the new legislation.

The statutory framework

The new framework has been established with remarkable speed. Thanks to a sustained programme of dissemination and in-service activities and in part also to the summary prepared by the DES for schools under the title *National Curriculum: from Policy to Practice* (DES 1989), it very soon became familiar to teachers. The curriculum as a whole in maintained schools is to be 'balanced and broadly-based' and is to promote the 'spiritual, moral, cultural, mental and physical development of pupils . . . and of society' and also to prepare pupils for 'the opportunities, responsibilities and experiences of adult life' (Education Reform Act, 1988, Part 1, chapter 1: subsequent details are quoted from the same section of the Act). These provisions do not differ sharply from the terms of the Education Act, 1944, except that it is now recognized, for a number of reasons relevant to primary humanities, that cultural development requires separate mention, and also that whereas the 1944 Act referred to the other four aspects of development as relating to the community, the 1988 Act distinguishes between individual development and social needs, and also between personal development and what may be regarded, in the broadest sense, as citizenship.

Of course, the principal difference between the new and the older framework is that the content of the curriculum is prescribed. Of this almost everyone in the teaching profession is now aware; more so perhaps than of the comfortable broad aims already mentioned. Instead of requiring 'such variety of instruction and training as may be desirable in view of their different ages, abilities and aptitudes . . .' (Education Act, 1944, clause 8 (1)), the 1988 Act states prescriptively that in maintained schools there is to be a basic curriculum consisting mainly of what is now technically 'the national curriculum', comprising:

CORE SUBJECTS	English, mathematics and science, and in Welsh-speaking schools, Welsh

FOUNDATION SUBJECTS
(strictly 'other foundation
subjects')

History, geography, technology, music, art, physical education and (at the secondary stage) a modern foreign language and, in non-Welsh-speaking schools in Wales, Welsh

The 'basic curriculum' is then completed by the addition of religious education (RE) which has the status of a foundation subject but is not liable to the same procedures for monitoring and assessment that apply to the national curriculum in the strict sense.

Outside the core and foundation subjects and RE there lies an area just within the perimeter fence of the curriculum where schools are permitted and in a sense encouraged to undertake anything that does not figure in the approved list, provided that it does not interfere with anything that does, and provided that it can be accommodated within the statutory hours of schooling and does not contravene any other aspect of the Education Reform Act. This completes the shape of the curriculum from the standpoint of subject knowledge, as it applies to maintained schools. In voluntary schools the nature of the requirements for religious education differ, as they have always done, from the position in maintained schools but the national curriculum applies. It will not, however, be enforced in independent schools. The position in grant-maintained schools and City Technology Colleges is less clear at present, but is relevant to primary schools in so far as they may cater for children who expect to proceed to either of the new forms of secondary school.

In view of the comparative recency of the terminology, it may be useful to emphasise that the subject components are to be related in the way indicated in Figure 5.2.

Figure 5.2 also indicates that there are also cross-curricular elements in the curriculum, that 'permeate' and interact with the subject components. These cross-curricular elements are not specified within the Education Reform Act itself, but represent aspects of policy that figured in the 1987 Consultation Document (DES/WO 1987) and in the *Policy to Practice* guide (DES 1989). They have come to be classified under three headings:

cross-curricular competences (or skills)
cross-curricular dimensions
cross-curricular themes

The first of these refers to matters such as oral communication. The second covers issues such as gender, multicultural education and related questions; they are thus defined as important for the management of the curriculum rather than for its content. The third, the 'themes' heading, covers matters that are more akin to subjects, such as health education, environmental education, economic and industrial understanding, citizenship, careers, and personal/social education generally, and for this purpose an Interim Whole Curriculum Committee of the National Curriculum Council established a series of Task Groups to keep an eye on these themes and their relation to the core and other foundation subjects, and to offer what is technically, if a trifle misleadingly, termed 'non-statutory guidance' to

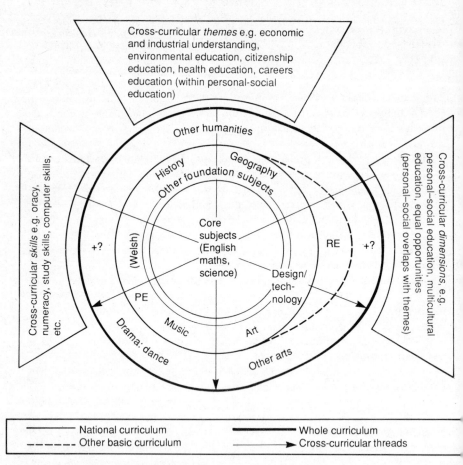

Cross-curricular *themes* e.g. economic and industrial understanding, environmental education, citizenship education, health education, careers education (within personal-social education)

Other humanities

History

Geography

Other foundation subjects

Core subjects (English maths, science)

Design/tech-nology

RE

+?

+?

(Welsh)

PE

Drama: dance

Music

Art

Other arts

Cross-curricular *skills* e.g. oracy, numeracy, study skills, computer skills, etc.

Cross-curricular *dimensions*, e.g. personal-social education, multicultural education, equal opportunities (personal-social overlaps with themes)

——————— National curriculum   ▬▬▬▬ Whole curriculum
– – – – – – Other basic curriculum   —————▶ Cross-curricular threads

Figure 5.2 Structure of the new national primary curriculum

teachers. There is thus some partial overlap between the peripheral subjects and the cross-curricular themes, and it has become evident that in the outer areas of the curricular system some issues were initially left open. This has provided an opportunity for some people, especially those concerned with subjects omitted from the core and foundation list, to put forward alternative strategies which may give their perspectives more scope: the social sciences are a case in point. By contrast, the functions accorded to the core and foundation subjects are to be quite precisely defined. The only element of uncertainty there is that (design and) technology, officially one of the other foundation subjects, sometimes appears to be regarded as linked with science and mathematics and thus to be a core subject in all but name. The National Curriculum Council has brought together the various components of the national curriculum, as they affect primary schools, in the first of their booklets of non-statutory guidance, *A Framework for the Primary Curriculum* (NCC 1989c), with particular reference to strategies of implementation.

An essential counterpart of the national curriculum (but not of religious education) is the national framework of assessment and testing introduced in order to ensure that the curriculum is successfully implemented or, as the term now is, 'delivered', like a baby or a parcel or a punch or a speech. For this purpose it is laid down that there must be in each subject Attainment Targets consisting of knowledge, skills and understanding, scheduled to be 'delivered' through Programmes of Study, and that there must be assessment arrangements that indicate how successfully the Attainment Targets have been pursued. It will be for the newly established School Examinations and Assessment Council to make positive recommendations on these matters to the Secretaries of State.

Although all this has become common knowledge within the teaching profession and to a large extent outside, it has taken some time for people to grasp that it is really going to happen to them. Among primary teachers, some of the more optimistic – or maybe the more indolent or overworked – believed that the full impact of the national curriculum would involve little more than *endorsement* of what they have been doing. Others, of a more doleful – or was it realistic? – cast of mind, feared that it would involve another word that sounds similar but means something very different, namely *enforcement* of something alien with which they basically disagreed. Both these reactions were probably unwarranted, but understandable. Meanwhile all primary teachers have been concerned, rightly, about the extent of change in role that would be expected of them, and in particular about the very considerable increase in workload and obligations that might arise. At the end of the Chapter 3, emphasis was laid on the demanding nature and range of primary teachers' existing obligations; yet here was the likelihood of still more, at a time when teachers' morale, which needs to be raised to meet such challenges, had instead been subjected to what amounted to a sustained and largely unjustified assault.

In addition to wondering how the new framework will affect them personally, primary teachers have joined in the more general scrutiny to which the new structure has been exposed. This scrutiny has concentrated on its principal aspects, one of which, particularly conspicuous to primary teachers, is that the new national curriculum is built on subjects. To those who are concerned with higher and further education, or with upper secondary education, this may appear self-evident, but in primary education it is not. To the supporters of a radical empiricist approach to the primary curriculum, indeed, it is almost the antithesis of what is desirable. To those, including myself, who adhere to the notion of an enabling curriculum, it is certainly important to take account of different perspectives, different ways of understanding and endeavour; but these only become definable as subjects as the children's development proceeds. Even to those who do maintain a subject-centred view of the nature of the primary curriculum, the actual list of subjects in the Education Reform Act may seem arbitrary and even biased, while the lack of definition of the relationship between subjects and cross-curricular themes, though it may open up possibilities, also leaves uncertainties. It has also been generally assumed, as Campbell (1989) points out, that the new framework should be built around what experts, working rapidly, have considered that children could or should learn or do, rather than around long-term investigations of what they can or do do; the thrust has indeed been 'from policy to practice' and not vice versa. Yet in one respect the intentions of the Act and of the events which led up to it have been fully vindicated. For there has been virtually unanimous agreement about the distinction between core and other foundation subjects. This is unusual among national systems, but it endorses Alexander's distinction between Curriculum I and Curriculum II at the primary level (Alexander 1984), according to which Curriculum I is the stronghold of prescribed, though not necessarily didactic, teaching, while Curriculum II allows more scope for autonomy but also for vagueness. Granted this distinction between core and other foundation subjects there has also been widespread support for what might be termed the promotion of primary science from Curriculum II to Curriculum I.

Primary humanities in the national curriculum

Primary humanities is thus embodied in the new framework in two different ways; through two of the foundation subjects, history and geography, and through different aspects of the cross-curricular elements. To use another term from the new vocabulary, these will form a part of every child's 'entitlement'. It will be in keeping with the priorities implicit in the framework itself if the foundation subjects are considered first.

The representation of humanities through two foundation subjects is considerably more than might at one time have been feared (e.g. DES/WO 1980). Those who feel comfortable with traditional subject names and have been critical of what is regarded as aimless social studies will be particularly reassured, though they may be obliged to remember that, as was indicated in Chapter 3, the relations between history and geography have not always been as amicable as they might. Those who hold an opposite view, namely that subjects are not an appropriate way of organizing the primary curriculum and that even a broad area like humanities should not figure recognizably before the secondary stage, are not so likely to be happy. This may be all the more so because a view has developed in some quarters that history, in particular, symbolizes a traditionalist approach to curriculum and even (in spite of Marx) an agent of social reaction and nostalgia. Between these two points of view, advocates of an enabling curriculum in which the three humanities' perspectives are represented will be pleased that at any rate two of them have been recognized within the foundation area, and that the new framework does not dictate how those perspectives should be translated into teaching methods, or even that the subjects should be separately taught at all. It only requires that they should be adequately represented in what is taught.

If we turn now to the cross-curricular elements, we may find that the attitudes of the three groups are reversed. It is the adherents of subject study who will least welcome the recognition that other ways of learning should figure in the curriculum. They may well recognize, among the cross-curricular dimensions, issues such as gender and ethnicity that could allow some elements of the social-science perspective to creep into the programme almost unnoticed. Yet they may still take comfort from the occurrence, within the list of themes, of relatively safe matters such as health and environmental issues (we are all green now), and from the fact that the social sciences are represented by economics, in the guise of economic and industrial understanding, and by a manageable approach to citizenship, rather than by sociology. Meanwhile the adherents of a more radical approach to curriculum may welcome the recognition given to some form of social studies with its progressive overtones and may also hope that the lack of specificity in the cross-curricular areas will allow the development of much more in the social-studies sphere than would be possible within the relative rigidity of the core and foundation subjects themselves. This time, the adherents of an enabling curriculum would virtually share the welcome given by the second group to the possibility of retaining the social-science perspective and a modicum of discretion for individual teachers, while being a little more enthusiastic than the 'radicals' might be about the specific involvement of the historical and geographical perspectives.

Thus there is something in the new framework for everybody. How far that outcome was intended must remain a matter for conjecture. In any case, the new curriculum will not give full satisfaction to anybody, for the element of discretion left to teachers, which the second and third group welcome as something essential to preserve in the new framework, might be seen by the first as perpetuating exactly what caused them disquiet in the first place.

In practice, the position of humanities will be further affected by the status of religious education as a necessary part of the basic or statutory curriculum but not of the national curriculum; something that must be taught like the rest but not assessed like the rest. A still further complication will be brought about by the embodiment of moral education within the important cross-curricular theme of personal/social education. In Chapter 3 I expressed my view that moral and religious understanding and endeavour are of basic importance but are conceptually distinct from the understanding of the social world with which humanities is concerned. As the new curricular structure implicitly recognizes, they are also conceptually distinct from each other, a point that defenders of both have to remember. What they both share, and share with humanities, is a concern with human values, attitudes, behaviour and belief. Matters such as worship and reverence are experiences that belong to religious understanding though not to moral understanding as such. They are partly – only partly – open to consideration within humanities as an aspect of the observed behaviour of other people and other societies. All of this implies difficulties for schools in which moral and religious education have hitherto been constructively combined with humanities in the primary curriculum. For the requirements of assessment will be confined to those aspects which fall clearly within the national curriculum, while there is likely to be an unwritten expectation that moral and religious education will be otherwise scrutinized; in voluntary schools this expectation may indeed be more clearly specified. For individual schools and teachers where the humanities umbrella has been extended in this way, the future assessment arrangements could present problems, even problems of conscience, that are not likely to arise in the core or other foundation subjects. Only in humanities might some teachers almost have to decide whether they are required to render unto Caesar the things that they believe to be God's.

There are thus several issues about the place of humanities in the new framework around which controversy could well develop. This in itself could be dangerous for humanities. For, if energies are dissipated, and publicly seen to be dissipated, in contention about those issues, the impression might be left that humanities has emerged once again as a problem area. And if, while the core subjects and the other foundation subjects move (admittedly with considerable nudging) towards unity of purpose, humanities continues for whatever reason to display disunity, then almost inevitably its status in the primary curriculum would be jeopardized.

This danger might be further aggravated by the intermediate status that humanities may come to occupy in popular esteem. It has already become apparent that art, music and physical education may be subjected to a less stringent approach than is to be prescribed for the core subjects (DES 1989, para. 4.17) while the position of technology remains uncertain. But there is no doubt that history and geography will be assessed quite positively, though without the status that will accrue to the other fully assessed subjects, because those are within the core. Thus there is a distinct possibility that humanities may come to occupy an uncomfortable middle position, regarded rather disdainfully from the standpoint of the core subjects, but bracketed with those core subjects as symbols of reaction by those, especially among infant teachers, who regard the arts as the essence of good primary education. This is a possible development that requires vigilance. Linked with this is another possibility, that full assessment might come to mean assessment in the manner, and even in the forms of understanding and endeavour, of the core subjects themselves. They are first in the field, both in time (two of their Working Groups were established well before the Act was passed) and at law, so inevitably they are defining that field. It is in relation to assessment that these issues will be seen at their most acute.

For all of these reasons, the place of primary humanities in the new framework cannot be regarded as entirely assured. It must be made secure, as the framework takes full shape. If it is not made secure, by a combination of clear thinking, good sense, negotiation, and sheer effectiveness in curriculum 'delivery' and assessment, then even the two foundation subjects themselves might become open to reconsideration when the Secretary of State comes to exercise his power 'to revise that curriculum whenever he considers it necessary or expedient to do so'. Fortunately, at present, that appears unlikely.

The TGAT Report

Before the Education Reform Act became law, the Secretary of State for Education and Science had established the Task Group on Assessment and Testing (TGAT) under the chairmanship of Professor Paul Black. It symbolized the determination of the government to link curriculum with assessment, and to single out specific 'reporting ages' for special attention: 7, 11, 14 and 16 have always been the prime favourites, and these are the ones for which the way has been further prepared by the statements of expected competence that HMI have embodied in the *Curriculum Matters* series. The work of TGAT, accomplished within a very short time-span, has already been referred to in Chapter 1. Eventually the Task Group produced a main *Report*, dutifully signed by its Chairman on Christmas Eve 1987 (TGAT 1988a). The report almost vindicated the speed with which these things are done nowadays, for it proved more influential than some others that have occupied months or even years of discussion.

Already, two of its features have acquired particular significance. First, it embodied proposals that went further towards meeting professional opinion and experience than many had expected (or hoped or feared) and had avoided the simplicities of benchmark testing so witheringly analysed by Thomas (1987). Second, its proposals laid down not only a framework for assessment, which was required, but also a radically new framework for the implementation of curriculum. Paradoxically, and somewhat to their embarrassment, many of those who had feared that the new curricular framework would be dominated by assessment, almost as it was under the nineteenth-century Revised Code and its system of 'Payment by Results', found themselves obliged, when they saw what kind of assessment was being proposed, to welcome that very outcome. TGAT took up the terminology (programmes of study, attainment targets) outlined in the 1987 Consultation Document (DES/WO 1987), as it was required to do. It then added further significant concepts, such as profile components, standard assessment tasks and levels of achievement which have already themselves acquired varying measures of statutory recognition. All of these were woven into a consistent and effective approach to curriculum that has now not merely become part of the provisions of the 1988 Act, but is also working its way into the professional language of teachers and even, sometimes inaccurately, into common parlance. It has necessarily been adopted by the working groups that have been proposing the detail of the national curriculum itself. Thus, by exercising the very powers accorded to them, the members of TGAT have succeeded in establishing an approach that would be politically very hard to gainsay. Their main *Report* has undergone searching professional criticism (e.g. by Torrance 1988 and P. Murphy 1988 and the contributors to a symposium in the *British Journal of Sociology of Education* (Kimberley *et al.* 1989)). In *Three Supplementary Reports* (TGAT 1988b), the Task Group answered some criticisms of the main *Report* and also sketched further details of how the programme might be implemented.

The main features of the TGAT recommendations, as they affect primary humanities, may be summarized as follows:

1 The ages of 7, 11, 14 and 16 are acceptable as special 'reporting ages'.
2 Assessment must include more than testing and must be: criterion-referenced; formative and diagnostic in intention; open to moderation; and related to progression in learning.
3 There can be positive educational value in nationally agreed procedures.
4 Assessment should be of a piece with teaching and should promote both feedback and 'feedforward' (i.e. to a new teacher or school).
5 Results for individual children should not be published beyond a limited circle; results for schools should not be published without reference to context.
6 Results of assessment should be presented as part of a pupil's profile.

7 Assessment should be substantially based on *standard assessment tasks* which would be related to the *profile components* which are to be the principal strands in the national curriculum itself. At the primary stage these components would be based mainly on the core subjects, but early in secondary education they would come to resemble more closely the full subject structure.

8 Subject groups would design profile components.

> We recommend that an individual subject should report a small number (preferably no more than four and never more than six) profile components reflecting the variety of knowledge, skills and understanding to which the subject gives rise. Wherever possble, one or more components should have more general application across the curriculum: for these a single common specification should be adopted in each of the subjects concerned.
>
> (TGAT 1988a, para. 35)

9 Standard assessment tasks should permit variation in *presentation* (oral, written, video, computer, etc.), *operation* (what the children can be expected to do) and *response* (what 'product' there will be to indicate what the children have done).

10 Teachers' informal monitoring should supplement standard procedures especially for diagnostic purposes and when catering for special needs. This form of monitoring or rating would be subject to peer moderation through procedures to be devised through LEAs.

11 Ten 'levels' of criterion-referenced assessment are proposed. At any one age, a pupil's overall profile of achievement would be 'aggregated' from the relevant data. A normal pattern, in the strict sense, would emerge empirically without functioning as a series of benchmarks. At the age of 7, only Levels 1 to 3 would be likely to apply and should be used, at that stage, mainly for diagnostic purposes.

12 There should be provision, by means of item banks, for further assessment of individual children where the initial procedure proves inadequate.

TGAT recognized, explicitly, that their recommendations would imply a new and exacting series of obligations for primary teachers. Their supplementary reports (TGAT 1988b) indicated something of the intensive in-service programmes that might be required for this purpose. A time-table for implementation was suggested and is being adhered to. Primary schools will have embarked, with one eye on assessment, on core-subject work with some young children before this book is published.

Primary humanities and the requirements for the core subjects

TGAT did not say much about primary humanities. In one sense that is beneficial, for it implies a freedom of action that the core subjects do not enjoy. Yet, as was indicated earlier, history and geography will be given a schedule just as prescriptive as theirs. This might in turn lead to pressure to concentrate assessment on the core subjects themselves, especially in view of the growing pressure to implement 8 above by means of cross-curricular profile components and attainment targets. Overpressed teachers might close gratefully for anything that relieved them of further assessment work in addition to what is to be required in the core subjects. Ironically, the more broadly based the core subjects become, the more readily they could absorb humanities in this way.

Actually, official concern appears to be concentrated not on the potential of the core subjects to absorb the other foundation subjects, but rather on the reverse possibility, that of the 'delivery' of the core subjects through those others. *National Curriculum: from Policy to Practice* (DES 1989) spells out this expectation:

> in primary schools, at present, most time is spent in acquiring knowledge, skills and understanding within the core subject area. The need to cover other curriculum ground means that *the possibilities for developing aspects of the core subjects in the context of the other foundation subjects and the whole curriculum* should be fully explored and reflected in the planning and delivery of much topic work.
>
> (para. 4.8: my italics)

The first sentence is probably premature as far as primary science is concerned. For the rest, there remains a danger that the 'other' foundation subjects in primary education might be judged by their capacity to 'deliver' the core subjects, rather than by their presence in their own right.

Consultation Report: Science, issued late in 1988 by the National Curriculum Council (NCC 1988a), represents the Council's considered advice on primary science in response to the working group's report. The general potential for cross-curricular development is evident. For example it is clearly stated that:

> Council's recommendations for draft Orders for science make use of the scope that exists for covering scientific aspects of other subjects and themes, and . . . these can be more fully worked out when other core and foundation subjects are in place.
>
> (p. 18, para. 3.18)

Much will depend on the way in which 'scientific aspects' are defined, and who defines them, and perhaps on what is implied by the quaint expression 'in place'. The proposed programmes of study in science and the related attainment targets include a number of examples where such issues might arise. For example, Attainment Target 5 within Profile Component II (Knowledge and Understanding of Science) for ages 7–11 proposes (p. 42) that:

> Children should study aspects of their local environment which have been affected by human activity. These may include farming, industry, sewage disposal, mining or quarrying. . . . They should observe and record the significant features of the process; the range and origins of any raw materials; waste disposal procedures and the usefulness of any product(s).

The definitive Statutory Order for Science (DES/WO 1989a, p. 69) endorses this recommendation among its 'detailed provisions' related to the Programme of Study for Key Stage 2. The recommendation itself is beyond criticism; yet it could so easily lead to a definition of the local environment in purely physical terms, with scant reference to its historical, social and cultural components which might well be the principal influences on the 'human activity' in question. There are many other instances, particularly in relation to physical geography and weather study, where similar issues could arise, in respect both of the process strands to be developed and of the knowledge to be gained.

Mathematics does not involve so direct a dispute about academic territories. *Consultation Report: Mathematics* (NCC 1988b) proposes programmes of study that are clearly mathematical in character. At the same time, these contribute importantly to aspects of humanities and to assessment in humanities. For example, Attainment Target 8, 'Measure', includes at Level 2 'Handling money: shopping activities in the classroom' (p. 45), though it does not emphasize the economic and social aspects of 'shopping activities'. Again, Attainment Target 12, 'Handling data', i.e. simple statistics, includes examples that relate directly to the geographical and social-science perspectives (p. 59), but mostly not at the Levels normally relevant to primary education. Another aspect important for humanities is Attainment Target 14, also entitled 'Handling data', but this time referring to probability (p. 69), which is related to the toleration of uncertainty that constitutes one of the higher thinking skills to be fostered through humanities. These recommendations now have statutory force (DES/WO 1989b, pp. 21, 31–3, 43–5). There could, of course, be other aspects of measurement relevant to humanities (map skills, time skills, graphing), but these do not in fact figure in the proposals for mathematics as clearly as they do in the case of science. However, the door is left open for further developments, since 'Council advises that cross-curricular aspects will be more fully worked out when other core and foundation subjects are in place (para. 3.22, p. 17).' Once again the expression 'in place' is used. Presumably it, too, is becoming part of the new vocabulary.

The relevance of English to humanities is immediately obvious. Tool skills proposed for assessment in the report from the Working Group on English 5–11 (DES/WO 1988c) included, for Level 4 (p. 43): 'Select and employ appropriate reference books . . . sufficiently to pursue a reasonably sustained line of enquiry', and at the next Level, within the range of some children in primary schools (ibid.): 'Begin, in discussion, to evaluate information sources and critically to weigh evidence and argument'. Again, the programme of study for ages 5–7 included (p. 44) 'folk tales, myths and legends' and for ages 8–11 (ibid.), still more pointedly, 'selections of fiction should range into other cultures and into history as well as extending children's understanding of the immediate world around them.' Again, in the profile component suggested as Writing, one of the descriptors for Level 2 includes (p. 48) '(pupils should be able to) Structure sequences of real or imagined events coherently in chronological accounts'.

These recommendations have been substantially embodied in a recast form in the National Curriculum Council's comments (NCC 1989a) and (in respect of Levels 1–3) in the subsequent provisional Order for English in Key Stage 1 (DES/WO 1989c) and its subsequent confirmation.

Taken together, these indications of the intentions of those who are concerned with curriculum and assessment in the core subjects do show that serious attention is being paid to matters that are important in humanities, and that everybody will have to take some notice of these in both teaching and assessment. Yet there remains a possible danger that, under pressure to bring the whole new framework fully into being as soon as possible, the separate claims of the humanities disciplines could be overridden. It could so easily be assumed that teachers and children have 'done' their history through their English, without recognizing additionally the kinds of understanding that belong to history as history. The same would apply to any assumption that all that is important in geography, and in the social sciences, could be 'done' as science. It is, however, encouraging that the radically new thinking developed by TGAT has been largely incorporated in the proposals for the core subjects, and that a case has been powerfully made for programmes of study which take children's development fully into account. An enabling curriculum can ask no less for primary humanities too.

The twin foundations: history and geography

Following symbolically after the core subjects and design/technology, the two representatives of humanities among the 'other' foundation subjects came on line for the setting up of working groups, and then for the whole sequence from Interim Report (nominally from the Secretaries of State) to public comment on a minuscule time-scale, to Final Report, to consideration by the National Curriculum Council, and finally to the issue of Statutory Orders. Of the two, history came first, preceding geography by a few months. As in the rest of the curriculum, HMI had already staked out a possible pattern of expectation for what are now Key Stages through the *Curriculum Matters* series, and especially in the booklets on geography (HMI 1986) and history (HMI 1988). Perhaps significantly, the later of the two spelled out more detail about what children might be expected to know and do at the ages of 7 and 11.

Meanwhile the two major relevant professional bodies, the Historical and Geographical Associations, had been preparing their own observations, including comments on the primary stage, and their statements covering the whole age-range 5–16 were published (Roberts 1989; Daugherty 1989). The Historical Association presented a well-reasoned case for history in the curriculum 5–16, bearing in mind earlier publications on the same theme, and recommended an approach based on this outline:

Profile Component 1 Knowing about and understanding the past
Attainment targets: – the local perspective
                               – the national perspective
                               – the global perspective
Profile Component 2 Exploring and investigating the past
Attainment targets: – using time
                               – using evidence
Profile Component 3 Explaining and communicating about the past
Attainment targets: – explaining about the past
                               – communicating findings about the past

                                                       (Roberts 1989, para. 4.3)

The much fuller document from the Geographical Association suggested a parallel framework:

> *Profile Component 1*   Understanding environments
> Attainment targets: – the local region
> – the wider world
> – landscapes and their formation
> – weather and atmosphere
> – ecosystems and resource management
> – people and settlements
> – movement of people, goods and
>   information
> – location and organization of
>   economic activities
> *Profile Component 2*   Investigating environments
> Attainment targets: – fieldwork investigations
> – understanding maps
> – sources of geographical information
> *Profile Component 3*   Evaluating environments
> Attainment targets: – environmental issues
> – the potential of places
> – environmental appreciation
>
> (Daugherty 1989: pp. 37–40)

The geography document also spelled out examples of how levels of attainment and programmes of study could relate to three of the attainment targets. To appreciate the full force of the arguments advanced, it is necessary to study the document itself, but it is interesting that the proposed sequence through Key Stages 1 and 2 involved a progressive expansion of horizons, in terms both of geographical arena (from the locality outwards) and of process strands. In the instances specified, the science and social-science perspectives were also represented.

It is encouraging to note that these suggestions from the two professional organizations are substantially compatible with what would be expected in an enabling curriculum. Other bodies such as the newly established Primary History Association also put forward views about what would be desirable in the national curriculum. Meanwhile, it must also be remembered that the humanities component in the cross-curricular themes will also become clearer as the National Curriculum Council continues to formulate different kinds of non-statutory guidance. Having been personally involved in one aspect of this activity, namely the Task Group concerned with economic and industrial understanding, I am encouraged by the quality and direction of its discussions which contributed to the general deliberations of the National Curriculum Council itself.

At the time of writing, neither of the Working Groups' reports has appeared, though both will be familiar before this book is published.* It would be all too easy

---

* The History Interim Report was published in August 1989, after this book was written. A brief comment on its implications has been included as Appendix 3, pp. 164–5.

to speculate in advance about their contents, but I shall not try. I shall confine myself to the sole observation that their forerunners in the core subjects gave full attention to the professional advice given to them and produced, eventually, recommendations that may have proved controversial but did not depart too abruptly from that advice. It will be for readers of the book to decide whether the same has applied to the reports on history and geography, for the future of primary humanities will be largely erected on these twin foundations.

Of course, when history and geography have run their course, art and music and PE will follow suit, and (secondary) modern languages, to which primary humanities could be a partial precursor. The place of religious education has also to be worked out in detail, while that of the cross-curricular elements has also to be finally decided. Meanwhile, a year or so behind the curriculum, the new assessment framework is also being assembled. So there is still flexibility in the framework, and humanities will not only need to adjust the parts where the mould is already set, but also to those where the plaster is still wet.

Making the best of it

The new national framework does seem to allow more opportunity for flexibility and for recognition of young children's ways of learning than seemed at one time likely. The emerging framework of assessment, including TGAT's emphasis on the importance of teachers' observation of children, is also more sensitive than the brash benchmark testing that was originally talked about. There will be scope for topics individually chosen by schools, and for continuous assessment with formative purposes, not confined to the 'reporting ages' at the end of the 'key stages'. Teachers will not only be allowed to take an active part in planning assessment: they may well be required to do so. They will need to 'make the grade', in humanities as much as elsewhere. Maybe professional opinion has made more impact than was acknowledged in the early days.

Part Three of this book will be concerned with what schools and teachers will be able, and obliged, to do within the new guidelines. The assumption will be that they should make the best of it. By that I do not mean whistling in the dark and hoping that, somehow, it will not be too bad. That would be a lame response. Nor do I mean resolving to oppose the new framework tooth and nail and waiting for some political or social change to tear the framework down, for it is quite unrealistic to look for support anywhere for opposition to what is now so generally, if perhaps too easily, supported. Rather I mean seizing the opportunity to make the grade, and in the process to make the future of primary education, since teachers are the essential agents of any change. They will retain considerable freedom of action, though they will be required to exercise that freedom with vigour and responsibility. Constructive implementation of the new curriculum will also entitle and empower the teaching profession to criticize, evaluate, and in due course help to modify and improve the procedures that are being so hastily introduced. This is a course of action that need not violate anybody's professional conscience. The greatest obstacle to making the best of it is likely to be the sheer size and novelty of the tasks that teachers will be expected to undertake, and the difficulty of generating the morale and providing the resources required for that task. Others have the power, maybe the duty, to reverse the downward trend in morale and resources. I shall try to show how schools and teachers can make the best of it and make the grade for primary humanities, even in the present circumstances. It could be much better done, even so, if those circumstances were radically improved, as of course they should be.

Part Three
Assessment in action

6 A school strategy for assessment

In the new framework there will be substantial scope and obligation for schools to develop their own policies for curriculum and assessment. Whatever profile components, attainment targets and programmes of study may be laid down, and whatever standard assessment tasks may be devised and approved, the whole procedure will, as the Department of Education and Science (DES) has emphasized (DES 1989, Chapter 9; NCC 1989c), depend for its success on the capacity of schools and teachers to implement it. Where, as may occasionally have been the case, schools lack any policy for assessment except in the limited sense of language and mathematics schemes and local education authority (LEA) require-ments, they will have to undertake, as a part of the preparation of National Curriculum Development Plans, what for them is a new kind of activity. This need not in itself cause dismay. There is in fact a precedent for this, since schools have already had to devise policies for curriculum, and for this purpose the Schools Council, in its last years (Schools Council 1981; 1983) and Her Majesty's Inspectors (HMI 1985c) provided relatively liberal versions of the emerging educational consensus as it applied to primary education and the primary curriculum in the 1980s. Although this may have caused some heart-searching, primary teaching has survived.

The arguments in favour of assessment, outlined in Chapter 4, should in themselves warrant the development of a positive policy in each school, whether or not there is any kind of national curriculum, including this one. That does not mean that a school's policy should be confined to implementing what will be the legal minimum. There will be plenty of scope for schools to go beyond that minimum and to develop their own strategies in a constructive and creative way, one that will be appropriate to an enabling curriculum and will empower schools, working as they must within the new framework, to seize the essential initiative.

This chapter offers an outline of how such a strategy might be designed. It is based on some experience of observing, teaching about and supervising research into the planning and implementation of curriculum innovation. There is a substantial literature on this theme, now accessible in particular through general sources on management in primary schools (e.g. Nicholls 1983; Lloyd 1985; Day *et al.* 1986) as well as through more specialized books and journals, but I have taken the liberty of writing this chapter without detailed reference to that literature.

Establishing the strategy

Any planning for assessment in primary humanities must, of course, form part of the wider strategy within the school which must in its turn adjust to the national framework as it takes detailed shape. One way in which this strategy could be developed would be by simply reacting to each new development as it takes place. Given the pace at which developments *are* taking place, together with the pressing everyday needs of school life, it will be very difficult for individual schools to do anything other than respond in this way. Yet if they do respond in this way, there is little chance of preventing the emergence of a ramshackle pattern dominated unintentionally but effectively by the core subjects. The only way of avoiding that outcome is through the deliberate drawing up, well in advance, and as a part of a National Curriculum Development Plan, of a co-ordinated strategy. that will accommodate adequately all the core and other foundation subjects and which will also go some way towards recognizing the contribution of the peripheral subjects and the cross-curricular elements. To do that will require considerable vision and determination. It will be difficult to do, because LEAs are being pressed to concentrate their advisory staff and material resources on the core subjects which are already relatively favoured. Yet the task must be attempted, if a 'balanced and broadly-based' curriculum really is going to be implemented; and some schools are managing it now.

The first step in any such planning must be taken by what I will call, collectively, the management. It is the responsibility of head teachers and deputy heads to be aware of what is going on nationally, and to master the sort of language and concepts that I have used in Part Two. This is in itself a very considerable task, and the official literature emanating from the Department of Education and Science can provide only a minimum of what is required. The professional press does keep its readers a little more aware of what is going on, and the changing scene is also borne in upon management through the appearance of new-style documents to be filled in. Yet there is a limit to what can be absorbed and understood from reading alone, within a busy professional life replete with the urgent problems of children, parents and teachers, as well as their own; for management has personal problems too. This printed guidance is to be helpfully supplemented by video material from the Open University, the BBC and the two national curriculum councils, the National Curriculum Council (NCC) and the Curriculum Council for Wales (CCW) (Moon 1989). However, it is in accordance with simple educational psychology to point out that the printed word, and even the multi-media approach, should also be reinforced by personal contact and discussion.

This is where meetings of management with their counterparts in local clusters of schools is so useful. Where they are organized by the LEA, they are even more useful. For this means not only that the arrangement and administration of meetings are easier and their legitimacy more evident, but also that advisers and advisory teachers can add their own expert knowledge and understanding to the deliberations. The advisory staff are themselves often thin on the ground and torn between multiple duties (Winkley 1985). Yet it is central to their role that they should be able to support schools in this way and, although they themselves are short of the time needed to catch up on the outpouring of official literature, somehow they manage to do it. At this level, as in discussions in which I have personally taken part, it is usually the case that one head teacher will have been impressed by a particular aspect of the documentation; perhaps a deputy head will have noticed how some suggestion would be particularly difficult in that school's circumstances and will thus alert others to the need for vigilance on similar matters, and an adviser will point out some constructive work that is under way elsewhere in the county or borough, one which will be of particular relevance in the new situation. Gradually, in such ways, the bare bones of official pronounce-ment take on the flesh of reality and enter into the professional consciousness of each school's management. In one sense humanities could gain from its position in the queue of curriculum change, for the machinery that is being invented in respect of the core subjects will already be 'in place' for other purposes; but that benefit will not accrue automatically unless the LEA's own procedures ensure that it does.

The next step would then be for each school to develop its own internal policies, in the light of this consultation between managements. Yet, as some readers will probably have noticed, there is a sense in which this sharing of experience between managements runs contrary to the democratic or collegial pattern of school organization (Campbell 1985) that is more appropriate to an enabling curriculum. It is therefore important that, once management has acquired the confidence to launch an initiative within a school, its members should incorporate the whole staff in the process. Probably they would want to. For everybody, including the newest member, is likely to have something to add, especially since newly qualified teachers nowadays have a high level of professional awareness; more so, in fact, than was available to some of their senior colleagues at the outset of their careers. Delicate questions of status and remuneration may, of course, also have to be taken into account, and it is a part of the skills expected from management that they should be effectively taken into account.

Staff conferences are likely to be the principal mode through which in-school policies can be evolved. It is intended that such days should be spent on matters concerned with the national curriculum, though once again it is necessary to watch carefully to ensure that the whole curriculum and not just the core subjects are catered for. Where possible, it is quite sensible to invite an external consultant to help in launches of policy at conferences of this kind, though not in such a way as to encourage dependency; a school must be able to proceed mainly under its own power. A popular structure for an in-service exercise of this kind is to start with a general introduction and then to follow with a workshop in which teachers, perhaps in pairs, hammer out suggestions for work with the age-groups with which they are directly involved, the whole day ending with a discussion of how to formulate an agreed, whole-school policy for assessment and record-keeping. It is valuable when such conferences can involve both infant and junior teachers, so that their different points of view can be aired and their differences reconciled at an early stage. In some cases it might even be necessary to emphasize that infant teachers are to be involved with humanities at all; for they will be.

The emphasis mentioned on *agreed* policy is important. There has been a tendency for some teachers to take part in occasions of this kind and then to resolve, intentionally or otherwise, singly or collectively, simply to go on as though nothing had changed. That human reaction is understandable, especially in the busy whirl of school; but it is going to be unacceptable. Indeed, it is partly in order to prevent that reaction that the Education Reform Act has been carried. If a school is to develop the creative and constructive strategy that I have referred to, within the national curriculum, then teachers must agree that the school's policy is binding upon its members. The counterpart of genuine discussion during the formulation of policy is that, once that process has been completed, management has the right to exercise authority in its implementation and to expect support in doing so. Where management is not arbitrary, it has more, not less, right to exercise authority.

A particular issue that might arise in some schools is the institutional division between the infant and junior departments or their equivalent. For historical reasons many infant teachers have felt that their work belongs to a distinctive tradition (King 1978; 1988), further removed from the 'secondary' or subject emphasis than is the case with junior teachers. Infant teachers may therefore be least inclined either to consider that subject areas should figure recognizably in the infant curriculum, or to come to terms with requirements for national assessment, even when they are statutorily binding. From the point of view of an enabling curriculum, this reluctance is understandable, but it could have unintended and regrettable consequences if it were to prove institutionally divisive within a 5–11 school. It could cause a different kind of result in a separate infant school, especially if a considerable number of the children are, as is now often the case, under the age of five and thus technically outside the national curriculum. For here the management may be required to introduce a policy about which they, as well as their staff, have basic reservations. First schools, which will straddle the first key or reporting age of 7, will be faced with further complications (DES 1989, para. 9.17). When school strategies are worked out in practice, all these issues are likely to be important.

Within the new national framework, it will also be necessary to secure the support of the school governors, who will have some responsibility for seeing that the national curriculum and assessment policy is carried out by their school. The overtones of those provisions are that, in the name of parent power and in the interests of the local community and especially of the local business community, any laziness, inefficiency, indifference or suspect ideology on the part of the school or the teachers should be eradicated. Combined with moves towards the transfer of some financial and administrative powers from Local Education Authorities (LEAs) to schools, the Act implies a considerable change in the pattern of accountability that primary-school management and staffs must now envisage.

However, those new provisions can also be more constructively used. Teachers need not necessarily be racked with anxiety that they may have displeased a coalition of assertive parents with nose-to-the-grindstone employers, any more than they formerly felt constrained by the assorted worthies elected to their LEA. In fact, the new provisions have given schools a new opportunity. Governing bodies are, by definition, interested in particular schools and must want to see their schools flourish, even when they differ from management as to what that means. Therefore they are rightly concerned about curriculum and assessment. In many places they are working hard to familiarize themselves with what goes on in schools in a situation in which, somewhat like jurors, they have more power than expertise. If they, as members of local communities, see that the management and other staff members in a school know what they are doing and try to understand the genuine hopes and fears of all the people in the area and not just some of them, then the governors' enhanced powers can be enlisted to support a staff rather than to discipline it. The process of mutual learning and understanding can also, when actively pursued by schools, result in greater comprehension by governors, and then by the general public, of what a 'balanced and broadly based' curriculum can be like.

Beyond this again, it will be increasingly necessary for schools to work together with other neighbouring schools, primary and secondary, not only at the management level but in more thoroughgoing ways. For this purpose too the support of the LEA and its staff will be needed. Such developments are already under way in an encouragingly large number of areas, especially where experiments in curriculum continuity are being developed (see also Chapter 11).

These developments can and should also lay the foundations for the introduction of the local and possibly regional moderation procedures that will be required (TGAT 1988a and b) both in respect of national testing and as a means of conferring credibility on the outcome of teachers' everyday appraisal, concurrent assessment and teacher-made testing, the issues to be explored in the next four chapters. Just as the establishment of school policies will involve some sacrifice of autonomy on the part of individual teachers, so will the establishment of inter-school co-operation require some surrender of independence by individual schools. This will eliminate some indefensible practices here and there, but will not result in wholesale capitulation of some schools to others. A genuine federation, reserving some freedom of action to individual schools, should be the aim and is compatible with the intentions of an enabling curriculum. I have visited one county area in which, before the national curriculum was introduced, a local compact had been negotiated between the primary schools contributing to one comprehensive school, whereby each primary school pursued for one-half of its time an agreed programme shared between them, while the other half remained at the discretion of each individual school. In such circumstances, assessment as well as curriculum rests on an agreed basis. That exact arrangement is unlikely to continue in the new framework, but I hope that its underlying principles will persist and indeed take root elsewhere. It is a sensible approach, compatible with the new framework itself, and equipped with the great advantage that it was substantially developed by the schools themselves.

Since the success of the national curriculum and its related pattern of assessment must depend primarily on those who are to operate the system, it seems evident that local arrangements should be built 'bottom up', with support, rather than 'top down', with resentment. On this TGAT at least left the options open. It also suggested a further option, that of regional levels which could in turn limit the autonomy of LEAs themselves, but could also act as a still stronger bulwark against dictation from the centre. A determined effort by schools and LEAs now to lay out the groundplan of such local co-operation will be tremendously beneficial in future, if only the effort and resources can be spared at this stage to ensure that it happens.

Applying the strategy to humanities

Once a school policy for assessment has been agreed, the next step must be to work out in detail its application to each aspect of the curriculum. Here curriculum consultants must be by definition involved. Since priority has to be given to the core subjects, both in the sequence in which policy is evolved, and in the status that core subjects carry, it is likely that in many primary schools the relevant consultancies will also be linked with the higher-salaried posts. If some other posts above the main grade are still available, their allocation may be a chance affair, depending on the preferences of the management and the LEA, especially the advisory personnel, and the relative influence exerted by different members of the school staff itself. In such circumstances humanities might gain in some schools and lose in others; but in every case somebody would lose out. Certainly humanities and the arts (except, in some ways, music) do not figure as shortage subjects in primary education and so have a low market value; yet they are to be foundation subjects. It will be lamentable, if almost unavoidable, if head teachers are virtually required to combine an appeal to idealism with the discipline of line management in order to ensure that teachers entrusted as postholders with the foundation subjects achieve, for them, outcomes as satisfactory as those for which others responsible for the core subjects are explicitly rewarded. Those teachers may be able to bask in virtue as well as in the company of children and perhaps the prospect of a good reference for a post elsewhere; but so can those who are paid for their additional responsibilities. I do not pretend that this is an easy issue to resolve; but there are ways of mitigating it.

The choice of policy for that purpose lies with the management. In fact, they are legally obliged to make that choice. On them rests, in practice, the obligation of seeing that the curriculum should be as 'balanced and broadly based' as the 1988 Act and its predecessors require it to be. For this purpose they do not have much room for manoeuvre, but they can do something positive. The easiest course of action, and the one that arises most naturally when market forces are given free play, is the one just indicated. It is also the one most directly calculated to defeat its own object, for it is a recipe for suspicion and resentment in a situation that demands teamwork and collegiality of procedure. A more constructive approach is that of 'twinning' consultancies, with each core subject linked with one of the other foundation subjects (e.g. English with humanities, maths with music, science with PE, or whatever combination may suit a particular school best). This arrangement at least ensures that somebody prominent is responsible for all the foundation subjects and rewarded for their trouble, though there is still the danger that each such consultant might regard their core commitment as the real essence of their job, and the other as an appanage, a minor power, as it were, whose diplomatic interests they were looking after for the time being. If such an arrangement proves unworkable, or even impossible to consider, as may be the case in many smaller schools, then as a last resort the management itself may need to take on consultancy roles so that no part of the curriculum is neglected. In very small schools, of course, even this means of defending the foundation subjects would not necessarily succeed, because the management provides the only personnel from which the core consultancies can be drawn. They themselves may indeed be the whole staff.

All of this applies to the curriculum as a whole. Assessment is an additional issue, in which the foundation subjects may emerge still less favourably. For the existing practice of assessment is largely confined to language and mathematics, so that many teachers feel more at home with those two core subjects than with others. It is likely that assessment in science and technology will be heavily resourced, so that the leeway can be made up. In the arts and physical education, it is not likely that rigorous assessment will be enforced. So once again it is humanities that might be in particular difficulties, with a legal requirement for assessment virtually as rigorous as in the case of the core subjects, but with advice about that assessment in the hands of consultants whose expertise in that quite difficult field has never been built up by substantial guidance.

So it cannot be assumed that the basis for adequate assessment of primary humanities will be universally found. Yet there will be opportunities, in many places, for a constructive approach. Humanities consultants will, in fact, need to pursue a course similar to that of management, and with the support of management. They too will need to plan ahead and not simply wait to be told what to do. For this purpose they will need to talk with their counterparts in other schools. As with management, such talking will bring to life many details of policy, and new ways of looking at policy. It may also add significantly to individual consultants' perception of the role of humanities and its assessment in the primary curriculum. The difficulty in these situations is always that of finding enough time to meet, but here again the support and urging provided by the advisory service are critically important. Unfortunately that support is also irregularly distributed, since some LEAs have no humanities adviser with primary knowledge and experience, and no primary adviser with expertise or personal interest in humanities. Yet, if enough consultants and management members are determined to initiate co-operation of this kind, it does take place.

The next step is one in which curriculum and assessment are both involved. It consists of agreement among those responsible for humanities in local primary and secondary schools about a common set of process strands for both stages – skills, concepts and perhaps attitudes – which can be agreed locally as necessary. If the existing guidelines, such as the HMI subject advice on geography, history and environmental education (HMI 1986; 1988; 1989) are borne in mind, it is likely that the outcome will run fairly close to, but will not be identical with, what will emerge from the working groups and the National Curriculum Council as the new national framework. (see Chapter 5). It may be possible to go further and to establish a bank of information, particularly about the locality, to help all the schools in the area (see e.g. Brown 1988).

Such collaboration can also be extended to form the basis for local moderation of the assessment procedures (DES 1989, para. 9.19). This will be required generally (TGAT 1988a and b) but will present particular issues for each area of the curriculum, including humanities. Some common form of reportage will be required for teachers' monitoring of development along the lines indicated in Chapters 7 and 8 and, if it is to some extent in place before it is legally required, then it will function more easily when it becomes necessary. The mere establishment of personal contact and trust counts for a great deal. The local, and perhaps regional, moderation process will involve readiness to make adjustments and concessions, but it will be easier to achieve this in partnership with those who are already colleagues than to do it in response to administrative directives. It is not yet clear whether these moderation procedures will in practice be arranged separately for each subject at the primary level, or whether they will be conducted on a whole-school basis. If the subject approach becomes established, it will be necessary for humanities consultants and others to be prepared for it. If not, then it will be important for humanities consultants to see to it that their aspect of curriculum is adequately catered for in whatever structure does emerge.

When external relations of this kind have been established, a humanities consultant will have the task of helping other colleagues to understand what is expected of them and to respond accordingly. There may be difficulties here. Some teachers may be reluctant to accept that humanities is to have a distinctive representation in the national curriculum through two foundation subjects and some cross-curricular elements. Some, while accepting in theory that this will and should be the case, will blanch at the work that they think it will involve for them in addition to the core subjects and the arts, physical and religious education. This is also one of the circumstances in which infant teachers might feel particular reluctance to participate in a strategy considered inapplicable to the children in their charge, although in fact it is unlikely that any discrete scrutiny of humanities would be required in the case of the youngest ones. It is even possible that, in some cases, there may be resentment at the responsibility entrusted for this purpose to what may be a relatively inexperienced member of staff. These points of view are not mere obstructionism. There is likely to be genuine anxiety among quite experienced teachers when they are required to undertake something so new to them. The only way for a humanities consultant to proceed is by reminding colleagues, with persuasive good humour, that these are now legal requirements, and to show by example and by explicit advice how curriculum and assessment in humanities can be carried out. For this purpose a consultant is entitled to the support of management, and to the exercise of leadership by management. Incidentally, if colleagues prove too reluctant to innovate, and management does not require them to do so, the national curriculum itself will inevitably act as a change agent. If, on the other hand, there are consultants, supported by management, who prove too arbitrary or dictatorial in their methods, the

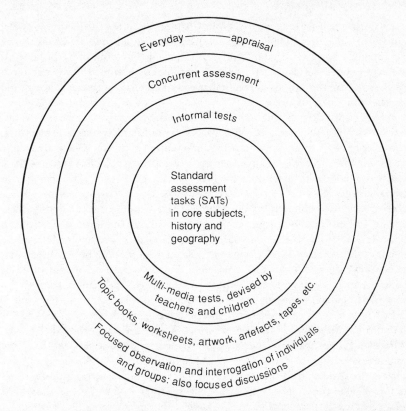

Figure 6.1 Focusing assessment in primary humanities in the new national framework

involvement of other schools and of LEAs in the moderation process should act as some check.

Consultants themselves may be expected to do more than share ideas with other consultants and external advisers and pass them on to colleagues. They should have their own ideas. Here, derived from the general principles outlined in Chapter 4 and in particular from the notion of the focusing of assessment, is one that may be suitable for an enabling curriculum.

A suggested plan

This plan involves the circles outlined in Chapter 4. Figure 6.1 indicates how the focusing of assessment outlined in Figure 4.1 could be adapted to primary humanities.

The low-level, continuing procedure in the outer circle, designated *everyday appraisal* in a sense modelled on Tough's use of the term 'appraisal' (see Chapter 4) is intended to monitor systematically every child's progress in the process strands and knowledge considered central to that child's part in a scheme of work in primary humanities. Everyday appraisal should be both diagnostic and formative in intention: it will be remembered from Chapter 4 that the distinction between diagnosis of difficulties and planning of work is not a simple one. It should also be self-referenced, so that each child's progress is profiled in terms of his or her own previous attainments and interests, and not in comparison with arbitrary criteria or with class norms, though the general capacities of children of the same age would be borne in mind.

Everyday appraisal should also be reinforced by *concurrent assessment*. This, which is roughly the same as what has been traditionally termed 'marking', involves comments, orally or in writing, on children's 'products', whether these are written work, artwork, or any other form of expression. The quantity of these 'products' would, of course, be greater as children grow older. The distinction between concurrent assessment and everyday appraisal is that the former can be looked at when the children are not there, so that it can be more intensive, less frequent, and more suited to summative assessment, although it too can be both diagnostic and formative in outcome. These 'products' can in fact constitute landmarks in children's development, related where possible to particular Attainment Targets (DES 1989, para. 6.9), and can be used subsequently as encouragement and stimulus as they move from class to class and even from school to school. It can be sobering to realize what one was once capable of doing, and to recall what comments were once made about it. It can also be encouraging to refer to it if, during subsequent years, that earlier work is ignored or dismissed. To many children and their parents, indeed, this concurrently assessed work *is* the humanities curriculum. This is what they keep in their desks or their drawers; this is what is displayed on the walls; this is what they take home when it is finished (and could well keep until later). This, too, is the arena of activity that will be transformed by Attainment Targets, Profile Components and Programmes of Study, but will remain of prime importance; a key aspect of growth toward self-assessment.

A school policy needs to make a place for both everyday appraisal and concurrent assessment and to follow up both with an effective system of record-keeping. How this can be done is discussed in Chapter 8, 9, 11 and 12. As Marsden (1976) indicates in the case of secondary geography, these procedures will also need to be supplemented by occasional positive *testing* of knowledge and of the transfer of skills and concepts. In Chapter 9 the nature and possibilities of such tests are considered. It is not suggested that they should be portentous in character; on the contrary, they can provide an excellent opportunity for a light-hearted approach to summative assessment, with important diagnostic and formative aspects too. What matters is that the staff as a whole should know just why testing is introduced, and that this understanding should be shared with parents and children and indeed governors too, so that they can appreciate its justification.

Chapter 10 also gives brief attention to the one element in any consultant's strategy that will not be optional, namely the *national testing programme* itself. Here, Standard Assessment Tasks, however stimulating and creative they may be, will become the characteristic mode. Teachers will be obliged to carry out the stipulated procedures. Here the role of management and of the consultant will not be to formulate policy so much as to translate it for colleagues, while endeavouring to ensure that it does not dominate the curriculum, especially at the reporting ages of 7 and 11. At present no detail can be conjectured about the actual procedures to be prescribed. When that information becomes available, there will be no shortage of guidance, though, as was indicated in Chapter 5, there may well be a shortage of time in which to absorb and apply its details.

Evidently, there will be no shortage of tasks for humanities consultants to carry out. The advent of the new national framework may have many consequences for their role but will certainly not lead to its abolition. There will be plenty for everybody to do within every primary school. I hope that the suggestions in the following chapters may be of some help in the initiation of that activity. Experience of curricular innovation warns, too, that progress towards a goal of change is rarely uniform and often meets with opposition that comes to a head, for one reason or another, after a few months. If this crisis is successfully met, developments thereafter should run smoothly. This could happen either to the innovations now being planned for primary humanities, or to the wider question of school strategy as a whole. It is a problem that may need to be met by advisers and teachers with vigour, tact and imagination. However, granted the national context, the proposed framework is bound to prevail in general, if not in detail. The hope must be that problems will be overcome amicably and constructively, rather than by confrontational means. In Chapter 12 I shall indicate some ways in which understanding of the processes of innovation could be taken further. Meanwhile, some further suggestions will be made about how assessment can actually be carried out in schools.

7 Influences on teachers' assessments

The Task Group on Assessment and Testing (TGAT) *Report*, and Department of Education and Science (DES) opinion as expressed in the *Policy into Practice* document (DES 1989) expect teachers to take a full part in assessment throughout children's schooling, with regular observation closely linked to teaching. The *Report* also recognizes that the confidence of teachers must be won if the national programme of assessment is to be successfully carried out. Chapters 4 and 6 have already indicated the importance of teachers' regular activities. In Chapters 8–11 I shall try to show how teachers can actually carry out those activities. That function will make considerable demands on teachers' professional skills and powers of judgement. Therefore, some attention should first be paid to some influences that may, unintentionally, affect their statements and opinions about children and their attainments.

The effect of learning about assessment

One of those influences is that teachers are not, and cannot be, totally objective assessors. That is a social fact, not a criticism of teachers. They are always learning more about children and about assessment. Therefore, what teacher M says about child A in relation to task Y is likely to differ from what she said about child A in relation to task X, not only because Y differs from X, or because child A has grown and developed a little between X and Y, but because teacher M has herself learned more about and become more skilled in assessment. A further complication arises when we have to consider what teacher N says about child A in relation to task Z, perhaps in the next school year, because now the difference in teaching styles between the two teachers and child A's response to each may also influence the outcome. If N is also more experienced than M, their respective initial 'baselines' for assessment will be different, and they may both move forward from those different baselines at different rates, so that they are not looking at either the child or the task from identical standpoints. The final complication arises when, in addition to these disparities, we have to consider assessment of child B by M and N on the same tasks, or on different ones. For B may trigger quite different responses from A in both M and N. Yet it is easy to establish a whole system of assessment which entirely overlooks such discrepancies or treats them on one simplistic level, such as by saying that N is a stiffer marker than M and ignoring the effects of longer experience.

This influence on teachers' assessments remains as a warning against setting too much or too permanent store on individual teachers' statements about Levels in the new national framework. Local moderation can reduce, but not totally eliminate, discrepancies of this kind. More effective, as a means of countering differences in the capacity to assess, is a policy according to which individual teachers are not sole judges of individual children's work over a prolonged period. A should not depend exclusively on M for assessment of X, Y and Z.

Assessment as negotiation

Everyday appraisal and, to some extent, concurrent assessment involve an element of negotiation. That does not, of course, mean simply proposing an assessment of children and then asking their agreement before confirming it. For teachers are bound to know, from their much greater experience and expertise, more about the quality of children's performance than the children do, and, as was emphasized in Chapter 4, children expect teachers to be experts in this as in other matters. Yet there is a sense in which negotiation is not only inevitable, but desirable, as an element in assessment.

It is inevitable because, as Becker emphasized in his own study of *Making the Grade* mentioned in Chapter 1 (Becker *et al.* 1968), assessment necessarily involves processes of social interaction. Whenever a teacher watches children working, asks them questions, draws them aside, encourages or rebukes them, or just looks meaningfully at them, their work is affected in one way or another. The effect varies according to age, and according to the degree of personal and cultural rapport between teacher and children, and also, as ORACLE (Galton *et al.* 1980) and Bennett, Desforges *et al.* (1984) have emphasized, according to teaching and learning styles. In addition, the matching of assessment to product is itself a matter for negotiation, implicit if not explicit. If 'she' expects too many products, indignation will be unbounded; if too few, then the impression gains ground that the children's efforts are undervalued and motivation falls away. So some sort of class norm of production (as distinct from a norm of performance) becomes established; not a national norm, but one that varies from class to class and from school to school. One class may have a voracious appetite for output, while another can collectively manage only a little.

For each of those classes, the establishment of a norm of production is an important part of the process of 'making the grade', because it affects the quantity of output on which concurrent assessment is based. So one class may have more to show than another, though the amount shown by individuals may vary greatly in both. It would be a realistic recognition of differences, however regrettable, within primary education to admit that the first of those classes would probably also show a higher average quality of work. It would also be realistic to consider that the gap between the mean performances of the two classes cannot be a matter for smug complacency on the part of the school, the teacher, the parents or the children involved in the first class, nor can it be reduced by sloganizing or pretence or by threatening the school, the teacher, the parents or the children involved in the second, but only by a sustained and well-resourced major strategy. However, this is where the temptation to fall into norm-referenced assessment must be resisted. For there will be individuals in both classes who do not conform to the general pattern. Thus there may well be some children in the second class whose work is comparable in *quality* with the best in the first class, but is less in *quantity*, because of the differences in norms of production negotiated with the two classes as a whole. Of course, this can be offset by a teacher permitting more work on an individual, 'enrichment', basis to potential high performers in the second class, but this too would exemplify discretion and negotiation. Thus it is inevitable that the outcomes of negotiation must be taken into account when assessments are made. Simple, across-the-board comparisons would necessarily be misleading.

I have already claimed that negotiation in assessment is not only inevitable but also desirable. That may seem to contradict the statement that teachers have the final say about assessment. It does not. Negotiation is a necessary part of learning self-assessment which, as indicated in Chapter 4, is a major justification for undertaking any assessment at all. Children may, in the short term, find it fun to try to fool the teacher with counterfeit work or to wheedle a better opinion and may thus try to practise negotiation of a dubious nature. A devil-may-care bravado may be put on to impress their peers. Yet that bravado often serves only to conceal deep-seated anxiety. In the longer run they, for the most part, really do want to know how they are doing. Once a teacher has made it clear that she is capable in everyday appraisal and concurrent assessment and more than a match for illegitimate tactics, then genuine negotiation becomes possible. Children can be asked their opinion about a piece of work and then can compare it with what the teacher says. If an individual has made what he or she agrees is a mess of a particular piece of work, then there can be negotiation about whether it should be repeated or indeed whether assessment of that piece can be traded in for a more demanding assessment of the next, when perhaps a more searching kind of self-assessment is required: 'No, David. I mean, have you really said why you think those farmers believe that they have to burn the forest?' In such ways negotiation can and should be built in to everyday appraisal and concurrent assessment so as to lead children towards a more realistic, if occasionally rueful, understanding of their own progress. They can become actively involved in deciding what is a good piece of work, and why, and what are the best features in it.

In some schools the process of negotiation is more systematic than this. Children are regularly required to state, after a piece of work, whether they individually have worked as well as they should. If they have taken part in a corporate study, they may be asked how they feel about the group's collective achievement and whether they, and the other children, have made an effective contribution. The success of such a policy depends, of course, on the prior establishment of suitable rapport, otherwise it can degenerate into a boring and meaningless exercise. Sometimes, too, teachers make parallel observations about each child, in the child's record, and then discuss any discrepancies with the child, on the assumption that the teacher's verdict is much more experienced than that of the child, but is still not infallible. The head teacher and the parents may see the outcome too, and in fully developed schemes of assessment they may also contribute to it. Where trust has once been established, this is the logical extension of negotiation in assessment, and the resulting improvement in children's motivation for their work and engagement in it can be impressive.

Professional knowledge about children's capabilities

One point mentioned in the discussion of the effects of learning about assessment was that teachers differ in their understanding of children's cognitive growth. Some display increased understanding through articulated thinking about children's learning; others prefer a more intuitive approach; each could learn from the other. It is a consideration that applies also to negotiation. For the confidence and capacity in assessment that teachers need in order to win the trust of children, as a basis for negotiation in assessment and indeed in curriculum planning, must be based partly on what teachers know about children in general.

This in turn gives rise to what can easily become a paradox. For a general idea of what, say, seven-year-olds are capable of doing soon becomes norm-referencing by the back door. Although none of them is likely to be capable of thinking of the national economy as a major concept, it does not follow that none of them is able to see what a local bank is for, or even how it relates to the bank's central facilities. Nor does it follow that every one of them can grasp the function of money. It is important to distinguish between *descriptive norms* which act as a general guide to teachers about the kind of work that can usually be undertaken with children of a particular age, and *assessment norms* which imply that all the children in a particular class ought to reach a certain stage in understanding, while any who go beyond that are culpably precocious. Descriptive norms do not and should not imply assessment norms. Parents are justifiably concerned about their own children's progress and tend to judge this in terms of norms within classes and schools as well as in the population as a whole. So do children; they soon work out who is 'brainy' and who is 'thick' in their class. Insistence by teachers on self-referencing may fly in the face of the social psychology of the class group as well as of society at large. The TGAT *Report* is helpful here, because it distinguishes clearly between levels of achievement and reporting ages and throws all its emphasis on criterion-referencing and quality of individual development. That is just as well, for in an enabling curriculum norm-referenced assessment must be opposed, in the long-term interests of all the children, and if that is to be achieved, teachers need plenty of support to counter the lay person's implicit belief in norm-referencing.

Teachers' personality and belief characteristics

Some teachers probably take more readily than others to the notion of self-referenced assessment. That may arise through inclination as well as through experience and may reflect deep-seated differences in personality and beliefs. The same may apply to readiness to conduct negotiation. The Bennett and ORACLE studies brought out differences in teaching styles in relation to pupils' learning, and it may well be that there are also different assessment styles related to individual make-up and professional ideology. For example, some teachers may derive particular satisfaction from the bustle of constant interaction with children and may feel that any requirement to assess their progress acts as a barrier between teacher and class. Others may prefer to maintain some sort of social distance between the children and themselves, seeing assessment as a symbol of that social distance. Again, some may feel happier with the summative, verdict-passing aspects of assessment while others prefer to emphasize diagnostic and formative purposes. All these issues reflect teachers' views of children and of themselves, and are bound to influence any scheme of assessment in practice. As with the effect of differences in the capacity to assess, there will be a tendency for the effect of different personalities and beliefs to cancel out over the years and over the children as a whole, a process that will again be assisted by moderation procedures, but it remains important to take such matters into account when placing emphasis on what a particular teacher says about a particular piece of work from a particular child: what M says about A's X.

Bias and stereotype

These personality and belief differences may merge into more general cultural attitudes that can also affect assessment in practice. This, at least, is an aspect of assessment that does not lack publicity. Teachers have been researched into for some years now in order to locate bias against particular children on grounds of social class, social attitudes, ethnic grouping and (most prevalent since it affects half the children) gender, and also in relation to special needs. Partly because of the way in which research studies have been designed, investigators have usually found some evidence of what they were looking for, though not always as much as they expected to find. Other possible categories of disadvantage, such as rural/urban differences, have not been given such extensive scrutiny. More recently, attention has been focused more adequately on the actual social processes that influence teachers' 'typification' or thinking about individual children, and their consequent actions (e.g. Delamont 1987; Pollard 1987; Troman 1988). Where social habits and thought habits have become entrenched in teachers' everyday procedures, they are bound also to affect how children are assessed, all the more so if the assessment is grudgingly regarded as an external demand imposed on an already overcrowded and stressful occupational role. Ironically, the more teachers are externally urged or even cajoled into watching themselves for bias and stereotype, the more they are likely to react negatively. The most successful attempts to eliminate stereotype and bias in assessment are likely to be those that arise from teachers' own collective efforts, rather than from obligatory awareness training imposed, like the national framework though with very different motivation, from outside.

The danger of considering influences on teachers' assessments

All of these issues are important to the actual processes of everyday appraisal and concurrent assessment. Yet there is a danger in stressing their importance. Emphasis on the subtleties and difficulties involved in teachers' participation in the national framework of assessment could have the effect of strengthening the hands of those who would prefer straight, no-nonsense testing as the basis for national assessment. Surely, it might be argued, that would avoid all these pitfalls of subjectivity and lead to the sort of sane monitoring that the Education Reform Act was designed to achieve. To accept that argument would be to deny the whole weight of evidence against reliance on testing that has been built up over a century and has been accepted by TGAT. It would also fly in the face of the principles of an enabling curriculum, as well as belittling the richness of evidence that stems from continuous contact with children in many situations. Yet it would be counterproductive to deny that difficulties exist. The only honest and effective policy is to admit and identify those difficulties and to develop means of minimizing or eliminating them. This, once again, is an issue in which LEA initiatives, especially in preparation for locally based moderation, can be critically important. Teacher participation, albeit in an improved mode, must be preserved.

8 Everyday appraisal and concurrent assessment

In this chapter and the next, attention will be focused on teachers' assessment activities, the ones in which the considerations raised in Chapter 7 are relevant. These comprise the concentric circles in Figure 6.1. From the outer circle inwards, the process of assessment becomes less continuous, more sharply focused, and more distinct from teachers' daily activities. Chapter 8 is concerned with the two outer circles, everyday appraisal and concurrent assessment, which are thus the ones which bulk largest in teachers' professional lives. They are also the ones which the Task Group on Assessment and Testing (TGAT) expected to constitute the basis of teacher's contribution to the national assessment procedures. Of the two, everyday appraisal offers the more complete, and concurrent assessment the more tangible, account of children's progress.

It is necessary at this stage to draw attention to Appendix 2. That Appendix embodies a scheme of work in primary humanities that was designed as part of an enabling curriculum in accordance with the principles of *Place, Time and Society 8–13*, and published in much the same form in the revised edition of my wife's *History in Primary Schools* (Joan Blyth 1989). It could be part of a possible national framework built on the principles of an enabling curriculum, though for that reason it would probably not fit into the national curriculum that we are to have. Nevertheless this scheme will be used to illustrate the approaches to everyday appraisal and concurrent assessment outlined in the present chapter and will also be referred to in relation to teacher-made tests in Chapter 9. In Chapter 10 one of the topics in the scheme will be more fully examined in relation to assessment as a whole, and in Chapter 11 it will again be mentioned briefly in relation to curriculum continuity and record-keeping. In this way the general suggestions to be made about appraisal and assessment can be given more point and substance.

Everyday appraisal

Observation

No teacher can teach without observing. Few teachers can manage the degree of focused and formative observation shown by Armstrong (1981) or Rowland

(1984). All teachers will be required to derive sufficient meaningful information from their everyday contact with children to be able to contribute effectively to their assessment. For this purpose they will need to focus their observations. This in turn means that in every topic or theme in humanities, or incorporating humanities, there should be emphasis on the most salient process strands – skills, concepts, task procedures and attitudes – that figure in the planned work. This in turn means that teachers need to analyse, in advance, which these are likely to be, and then to amend their analysis as the work proceeds.

Suppose that a class of seven-year-olds is looking at the topic 'Folktales', as outlined in Appendix 2. They begin by listening to a folktale from Homeric times, and then doing some work based on it, such as making up a little poem illustrated by artwork. Then this is followed by a contrasted folktale from their region of England or Wales, and they do something rather different this time, such as acting out the story. At that stage there is a brief class discussion about the two tales. How did we get to know them? Are they true? If not, are they still important? When and where were they first told; and how do we know that? Can we find those places on the big map, using the gazetteer index, and can we see where those folktales come on this time-line? The final part of the topic could be the selection of a current incident, perhaps from the class's or the school's own doings or else from some current happening in sport or society, and the making of a collective ballad or a set of individual ones about that event, ending with a brief but quiet reflection on why it might be that folktales have survived but our story probably won't.

In the course of this scheme of work children will have been busy writing, drawing, moving, discussing and creating something new, and in each sphere their general skills will have been in action and observed. In addition, they will have used two kinds of skills particular to humanities. One of these is fairly obvious: the skills of mapping and time-location will have been introduced, with emphasis at this age on finding places and on putting events in the correct sequence. Such skills could be called *overt skills*, and any systematic observation would entail looking at how individual children master them; some will not and will require particular help and advice. In addition there will be *implicit skills* such as capacity to reason and to question: 'Suppose somebody who wrote that book made up the story?' It is less easy to plan observation for that purpose, because it may come up at any time without warning. Striking examples can and should be noted after any discussion, though for a teacher this is one of the most difficult situations in which to make focused observations because, with children at this age, the teacher has inevitably to remain centre-stage during discussions.

Alongside skill development can be found concept formation. The concepts peculiar to folktales for seven-year-olds are limited, but they include the label 'Folktales' itself, the idea of story-telling, an extension of the ideas of 'long ago' and 'far away', and the mobilization of concepts in order to compose something about events today. Children's use of these terms and ideas should be watched for. At the same time, social/emotional aspects should not be neglected. The choice of event for the final ballad stage is obviously important, for, if it were directed against any individual or group, it could trigger reactions that are unhelpful either in teaching or in assessment. Meanwhile any unexpected instances of tittering or incomprehension or tension or terror should be noted, for all of these have some kind of significance for learning. It was probably wise of the TGAT *Report* to advise against reporting attitudes, but it is essential that teachers should bear such matters in mind, both formatively for planning further work and also diagnostically to cater for individuals.

The extent of actual knowledge involved in 'Folktales' is not great, but it is important that it should be grasped. The nature of such tales is itself helpful here, for they would not have survived if they had not been structured in such a way as to chime in with folk memory. Children take to stories with that kind of structure and are themselves likely to insist on getting the detail right and remembering it in exactly the correct sequence. In the course of telling and retelling, as they were used to doing in the infant years, children come to retain folktales, some of them for a lifetime. As they learn, teachers can observe how effective that learning has been.

All of these matters can be noted through focused observation that requires no other kind of planning. However, the normal experience is that only some children pick themselves out during such observation: this one knew exactly what to do; that one hadn't a clue; those two were so uninvolved and silly that they had to be made to sit right in front of the teacher; one was so tense and upset (though trying to conceal it) that he/she might have cried or felt sick if we had gone on any longer. Yet when the teacher came to recall the humanities or topic-work time that day, half the class had done nothing that could be remembered. Nevertheless all of them have to figure somehow in everyday appraisal, and so it may be necessary from time to time to supplement focused observation with something more directed. Two strategies for that purpose are interrogation and focused discussion.

Interrogation

By interrogation I mean more than chance questioning, but rather something like the research worker's focused interview. In the 'Folktales' example it might involve talking to perhaps four or six children sitting round a table or, if necessary, taking them specially aside, and asking them particular questions about the tales, shaped in such a way as to probe their understanding: 'Let's see which of you can find where Crete is. What did we have to remember about looking places up on the map?' It does not take very long to introduce that kind of interrogation into everyday procedure, but it does make it more possible to check up on the understanding of the less evident members of the class.

Focused discussion

This is a similar and very familiar procedure which may involve more of the class and is intended to concentrate on particular ideas. It may involve introducing new ideas, for example in the final section of the 'Folktales' example where a ballad or something similar is being planned. Questions are directed to particular children chosen because they represent gaps in the teacher's existing tally of observation. Such discussion is, of course, a piece of teaching as well as a piece of everyday appraisal; in fact, it is never possible to distinguish the one entirely from the other, and TGAT stressed this as an essential ingredient of the national strategy: standard assessment tasks are to be part of teaching rather than something separate.

Another example: 'Workplaces'

The actual array of skills, concepts, task procedures and attitudes that can figure in everyday appraisal obviously varies according to the age of the children and the nature of the topic. A quite different set of process strands would be involved in handling another of the topics from the scheme in Appendix 2, namely 'Workplaces' with children aged 9. Once again, the strands would be specified beforehand and modified as the scheme developed. General study and other skills would again be involved, though now at a more demanding level. Among particular aspects to be chosen for appraisal, overt skills would include interviewing, mapping, and also the manipulative and practical skills involved in production in a mini-enterprise. Implicit skills would again include the capacity to ask questions and to formulate hypotheses and generalizations about economic life in the shape of a single workplace. Concepts to be monitored would include those related to production and to distribution as well as the more specific ones applying to the particular workplace itself. The grasp of task procedures can now be added to the list for observation, since the organization of a mini-enterprise requires observable collective behaviour on the children's part. Finally, knowledge of the actual workplace or workplaces studied can be plumbed during informal talk during or about visits.

The combination of focused observation, interrogation and focused discussion used for 'Workplaces' may differ from the arrangements found useful in 'Folktales' for younger children, but the idea of combining them remains the same. It could be applied, with adaptations, to any of the themes listed in Appendix 2, and maybe some teachers would like to try their hand at working out how everyday appraisal could be used in one of those or, better still, in a scheme of work that is now in progress or being planned in their own school. Other topics from Appendix 2 are also mentioned in the following section which complements the discussion of everyday appraisal.

Concurrent assessment

In any system of national assessment which allows for a substantial but moderated initiative on the part of teachers, concurrent assessment is likely to be the most salient component. It is less subjective in nature than everyday appraisal, but more flexible than any programme of testing can be. It requires particular attention.

The difference between everyday appraisal and concurrent assessment was indicated in Chapter 6. Concurrent assessment is take-away assessment. It is something that can be carried out on the children's products when the producers are not there. It may have to be done in the staffroom, perhaps spiced with occasional bursts of laughter or astonishment for the apparent benefit of colleagues. It usually involves prior negotiation about the nature of the product, and subsequent negotiation about its quality, but it is something that a teacher does initially away from the children.

Because it originates through planning and negotiation, any product of this kind is unique to a particular scheme of work; and that will probably continue to be the case within the national curriculum. Sometimes and in some situations there will be written work of various kinds on worksheets or in topic books, suitably illustrated and presented; these are likely to be the most prevalent instances. At other times, especially with younger children, the emphasis will be on artwork or modelling with, say, an appropriate written sentence. Occasionally there can be a taped discussion or a printout from a word processor. In a world of untold luxury, there might be an occasional video-recording in which individual participation could be noted. Each of these possible forms of product requires consideration. It may be useful, in discussing them, to include references to concurrent assessment that might be expected in the two topics already considered: 'Folktales' (age 7) and 'Workplaces' (age 9).

Topic books

These come in many shapes and sizes and embody many purposes. A usual one is made of sugar-paper sheets with a cover designed by the child, in which everything that this child has written or tried to write on a particular theme or themes is entered. Teachers often assist younger children in the process of sticking artwork or written work into the book. The contents comprise everything from drawings with words or sentences from younger children, to painstaking pages written and illustrated by top juniors. Topic books contain what children put of themselves into a piece of work and deserve serious consideration.

One kind of consideration must be that of general quality. Questions of neatness, legibility, presentation and that bugbear, spelling, are not negligible and it is a legitimate expectation that these should show steady improvement on a self-referenced basis as children grow older. It is also reasonable to expect that children will grow in appreciation of the need to take these issues seriously, as their self-assessment develops. The danger is that relatively too much attention may be paid to these general quality issues, at the expense of the particular aspects of humanities that figure in the topic. For the purpose of assessing humanities topics must be, largely, to assess understanding and endeavour in humanities.

For that purpose, as for everyday appraisal, it is necessary first to be clear about the process strands and knowledge involved in a particular topic, as Tann (1988: Appendix) and Kerry and Eggleston (1988) emphasize, and also about how these could figure in the topic book. For example, in 'Folktales' it might be expected that Susan would make a drawing to represent Icarus, or Robin Hood, with an explanatory label or sentence. The drawing and writing would often be accepted in the rather wispy and irregular idiom to be expected from seven-year-olds, but the ideas behind them would be scrutinized purposefully. If Icarus were portrayed as an astronaut, or Robin Hood as an assistant to Batman, that would not do.

The next step would be important: what sort of comment should be made to Susan, and how? For lower juniors, and for infants, it is rarely appropriate to write much in the way of comments, though some symbolic mark or seal of approval devised in collaboration with the children to indicate that a piece of work has been seen and accepted, such as the smiley face that I have seen used – and its opposite – may be useful as a means of cementing 'we-feeling' between teacher and class. Actual comments of a meaningful kind have to be oral, and that means finding time for the comment within the teaching programme, even if the concurrent assessment itself can be done outside. This is where negotiation, and indeed the other issues raised in Chapter 7, are important. If a brief word with Susan – all that can be spared – is to be effective, then it must be couched in terms and in a tone of voice that communicates with her. This is a skill that teachers acquire anew with each new class that comes to them, and often they show an almost uncanny capacity to do so with all, or nearly all, the children. This is necessary for any part of the teaching, of course, but also for concurrent assessment. For if the teacher has the right rapport with Susan, then Susan will be motivated to make a genuine reply, and it is that reply, rather than her questionable Icarus or Robin Hood, that is the basis of her assessment. It is diagnostic in so far as it shows what she has or has not understood. It is formative in so far as it indicates what help or advice she needs. It may also be summative if this is her final effort in that topic.

In 'Workplaces' more could be expected. Each child could report on an aspect of a class visit and could perhaps also illustrate and write about his or her own contribution to a class mini-enterprise. Written comments would be more in place with upper juniors, though still with oral supplementation. At this age-level, too, a sharp focusing of process strands and knowledge would be necessary as a basis for assessment.

For example, suppose that the class visit to a workplace had involved the social skill of interviewing. Jason had been detailed to ask questions of the quality supervisor and had done so, duly entering answers on his clipboard. The teacher would set Jason on the task of interpreting what he had found out, reminding him to comment on how he found out and how far he thought it would tell the whole story. Then, in reading over Jason's account, she would expect more than a description of the quality-control supervisor's work. She would also expect to find some reference to the reliability of Jason's own evidence. Similarly, if each of the children wrote a small description of the class exhibition or presentation to the rest of the school, the teacher would look for more than 'We did this and then we did that'. There would need to be at least some reference to the small number of economic ideas emphasized. Then, as with the younger children in 'Folktales', time would need to be found for at least a passing, but meaningful, oral comment and brief discussion, for in that way the measure of the children's understanding can be more directly revealed.

Of course, as such topics become more complex with increasing age, the actual process of concurrent assessment also becomes more complex. It should, increasingly, require children to consider and evaluate different accounts and interpretations of events, places and situations, past and present, and to deploy higher thinking skills and toleration of ambiguity. It also becomes more open to the influences described in Chapter 7.

Worksheets

Worksheets often figure in topic books, though they can have an independent existence too. Their distinctive feature is that they are largely predetermined. They can cover anything from straight recall questions to opportunities for quite ambitious lateral 'transfer' thinking. Indeed, so they should, for their potential is only fulfilled if they afford much more than the humanities counterpart of a set of arithmetical examples. Jason's clipboard probably carried a worksheet prepared by his teacher, or better still by the teacher in concert with the children. It might begin by covering some of the factual data from the particular workplace and some questions requiring skills such as sequencing and ordering, but could go on to provoke higher thinking and interpretative skills and concept formation. One advantage of worksheets is that they can be closely tailored to the particular process strands and knowledge involved in a topic and thus quite directly be used in assessing individual children's grasp. It is for such purposes that they should be devised, and not as a vademecum for everything to do with humanities, one reason why they have sometimes acquired a bad name.

Maps and time-lines

These are so directly linked with basic skills in humanities that they merit special discussion. Mention was made of both in relation to 'Folktales' and 'Workplaces' when discussing everyday appraisal, but neither would be sufficiently central to those particular topics to figure significantly in their concurrent assessment. For this purpose another topic from the Appendix 2 scheme will be more appropriate, namely 'Knowing Our Place' with children aged 10–11.

The aim of this topic is to bring together the different humanities perspectives in a synoptic study of the locality around the school. The physical configuration of the locality must first be understood. This can be approached through group work involving compilation of maps showing, in simplified form, the surface geology and landforms, rivers and streams (always important) and major plant-life distributions, and then different aspects of local economic and social life. These aspects would include settlement and housing, land use, transport, and cultural features such as civic, political, religious and leisure provision, and a sensitive reference to social differentiation. These maps would show the locality not as a discrete unity, but in relation outwards to other places, and would thus collectively convey the key concept of interrelation, between features but also between places, when the maps were compared, and related to a local model made by the children.

The historical perspective should also be considered, partly because it is so closely involved in the present landscape and social scene. One useful device for this purpose is the making of a 'historical map' in which surviving archaeological, architectural and other remains of earlier historical periods are plotted, much as remnants of different Gothic styles are often shown by different shading or colouring on plans of castles or cathedrals. Meanwhile significant local events, distant and recent, and periods of time such as the years during which the railway was the chief means of local transport, can be entered by children on a cumulative time-line that can be expanded into a time-chart.

Each child would contribute to these collaborative maps and the time-chart something of their own work: an illustration, or a piece of writing. In addition, each would be asked to select one local feature, or incident, or issue, past or present, that interests them particularly, and to illustrate it with a map and time-line of their own. In this way the teacher can learn not only what each child knows about the locality, and about how to use map and time skills, but also something about the child.

Taped teacherless discussions

Here, the medium for assessment would be tape recording, set up for a small group of children holding a discussion in a separate room or bay. Such discussions represent a rather different kind of product from those hitherto mentioned. By definition, no child contributes continuously to a discussion, though some may come perilously near to doing so. For those who have plenty to say, a taped discussion represents a concentrated form of what emerges from focused discussion within everyday appraisal. The teacher can listen and note their performance without herself having to be a participant in the discourse. For the others, the more mousey ones who contribute little to the actual talk, concurrent assessment becomes more of a problem because they may have ideas which they cannot manage to inject into the conversation. Or their ideas may be concentrated into a single sentence that could easily be overlooked when the tape is played back. So this form of concurrent assessment can be used only to supplement the others and not as itself the main basis. For that supplementary purpose, however, it may be very valuable, revealing in some children a capacity for thought and indeed for leadership in thought that, sobering though this may be for teachers' self-esteem, does not emerge when teachers are around (Biott and Clough 1983; Biott 1984; Prisk 1987). A further reason for using taped discussions is that this may be the only practicable way of actually accommodating the assessment of all the children within the time and space available.

In respect of the content to be assessed, this depends on how the taped discussion is set up. Probably the most useful approach is for the teacher to set a provocative task and then leave the children to it. 'Folktales' might figure at too young an age to warrant use of taped teacherless discussions, but in 'Workplaces' this approach could be readily used. For example, the teacher could present a small group with a damning report on the product of the class mini-enterprise and then go away, leaving them to make a fight-back answer. The various kinds of response could reveal much about attitudes as well as about deployment of task procedures and concepts and use of cognitive skills. Discussion of a proposed bypass, involving demolition of seventeenth-century cottages, could achieve much the same effect in 'Knowing Our Place'.

Assessment of other products

Some place must be found within any assessment strategy for the more unusual and ambitious kinds of product. If, in 'Workplaces', one child produces an elaborate but accurate flow chart of processes and can explain just what it is about, credit must be given both for the flow chart and for the explanation. Similarly, if in 'Knowing Our Place' there emerges a model farm or church, lovingly and almost accurately reproduced, that too must be rewarded. In some topics, such as the perennial 'history of transport', individual or group models may figure as a regular feature rather than as a *tour de force* by a few. In all these cases there is a great incentive to reward the artefact itself, simply because it is so impressive and because the children who made it would be so disappointed if it were not fully appreciated. Yet, as a part of concurrent assessment in humanities, it must be combined with searching questions about why that farm or that church is important, and not just an agreement that it looks nice and is fun to copy.

Much the same is true of board games that children may design, and of another and, at present, still more unusual product, namely insertions on a computer programme. Where children can make a game embodying the essence of what they have learned, this constitutes an excellent basis for concurrent assessment. When they can secure a printout of responses to a stimulus program, or, better still, make a program of their own, this can be a genuine example of concurrent assessment for an age of information technology. Here again, there is a need to ensure that the procedure achieves, like the board game, more than mere recall. It must be designed in such a way as to call for thinking skills too.

Running records

Everyday appraisal can, and should, do more than provide formative guidance and a vague impression that children are doing nicely. It should also contribute meaningfully to knowledge about their progress and development in the process strands and understanding associated with primary humanities as a whole. Concurrent assessment should in turn sharpen this knowledge in a more focused way. If full advantage is to be taken of the outcomes of everyday appraisal and concurrent assessment, some sort of record-keeping is essential. This should be started while a scheme of work is actually under way, and not left to chance or memory alone, since memory, however vivid, soon becomes overlaid with new events.

For this purpose, it is important to have *running records* of a kind that a teacher can use for her own purposes. Most teachers would prefer to design their own. There is also a place, and will in future be a still more established place, for more systematic records, and in Chapter 11 attention will be paid to how these more systematic records can be compiled, using the running records as part of the necessary basis. For the present, it is the running records themselves that must be considered. Irrespective of a teacher's preferences for their nature, certain general principles should be borne in mind.

The first step should be taken at the very start, for it records the *baselining* referred to in Chapter 4. It is important to take full account, at the beginning, of every child's starting-point. This would be done almost without question in primary physical education or arts education and is just as important in humanities. Here is one situation in which the establishment of a national set of requirements for recording progress will be of positive value, for there is likely to be, within any school, a reservoir of information about individual children's progress in the core subjects and, later, in the foundation subjects too. So, in designing any particular piece of work, a teacher could gain a fair impression of the minimum to be expected from a class, and of the individuals above that minimum (and occasionally below it). This is *general baselining*. When the national assessment in history and geography is under way, it should be possible to extend that information to cover competences and understandings more directly involved in humanities. Therefore, the actual baselining to be carried out with the children directly in connection with a particular topic can be focused specifically on the topic itself. (A more formal summary of this same procedure is given in Chapter 11, where it is discussed in relation to systematic school records.)

This *specific baselining* can be approached through general discussion and questioning, supplemented by particular questions beamed to individuals on the topic, and followed by the first piece of concurrent assessment so that, as with general baselining, a picture again emerges of a minimum equipment, interest and enthusiasm of the class as a whole, together with some idea of the extent to which some individuals exceed that minimum or, occasionally, for specific reasons fall short of it.

In accordance with the principles of an enabling curriculum, it is necessary next to form some idea of what each child might gain from taking part in the topic. This too should be quite thoroughly carried out and recorded, otherwise much of the value of the work itself could be squandered. It is important to emphasize the distinction between this formative forecasting and the prespecification of objectives. For with prespecification, there is an assumption that the whole procedure can be designed in advance, whereas, in an enabling approach, the nature, direction and pace of an individual's work is something to be decided gradually, through negotiation.

The third stage in the maintenance of running records is the actual recording of progress in a topic. It is probably even more important now than in the baselining stage that teachers should record progress in ways that suit them best, thereby retaining the assurance that they are doing only what they personally find useful. So, having an idea of where the individual children are heading, the teachers can keep trace of what they observe through everyday appraisal and concurrent assessment. Their comments should include remarks not only about learning in the stricter sense, but also about interests, emotions and behaviour, especially where these manifestations are unexpected or challenging, since all these aspects of children's lives are important for the formative guidance of individuals. Eventually, having perhaps also supplemented their observations with testing of the kind discussed in Chapter 9, teachers can be in a position to form some impression of what each child has gained in depth, in relation to expectations, when the topic work is complete. They may even be able to incorporate the children's own views about the progress that they have made, as a step along the road to self-assessment.

It is important to clarify the status and purpose of these running records. On the one hand, they are intended to tighten up the rather casual system, or even absence of system, of recording which has too often characterized primary humanities. On the other, they are essentially for the teacher's own use, for diagnostic and formative, and eventually summative purposes, within a particular topic. Subsequently, as indicated in Chapter 11, they should become the basis for parts of more systematic (and more carefully circumscribed) records, covering a child's school life in all its aspects, and intended for use within and between schools. These systematic records would themselves also require some form of 'translation' into a format required within the new national framework. In Chapter 11, an attempt will be made to show how these further aspects of record-keeping could be conducted. Without those further stages, running records could not be related to the national curriculum; without running records, the essence of learning in primary humanities would remain unreported and undetected; and without the freedom to keep running records the way they want, teachers will not keep them. But if they are useful rather than burdensome; if they are seen to be a part of teachers' roles in the way that they would be perceived in the social-work or paramedical professions; if time is allowed for teachers to keep running records; and if dignified and appreciative attention is paid to the outcome, they will do so. So running records must remain a bastion of teachers' autonomy, though not of their isolation from the rest of the profession or of the world.

What about the infants?

very important

As must already have been noticed, the focus of this chapter has been on the junior years. To some extent this is inevitable, because the scope of teaching and assessment expands markedly during those years. Yet emphasis is now being increasingly laid on the nature of curriculum and assessment at the infant and even the nursery level. In addition, the ages 5–7 are included within the national curriculum, and 7 will be the first reporting age.

It is unlikely that this will imply separate assessment of each foundation subject, or even of process strands or knowledge specific to humanities as a whole. It is, however, important to ensure that historical, geographical and social ideas should figure in some form in the topic and other work of infant schools and classes. This can and should include story, drama, local exploration, looking at families, experiences with artefacts or 'things' from long ago and far away, some social encounters to widen horizons and to combat stereotyped or racist attitudes, and the beginnings of relevant skill development such as purposive observations, mapping (Catling 1979), sequencing, for example through picture study (Joan Blyth 1988), and the beginnings of the use of the vocabulary of humanities.

Although, technically, four-year-olds are outside the national curriculum, their teachers are bound to bear its requirements in mind. Five-year-olds are however 'in'; they have an entitlement to claim. Yet, qualitatively, these younger children are differently placed in comparison with 'middle' and 'top' infants, as they may continue to be called within the new framework. For the most part, they are less open to any kind of formal teaching, and still more so to any externally imposed assessment. Socialization into school is still a central consideration for them. Yet, as Blenkin and Kelly (1987b) have emphasized, purposive intellectual development within schools begins with these youngest children and can (Whitehead 1987, in Blenkin and Kelly, op. cit.) lay important foundations, especially through language experience, for subsequent education in humanities.

Older infants continue and expand this potential, and show a considerable

very   *important*

increase in intellectual and social understanding. It becomes possible to detect different process strands. Roald Dahl's *Charlie and the Chocolate Factory* (1985) can provide a whimsical introduction of sorts to industry education, in combination with experiences of economic reality. Stories about comic beasts and weird but friendly characters are almost always scrupulously remembered in the correct order, thus providing early experience in sequencing. Stories involving imaginary places almost demand some kind of mapwork to set alongside the first explorations of school and locality. In addition to teachers' wall maps, children can and should make attempts at their own. Older infants become ready for more 'real' stories from the past and from distant lands which can generate more specific historical, geographical and social ideas, bringing them near the level of understanding expected of the seven-year-olds embarking on 'Folktales'. Some individual children may volunteer, and be encouraged, to go further and develop interests of their own, sometimes quite sophisticated in character, as the work develops.

That does not imply that there should be separate assessment of history or geography or of particular cross-curricular themes before the children reach the seven-year-old frontier. The arguments put forward for distinguishing the three perspectives in humanities in Chapter 3 have less force in the infant years. In those years everyday appraisal is likely to be focused on more general development, though signs of particular capabilities and interests in humanities – or of their absence – should be noticed and noted. The capacity to sequence can be noticed through listening and probed through questioning. The same applies to vocabulary acquisition. Concurrent assessment of 'products' has its place too, especially where artwork and mapwork are concerned, though less so than with juniors because imperfect mastery of pencil and brush work ensures that each product takes a long, sometimes painfully long, time to complete. Yet it is better to have a slow than a slipshod outcome. For infants, then, the whole process of appraisal and assessment from baselining onwards is bound to be more rudimentary than with juniors, and less specifically focused on humanities. Yet it is never too soon to detect the beginnings of specific process strands and knowledge which can act as a springboard for subsequent development in that field.

What about special needs?

In Chapter 1 I pointed out that the important issue of designing assessment in humanities for children with special educational needs would not be treated in this book, both because it is a large question in its own right, and because I do not feel competent to handle it. However, it cannot be entirely ignored in a discussion of everyday appraisal and concurrent assessment in the primary years, if only because some children's diagnostic assessment in humanities will contribute to their classification, even statementing, as pupils with special needs. This will depend both on national policy which will elaborate the suggestions made in the TGAT *Report* about diagnosis, about sensitive external assessment, and about the possibilities of exemption from national testing (DES 1989, Section 8).

In addition, it is important to recognize that, especially for children with special needs other than severe learning difficulties, humanities will play an important part in the curriculum. It is not possible to do more here than to stake that claim in broad terms, and perhaps to add that everyday appraisal and concurrent assessment could play an important part both in revealing aspects of perceptions of other people by children with serious sensory handicaps or behavioural problems, and also in providing evidence on which recommendations could be made for their return to mainstream schooling.

9 Testing

Since the advent of the new national framework, the notion of testing usually awakens first in teachers' minds the spectre of externally imposed tests. Certainly it is intended that there shall be some kind of external testing. Already, Standard Assessment Tasks (SATs) are being developed for the core subjects. Some people probably hope and believe that testing of this kind will be the dominant, and maybe even the exclusive, feature of assessment in the future. It is a central argument of this book that teachers' in-depth understanding of children's growth should figure prominently in any national assessment programme and that the Task Group on Assessment and Testing (TGAT) recommendations to that effect should be upheld. For this purpose, everyday appraisal and concurrent assessment are important, but not quite sufficient. In order to make up the tally of teachers' positive contributions to assessment in primary humanities, I want to draw attention to another kind of testing, the kind that teachers can design for themselves, or failing that, at least choose for themselves. In doing so, I shall draw on some of my own recent experiences in schools, not in order to assert that teachers ought to use the same or similar tests, but just to pitch in a few ideas that teachers may like to think about when devising tests for their own purposes.

There are three reasons why such teacher-made and teacher-chosen tests are not very popular at the moment. First, from the standpoint of the national assessment programme itself, they may appear rather lame and subjective. Even with due moderation (in both senses of the term), an initiative by one teacher may appear lacking in the refinement available through SATs, especially since it seems likely that those will be ingeniously beamed at children's learning and enjoyment as well as at their assessment. On the other hand, those who have serious reservations about any kind of national assessment may well regard teacher-made tests as almost a case of collaboration with the enemy. As for teachers themselves, whether or not they admit to occasional testing as though it were a secret addiction, they may well believe that in the maelstrom of the national curriculum they are unable to contemplate any commitment of time and effort additional to what is required for everyday appraisal and concurrent assessment.

I believe that the first two objections are answerable. Subjectivity can be positively valuable, provided that its limitations as well as its advantages are borne in mind. Nor is testing intrinsically harmful, provided that it is conducted within a supportive environment and without overtones of condemnation. But I do have some sympathy with the third objection, and so I hope to indicate how and why teacher-made tests can have a significant place in primary humanities.

Teacher-made tests are useful for two reasons. Firstly, they can promote immediate reinforcement of learning. Secondly, they can provide a useful diagnostic and also summative check on particular process strands, especially skills. They may be administered in several ways: orally with verbal or nonverbal answers; orally with written answers or with answers depending on graphicacy; and tests of a worksheet nature. Each of these kinds of test can be adapted to particular purposes, levels of sophistication, types of material and indeed to the social characters of different classes. For present purposes they will be classified according to type of material.

Map skills

One of the simplest kinds of map test involves probing children's notions of direction. It can be borrowed from the repertoire of physical education rather than of literacy, and can be used, for baselining purposes, to diagnose existing ideas held by a class and by individuals in a class, or alternatively as a summative check on new learning. First, north must be located through reinforcement of previous learning and perhaps through a compass rose in the classroom itself. Then the tables are cleared and two children are placed together in the middle of the floor while the rest form a continuous ring round the outside. One of the two is then invited to call out a direction (taken from the cardinal and half-cardinal points) in which the other child should move, and a number of paces in which they should move. That child is the next to be 'on', summons a third and issues instructions to the newcomer, and so on. Thus two children are under the teacher's observation at any one time, and their understanding open to inspection. The idea of the exercise is that instructions should always be given so that the 'cursor' child of the moment never touches the human ring round the outside, and that everybody should carry out his or her instructions correctly. Those who break either of those conditions are immediately 'out', and the teacher nominates somebody else to take over. Those who then remain have presumably mastered the relevant NOFAN sequence and the test can then either be terminated or carried on to a climax by speeding up the giving and carrying out of instructions. Another possibility, more suitable for outdoor use, is to turn the test into a team game in which two or more roughly matched teams pace each other, though that is more difficult for a teacher to monitor unless each team has a trusty umpire to share the task. I give this example, almost at random, as one of many which make it possible to test every child's concept attainment from the age of 6 or 7 without making any demands on writing skills. Many similar ideas can be found in standard books on primary geography or environmental studies.

From a start of this kind, it is possible to move to something more demanding.

For nine-year-olds, for example, it may be useful to set a Treasure Island pattern of exercise, whereby each child has an outline map with some features and a simple instruction sheet by which to find the 'treasure'. If there are objections to doing this kind of test in a rigid, disciplined way, it can be given to children to do in those times when they might otherwise 'get out their reading books', or whatever a school's practice may be. In such cases, where for the time being collaboration is not called for, it may be possible to vary the exercise slightly for each individual, so that all the children have to think for themselves.

Mapwork skills also involve a developing familiarity with the 'use of globes' as it was once called, and also with atlas, wall and sheet maps. Similar individual tasks can be set for these purposes. In addition, whole classes can take part together in atlas and map quizzes and similar games involving increasing degrees of complexity. In the simplest case, involving atlas or sheet-map facility, children can write down the name of a place whose co-ordinates are named by the teacher; this procedure too can be speeded up when required. Conversely, a place-name with its co-ordinates can be called out, thus basing the exercise on the gazetteer index, familiarity with which should be a reasonable expectation before the end of Key Stage 2. In due course, relief and other features can also become involved. Further elaborations could involve giving names in anagram form; locating two places and naming a third on the road or railway or coastline between the first two, and so on, the primary aim always being to develop skills, though some actual knowledge would also probably remain. This mode of test is also applicable to the globe, either with mini-globes for major features of the earth's surface, or by taking turns individually or in pairs at the 'big' globe, in much the same way that they are accustomed to do with the mini-computer.

At the end of primary education, a more summative procedure may be called for, one which can also be used diagnostically at the beginning of secondary education. My own work led me to devise a 'Golden Island' test for children aged 10 and 11, one which proved fairly useful for these purposes. The questions were worked out with previous studies in mind but they also involved, as all such tests must do, an element of invention. They were mixed, in such a way as to reveal some understanding on the part of the humbler performers while also extending those with higher attainments. 'Golden Island' itself is shown in Figure 9.1. I would not now advocate using as many questions as I originally included, even though all of them did produce interesting and revealing answers. Five is probably enough, and I suggest that these are the most useful ones:

1   Look very carefully, and then write down the direction you would have to go from Atford to get to the highest point on Golden Island.
2   If you could walk six kilometres an hour, about how long would it take you to walk along the road from Bainbridge to the ferry?
3   Imagine that you were looking at Silver Island from the Golden Island end of the ferry. Where would you see the highest land: at the eastern or at the western end of Silver Island?
4   (Be very careful about this one.) Which is the highest town on Golden Island?
5   The government of Golden Island can afford to build either a road or a railway to Cattlebay, but not both. Say which you think they would build, and why.

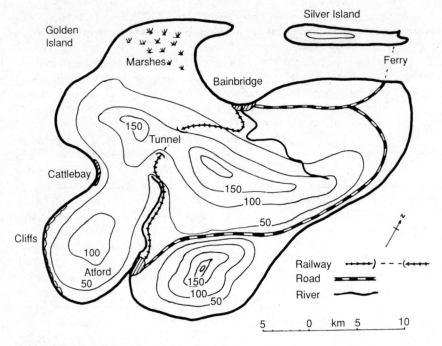

Figure 9.1   Sketch map for 'Golden Island' map test

These questions test different kinds of map-reading and map-interpretation skills. They are not intended to resemble a standardized test, with its pre-agreed correct answers; anybody could use or modify it as they wish. (In case anybody is perplexed by it, the correct answer to Question 4 is that they are all the same height, so none of them is the highest. Some children got it right, but not many.)

It may be of interest to know that among the other questions in my earlier versions were two that depended on graphs and thus were directly related to mathematical skills as applied to social data. One was a piegraph showing the proportions of total population in the towns and elsewhere, and the question based on that – 'Do more people live in the countryside than in the towns?' – was often well answered; it also made little demand on verbal skills. The other showed mean monthly noon temperatures, with the highest figure for February, and the children were asked to speculate where in the world Golden Island might be. This proved difficult for most children of this age, but not for all; a few answers such as 'near Australia' or (in 1982) 'near the Falklands' were acceptable, and serve as an encouraging reminder that some children can, at the beginning of secondary education, show understanding of concepts that may still baffle others at its end. I hope that their Levels in the national programme will allow for this, without docketing them as 'clever' or as precocious snobs.

Mapwork is also one of the few humanities fields in which some published tests have been devised, notably the *Bristol Achievement Tests* (Brimer 1969) and the *Richmond Tests of Basic Skills* (France and Fraser 1975). It is not always easy for teachers to gain access to such standardized tests, though LEAs have often used them as a part of their regular programmes. From the standpoint of cross-curricular assessment, it is noteworthy that the mapwork element is often linked with the core subjects and that the very nature of the scoring codes tends to throw emphasis on right answers rather than on toleration of ambiguity.

Many other kinds of mapwork tests, suitable at different ages and for different purposes, will occur to teachers as they work in this field. They are likely to be much more ingenious, and appropriate to particular classes, than the examples that have been mentioned. They could include 'creative mapwork' through the planning or replanning of real or fictitious neighbourhoods, using three-dimensional material of the type developed by Gibson in his *Education for Neighbourhood Change* project (Gibson 1989). (This material can, of course, also be used in everyday appraisal and concurrent assessment.) The most important criterion to observe in any of these test procedures is that they should monitor the development of the particular process strand over the years.

Time skills

A parallel series of tests can be devised to probe children's grasp of the conventional time-scale. In the early stages, when the emphasis is on sequencing, children can be labelled with particular events in a story and then lined up between two chosen as markers. Each one can then be called in turn and required to fit into the line in the right place. As with the 'human direction' idea, this procedure can be speeded up or turned into a team game, according to circumstances.

A more demanding kind of test is one in which the events of a fictional tale, or of a genuine historical story, are told in such a way that their sequence can be worked out with a little effort. This may be appropriate for children who can read reasonably fluently. A worksheet can then be given to each, with cloze-procedure blanks to be completed in writing. Alternatively an outline strip cartoon can be distributed, with balloons to be filled in to show the utterances of particular people or of representative individuals; this could be used to consolidate a narrative through something like a personal Bayeux Tapestry. A valuable addition to the repertoire of time- and sequence-testing is the sorting of cards representing different past ages, as developed by West (1986). A more comprehensive testing of time-learning might take the form of a blank time-line or time-chart marked in an appropriate combination of years, decades and centuries, on which individuals could mark in colour code some dates and date-spans of the major events and subdivisions of their recent topic, such as the development of road transport. Such procedures are, of course, also appropriate to concurrent assessment; the test situation would be different because they would be carrying out a task at a particular time. It should be noted, however, that testing need not always be conducted 'unseen'; sometimes the capacity to use material in an 'open book' situation can be separated from what amounts to memory testing.

My experimenting with time skills among children between 10 and 12 led me eventually to devise two separate tests, both entitled 'In Time', with one covering a short and one a very long time-span. The shorter was deliberately beamed at the children's own past, present and future experience, and I worked out five questions suitable for brief written answers. Figure 9.2 illustrates the method used. Of course, the actual dates require regular updating. If this test were to be regularly used, the time would come when such questions would be more suitably related to the Prince and Princess of Wales than to the Queen, if only because the arithmetic would be easier. That suggestion is not, of course, intended or likely to make them sing 'Long to reign over us' with any less zeal. Meanwhile I think it would be hazardous to select any alternative claimant, however prominent, from outside the Royal Family.

The other test of time skills did not involve a time line. It consisted of five short questions: no. 3. has been slightly adapted:

1   The full date of this year is 1990 AD (or whatever). What does 'AD' stand for?
2   Write down the date of the year at the beginning of the twentieth century.
3   Write down the date of the year when you will be thirty.
4   Halley's Comet comes near to our Earth once every 76 years. It came this way in 1985 and 1986. When will it come again?
5   (Be specially careful with this one.) Write down the date of the year that was 2390 (or whatever) years ago.

Of these questions, the first does appear to depend on specific teaching. Some answered it perfectly, Latin and all. Others made possibly creditable guesses, such as 'After Death'. Question 2 caused puzzlement, not because of the pedantic argument about 1900/1901 but because so many gave 2000 as the answer. As for Question 5, this proved a real challenge, but a few got it right, in this field of skill study where, in contrast to much in primary humanities, 'getting it right', as well as concept formation, is genuinely important.

It may be objected that these 'In Time' tests are basically tests of mathematical understanding rather than of the understanding of time past. That is true. But I would defend its use in humanities on the same grounds as I would defend specific map testing. For map testing is in a sense recall and cognate-transfer testing of a particular kind of geometry, just as time-scale testing is recall and cognate-transfer testing of a particular kind of arithmetic. The aim of such testing is to establish and confirm the attainment of NOFAN sequences in representational skills, and familiarity with their use. The concepts related to place and time are a different matter, requiring a different kind of testing to be considered subsequently.

Unlike mapwork, this kind of time-scale testing does not figure much in standardized test series. Like mapwork, it requires to be supplemented by some opportunities to work out probabilistic answers. One such opportunity that I followed up was by seeing whether children could detect absurdities.

Name...

In the space below are some dates on a line. Copy these sentences so that each of them is opposite the right date.
I first started school.
I expect to be 16.

2010
2009
2008
2007
2006
2005
2004
2003
2002
2001
2000
1999
1998
1997
1996
1995
1994
1993
1992
1991
1990
1989
1988
1987
1986   Queen Elizabeth II is 60 years old
1985
1984
1983
1982
1981
1980
1979
1978
1977
1976
1975
1974
1973
1972   Queen Elizabeth II has been Queen for 20 years
1971
1970

Then answer these questions.
1   Were you at school in 1976?
2   Will you be 16 before the Queen is 70?
3   How old will the Queen be when she has been Queen for forty years?

Figure 9.2   One kind of time test

Thinking skills and concepts: absurdities tests

One kind of absurdity that has figured both in studies of intelligence and in examinations of children's capacities for historical thinking is the anachronism. It is to be found in some tests in the Binet-Simon tradition and also in early work such as that by Oakden and Sturt on understanding of time (Oakden and Sturt 1922). A parallel kind of absurdity is misunderstanding of spatial arrangements, a field initially explored by Jahoda (1963a and b). It is possible to conjecture other kinds of absurdity in economic and social affairs, such as those revealed in some of Schug's work (e.g. Schug and Birkey 1985). In one sense, the detection of such absurdities indicates the degree of success in NOFAN sequences, for the final 'naturally' level is often revealed by laughter at the very idea that anyone might get it wrong. Therefore absurdities tests are in a sense tests of 'intelligence in action', just as tests of mapwork and time skills are tests of mathematical understanding in action, but they are also tests of the acquisition of particular concepts in humanities. Most children like such tests and are amused by them, if they are suitably matched to learning and not used to penalize slow triers. Teachers, too, can enjoy devising them, perhaps for similar reasons, for they can denote success in promoting children's understanding and thus the completion of NOFAN sequences in teaching skills.

Absurdities can be probed at any stage from the infant years onwards, though less suitably then by testing than by everyday appraisal. We can all laugh at the drawing of the silly person who tried to grow roses on a glacier, or to drive up a mountainside in a sports car. With a little practice it is possible to think out other examples for lower juniors, related to the actual work undertaken, such as one-word or cloze-procedure questions about why Livingstone did not radio for help from Ujiji, or why the management of a car-exporting firm could not keep making money by building more factories and employing more people. For my own summative probing of children's understanding at the end of primary education, which I termed 'Deliberate Mistakes', I bore in mind earlier attempts such as those by Oakden and Sturt and others, without using their actual examples. My instances, as I would now phrase them, were:

1   Queen Victoria was named after Victoria Station, which is near Buckingham Palace.
2   An American museum has just paid thousands of dollars for the typewriter that Shakespeare used.
3   The hottest places in the world are the places where they have the longest days.
4   The explorer Roald Amundsen was the first man to reach the South Pole. If he had gone just a little way further, he would have gone further south than anyone else has ever been.
5   One British pound is worth a lot of Spanish pesetas. That means that British people are much richer than Spanish people.

After each statement, a question was put: 'What is wrong with that?' Similar items could be devised to examine the grasp of other concepts. Clearly better ones could be invented, but these proved encouraging in that the most capable children found no difficulty in identifying the 'deliberate mistakes', while those who did not sometimes afforded, through their efforts, some interesting clues about their reasoning strategies. For example, some thought that Amundsen would have fallen off; a few suggested alternative explanations such as that Shakespeare, being a poet, would not need a typewriter, or that, for them, Victoria Station is not near Buckingham Palace but in Manchester. Occasionally, children affirmed that there was nothing wrong with one or more of the statements. In general, these answers underlined the importance of looking not for right/wrong answers but for quality of thinking and reasoning. In systematic assessment, it would be necessary for teachers to agree some system for picking out such levels of reasoning, somewhat on the lines of the Assessment of Performance Unit (APU) language-assessment procedures (APU 1982). An extension of such procedures would be necessary in any local system of moderation in the national assessment framework.

Thinking skills and concepts: other kinds of test

There are many other ways of testing thinking skills and concepts at any stage in primary education. From my own investigations, however, I am sceptical about their value for across-the-board summative purposes. It seems to me that, unlike the free-standing skill and concept tests hitherto considered, these others should be geared closely to particular pieces of learning. For this reason I found it helpful to undertake some teaching in school before finally trying them out with the same children. I will limit these examples to what I found feasible with 'top juniors', suggesting only that the same principles can be adapted to testing with younger age-levels.

One of my examples was based on *deduction*; the title was 'Tombstone'. After some practice with similar data, children were asked to think about an inscription from a tombstone duplicated for their benefit. They were also given three statements made by a (fictitious) boy about the tombstone: the names given here are also fictitious, though adapted from a real example:

- All the men in the Smith family were officers in the Armed Forces.
- Mary Smith lived longer than any of the other Smiths.
- William Smith had a grandson before he died.

This of course involves the intelligent application of arithmetical understanding to dates, but is also an exercise in sifting historical evidence, and proved quite effective for that purpose.

A second example was based on *paradox* which touches on much the same kind of thinking skills as absurdities testing. It was entitled 'Topsy Turvy', and, following the introductory teaching, asked: 'Some of the most expensive houses are in the middle of towns, and some of the most expensive houses are on the edge of towns. How can that be true?' Needless to say, this gave rise to long rigmaroles of attempted reasoning, and was pitched rather high for these children, but showed evidence of genuine effort, and of the appreciation of some aspects of locational advantage such as the concentration of shops and other facilities in town centres.

The third test attempted to probe reasoning and evaluation of evidence in a different way, by looking for missing steps in a chain of reasoning about a humanities topic. It was termed 'What Had They Forgotten?' and ran thus:

> Two children found an old building. They noticed that the doors and windows were a special shape. They looked in a book, and found that doors and windows that were that special shape were very often made three hundred years ago. So they told everybody that the building was three hundred years old; and they told their teacher too. But their teacher was disappointed, because they had forgotten something. What had they forgotten?

For the most part, this revealed a capacity to reason along the lines I had expected, though some paid more tribute to their personal/social education than to my prognosis by emphasizing that you should not go into old buildings because it is dangerous to do that. I mention this because, if I had been preparing a standardized test, I would then have needed to amend or eliminate this test, but for a class teacher it would only be necessary to follow up individuals with a supplementary question at an odd moment. One of the beauties of this kind of work is that all testing yields something unexpected, but in teacher-made tests that is relatively unimportant, and in any case it has a diagnostic bonus, as a piece of experimental teaching, showing more about how children think and where they, as well as the teacher, need to develop more acute perception.

One other test is worth mentioning. It was intended to probe toleration of ambiguity and was called 'Think It Out!' The whole test, which again followed a piece of teaching on similar material, is reproduced in Figure 9.3. Here, concepts are a little more directly involved. The test was designed both to indicate how far notions of a hierarchy have been acquired and to see how possible children find it to distinguish between what *must* be true and what is *likely* to be true, though in a different context from that of the tombstone. The logic may be similar, but the knowledge context is different. It also touches upon the further question of task procedures, since it challenges children to decide how they might organize their operations to look for further evidence.

This test proved suitable for the age-group, but such approaches could be adapted for younger children too. A worksheet with three or so multiple-choice questions requiring only ticks would reduce dependence on writing skills. Artwork could be used too. Following a brief verbal account by the teacher, say of a harbour, children could draw or felt-pen a simple picture to include the three or four points that the teacher had included in her description. Such an approach can also be combined, for younger children, with the 'What had they forgotten?' method: the teacher could forget to mention the water in the harbour and then ask the children to try to include the thing she had forgotten. She might well find that she had genuinely forgotten something else too; no matter, for once again this is not a standardized test with a numerical result. There is, of course, a huge range of possibilities here, across topics and ages, and the greater the variety and frequency with which they are encountered, the more sensitive are the antennae with which the teacher can monitor, and the less threatening any one test becomes.

Name...

THINK IT OUT!
(Are you quite sure?)

In this clothing factory there are:

machinists	supervisors	secretaries
a manager	and an assistant manager	

Look at these sentences and decide which of them is *almost certain* to be true, and put a tick in the box after each of those.

1   All the people in this factory are women.   ☐
2   The clothes made in this factory are made by the machinists.   ☐
3   The manager is the one who tells the others what to do.   ☐
4   The secretaries work in an office.   ☐
5   The supervisors earn more than the machinists but less than the
     assistant manager.   ☐
6   A machinist who works hard will become a supervisor.   ☐
7   The assistant manager does the manager's job when the manager
     is away.   ☐

Now look at the sentences without a tick. Suppose you visited the factory. You might be able to find out which of those sentences is also almost certain to be true, just by going and asking.

Are you quite sure? If there are any that you might still not be quite sure about, put a cross in the box, and then write down under here why you might still not be quite sure.

Figure 9.3   A test to probe concept attainment and toleration of ambiguity

Testing of other process strands

The tests so far mentioned touch only indirectly upon concepts, and hardly at all on attitudes, including task attitudes. To approach these strands more directly, a different set of tests might be in place. The models of open and closed concept formation mentioned in Chapter 3 could generate models of testing, notably the Gunning-Wilson concept ladder linked to particular NOFAN sequences (see Chapter 3, above; also Antonouris and Wilson 1989, Chapter 2), while the work of Smith and Tomlinson (1977), of Knight (1989) and of Hilary Cooper (forthcoming) on historical concepts may suggest further possibilities. In general, it is important to avoid placing too much emphasis on any one such test unless it is corroborated by the outcomes of everyday appraisal and concurrent assessment, because only then is it possible to maintain that the 'A' or 'N' stage in the NOFAN sequence has really been attained: the 'O' and even the 'F' stage may result in a lucky guess once but, by definition, not consistently.

Attitudes are excluded from the TGAT reporting recommendations and, as was discussed in Chapter 4, attempts to assess attitudes and attitude change in primary education may be both undesirable and impracticable. But task attitudes can be inferred from everyday appraisal and can be built, at least for older children, into concurrent assessment and into testing. It is particularly useful to present children with brief but contrasting accounts of local and other topical events and issues, and also of others remote in place and time, and to invite them to identify and try to explain and evaluate the differences between them, hoping that they will manifest a desire to work on these lines. As for more general attitudes, they can reveal themselves tellingly as asides within other assessment procedures, and it is important that they should be carefully noted and followed up as a part of personal/social education which is likely to be a major cross-curricular element in the national curriculum itself.

Testing of knowledge

There is also a case for testing, summatively, the knowledge expected to be gained from a scheme of work. Such testing need not be a solemn or decisive matter, but it should be both searching and enjoyable. Although my own explorations concentrated on summative process-strand assessment with ten-year-olds, I did experiment with knowledge testing related to local environments and other themes, and became convinced that certain general principles should be taken into account by teachers devising something appropriate for their own classes.

One of those principles is that simple recall should be tested as little as possible. Any knowledge testing will depend on recall in any case, but if a test really is to be searching, then it should involve the use of the kinds of thinking skills that are associated with transfer, and even with generalization. For example, in a shopping study with older infants or younger juniors, it would be preferable to ask 'What is the name we give to the kind of shop that Mr Ali runs?' than to enquire 'What is the name of the shopkeeper that we met?' This applies irrespective of the length of the answer given, which can well be a single word, perhaps selected from a short multiple-choice list, or inserted into a cloze-procedure blank space. It also applies whether the stimulus is spoken, or given in worksheet form. Similarly a question to older children about Italy would not require them to give or even to explain the Italian name for the south of the country, but might ask them to choose which of three reasons is most likely to account for the poverty of the Mezzogiorno.

A second principle is to use nonverbal stimuli widely, and not only with younger children or those with particular verbal difficulties. As was mentioned earlier, picture study has had a long tradition in the teaching of history and geography, as a means of opening up a theme, and it can also be valuable for consolidation of knowledge and for summative assessment. One such instance could be taken from the second of the three fourth-year junior topics in the scheme outlined in Appendix 2, 'Here and There'. This involves a visit to a different but reasonably accessible locality, to emphasize comparisons and contrasts. While there, a teacher could take photographs or even a ciné-film or a videotape for subsequent use, and bring it into play at the end of the study. Again the questions would be of the pattern 'Why was she doing . . .' rather than 'What was she doing . . .' and 'What is there near here that reminds you of . . .' and 'Is it quite the same as . . .?' and 'Is there anything about it that is the same everywhere . . .?' Once again, recall is not enough. A further obvious refinement is for the children to be challenged to produce relevant sketches or pictures or to take stimulating and puzzling photos that may have each other, and the teacher, guessing, provided that they conform to the general rule that those photos must be about the topic and not about some other themes of the kind that might readily suggest themselves to groups such as Pollard's 'jokers' (Pollard 1985), and also that the puzzlers must take turns at being puzzled. It should be noted finally that, although nonverbal stimuli are so important, the test answers can be given orally or in one-word written answers or in more extended writing.

The third principle is that testing should concentrate on the essential features of a topic, the parts calculated to stimulate development in the process strands as well as to bring out the intrinsic importance of the topic. This is the part of the subject that everybody should know, even though individuals will display and develop that knowledge according to their different capacities, their NOFAN development, and what they have previously learned. The content of knowledge itself represents a new NOFAN sequence for everybody to follow, irrespective of their capacities. An analogy might be that of some playgoers meeting in the bar after a performance. They would all have shared a learning experience, even though some hardly ever went to the theatre, while others were drama students or professional critics, and they could all be expected to have something to say about the play. So here, for once, the children would be justifiably treated as a class unit, which may well become a useful experience within the national curriculum, especially if differentiation by 'levels' becomes a customary experience. Alongside this common-knowledge testing, differences in process-strand development would of course continue to be monitored through everyday appraisal and concurrent assessment, so that the danger of regarding the class more generally as a homogeneous piece of test fodder would be avoided, as it should. The common test should be strictly focused on the particular common experience.

In addition to the testing of specific knowledge, there is a case for keeping some kind of check on children's developing awareness of that 'backcloth' of place and time that was mentioned in Chapter 4, together with a few salient features of contemporary society. It is important to remember where Australia or the Arctic Circle can be found on the globe or in the atlas, and to build up some sort of memory of the world map as shown on a customary projection. Similarly, it is of some importance to know that the sixteenth century in English history corresponds more or less to Tudor times. It is probably less necessary, but still valuable, to know what happens at, for example, a bank or a post office or an airport, information which some children may acquire very effectively from homes and families, while others may not. West (1981) emphasized the importance of learning in the family context as a contributor to the learning of 'school' history, a consideration that really applies to humanities as a whole, a point to be borne in mind as the implications of national policy on curriculum and assessment are worked out.

It may also be important to know what families themselves stand for, or have stood for, in our society, even if individuals and cultural groups differ from that position. It should be emphasized that knowledge of these kinds should arise through an enabling curriculum designed primarily with other ends in mind, rather than from direct fact teaching. Specific information such as places and dates should gain entrance only in conjunction with more meaningful learning. No doubt those who are concerned with SATs in history and geography, and with the representation of cross-curricular themes in the national testing programme, will bear such considerations in mind.

There are many other ways in which teacher-made testing can be relevant and helpful. Of course, any such tests should be used sensibly and with well-considered justification. Nobody would think of trying to use all of them, certainly not with the same class. Many teachers will have their own extensive and well-tried repertoires, suited to their own personalities and experience, that go beyond anything that I have mentioned; and so they should. The examples suggested here are simply offered, like the rest of the book, as something to start with for those who have not yet made a start for themselves.

Tests and records

In general parlance, as well as in the literature about the new national framework, testing and record-keeping are closely associated. In addition, there is often an assumption that tests will give rise to scores, often of a norm-referenced kind, and that these will 'be inserted on records and perhaps subjected to statistical procedures that can be applied only to norm-referenced data. Tests of the kind hitherto discussed could not be used in this way, and since SATs for the national reporting ages, with their arrays of Levels, may be expected to display some such features, it is probably appropriate that teachers' own tests should comprise material of a different nature. Yet it is legitimate to expect that those tests should contribute in some meaningful way to a purposive kind of record-keeping. The most promising approach to this purpose of testing is to follow the same general principles as with everyday appraisal and concurrent assessment. This entails viewing learning and development during any episode of schooling as a process in which each child moves forward from his or her individual baseline. The direction, as well as the speed, of the movement is unpredictable, but summative testing can help to suggest what point each has reached, and to record children's progress not by comparisons within or beyond the class, but by the improvements that each of them shows during the work in question and, where possible, by the advance that they show towards fuller self-assessment, strenuous self-direction and self-knowledge. More specific suggestions about this kind of record-keeping will be found in Chapter 11, where the problem of 'translation' of records relating to process strands into terms appropriate to the new national structure will also be faced.

National testing

Soon a programme of national testing in history and geography will be promulgated, and humanities will be represented somehow in whatever approach to cross-curricular themes may secure the approval of the Secretary of State. This is likely to take some time. So it is not yet possible to indicate exactly what teachers will be expected to do in the assessment of primary humanities. They are promised a significant part, though it is not clear how autonomous that part will be. Naturally teachers would like this book to give them the answer, but at this stage, in the nature of things, it cannot. Whatever the outcome may be, teacher-made testing will have its part to play on the educational grounds already indicated and will help to soften the impact of external testing on schools, teachers and children alike. In any case, it is certain that constructive expectation will be more helpful than panic. For the successful operation of national testing will require a confident, though not uncritical, primary teaching profession to carry out the major part of it. This in turn requires the support of an administration more concerned with human feelings and capabilities than with enforcing policies and implementing schedules. Any future book on a theme similar to mine, published in, say 1995, will be obliged to include a whole chapter, rather than one bare paragraph, on national testing in primary humanities. It will be interesting to see what there is to say then about the national assessment framework, about how far history and geography will have their own Standard Assessment Tasks, and especially about how the system works in practice.

10 Putting it together: an example

The last few chapters have been concerned with various aspects of assessment in primary humanities. It may now be useful to follow an example of how the process can be fitted together.

For this purpose I have chosen a further topic from Appendix 2, namely 'Exploring', the second of two suggested for eight-year-olds. This is the age-level, now to be known as Y4, which is just after the middle of primary education and pitched between the testing ages of 7 and 11. The topic itself is described as covering:

> children's own explorations, under adult guidance and otherwise; eminent explorers past and recent; detail about at least one major exploration and its consequences; relations in place and time.

This is a topic that touches upon central concerns in history and geography and may well figure, in some form, in the national curriculum. It is also appropriate to the expansion of experience appropriate to an enabling curriculum, though for this purpose it would include also a central emphasis on process strands and on the children's own experience which may not occupy so crucial a place in the national curriculum itself. In this chapter some indication will be given of how this topic of 'Exploring' could be developed from the initial planning stage to the completion of assessment.

The planning process in topic work usually begins with something like a topic web, or rather three webs. The first of these is a fancy-free outflow of ideas, almost like Jungian free association. The second is a more disciplined 'editing' of those exploratory ideas in the light of general knowledge about eight-year-olds, and of particular familiarity with one class of eight-year-olds, also of a teacher's knowledge about exploring, or at least knowledge of where to go to find suitable material on that topic. The third web involves a further 'editing' process, this time in order to ensure that Attainment Targets and Programmes of Study, the official representatives of process strands and knowledge/understanding in the national curriculum, are adequately represented. It is, of course, possible to reverse the order of these two webs, but the first of the three must remain first. Tann treats these processes of teachers' thinking quite fully in her recent study of topic work (Tann 1988, Chapter 2), indicating in more detail how they can relate topic planning both to children and to basic elements in curriculum.

As was indicated in Chapter 3, proportional representation of subject perspectives in the primary curriculum is important in the maintenance of overall balance, but not in the structure of individual topics, where it can verge on the absurd. Tann, following and developing an approach outlined by the Schools Council in *Primary Practice* (Schools Council 1983, Chapter IX) prefers to think in terms of process strands, looking at a topic for its potential for developing skills, task procedures, concepts and attitudes as well as knowledge considered important in its own right.

I believe that it is possible to take that analysis a little further and to consider a topic such as 'Exploring' along the lines already indicated in Figure 4.2. There the process strands, organization of the work, and strategy of assessment were all considered together. Figure 10.1 embodies a suggestion of how this approach could be applied to 'Exploring' with eight-year-olds. In future, some such strategy may well be necessary in order to sustain the different features of the national curriculum in action.

In order to work out how this strategy could be applied, it is necessary first to decide what process strands and knowledge are likely to figure in the topic itself, and then to decide upon the organization and assessment of the work.

Process strands

Map skills

It is desirable that eight-year-olds should have done some mapwork already, especially in the locality. However, 'Explorers' would introduce something new in relation to the globe, atlas and perhaps a collective wall map. The problem of map projections would arise almost inevitably; Mercator's projection itself derived from the needs of navigators during the great age of Renaissance exploration. A new series of NOFAN sequences can thus be initiated; its extension could be stimulated by asking such questions as how it might be possible to represent, on a plane surface, the voyage of astronauts to the moon.

Time skills

Children at the Y4 age should normally have become practised in sequencing of events and artefacts, in relation to their own lives and more widely. Events touched upon in 'Exploring', especially those of the exploration selected for particular study, would be treated in this way and sequenced both on a clothes-peg time-line such as West recommends (1982, 1986; Joan Blyth 1989, pp. 106–9) and in the children's individual files. The next step would be to relate these events in one exploration, together with some other important expeditions, to the conventional time-scale itself, on a permanent classroom time-line ranging from,

Figure 10.1 Topic development and assessment in primary humanities: an example: EXPLORING

Aspects	Week	0	1	2	3	4	5	6
Aims			Extended knowledge and understanding of exploring, in relation to attainment targets				Involvement of children in planning the topic		
Process strands	Skills		Personal mapping	Discussion	Reference (retrieval) (library and other)	Social skills; Thinking skills	Expressive (display)	Map skills; time skills	
	Concepts		Communication:		Power: Exploration, discovery, expedition, navigation, astronaut: Continent, ocean etc.	Categorical and methodological concepts			
	Attitudes				Respect for accuracy	Courage: Attitudes to unfamiliar people			
Knowledge and understanding			Rendering own explorations explicit			Learning about one major exploration (or more)		Placing specific explorations in historical and geographical contexts	
'Delivery'			General discussion of exploring / Related to personal experiences / Baseline first 'products'	Widening view of exploration in 'world' context: choice (through discussion) of one major exploration, possibly more, to investigate	Illustrated narrative of the chosen exploration / Group work / Some 'expansion' individual tasks	Second 'products': topic books worksheets, artwork, etc.	Presentation of outcome of exploration study (third 'products')	Placing of chosen (and other?) explorations in context in globe, atlas and time line	
Assessment	Clients				Children; parents; governors; own and other teachers			
	Purposes		Diagnostic/formative			Summative			
	Referencing			Self-referencing as far as possible					
	Baselining		Knowledge of individuals: questioning; interrogation		'Expanding': challenges to individuals and groups (Baselining of newcomers/absentees)		New baselining from summative testing		
	Focus		1st concurrent assessment	Everyday appraisal		2nd concurrent assessment	3rd concurrent assessment also testing		
	Range		Recall (and interpretation)	Development of transfer	Recall of new information	Generalization of ideas about exploring	Tests involving transfer		
Relation to national curriculum			Use of standard records	Relation of 'exploring' to attainment targets, profile components and programmes of study (core, history, geography)					
	Week	0	1	2	3	4	5	6

say 1000 BC to AD 2000. This would show visually how what counts in most people's minds as major exploration has been concentrated in time, much of it in the past two hundred years.

Reference (retrieval) skills

One important aspect of study skills needed in 'Exploring' is that of accessing information. There have been for many years books on exploration written for younger children, and these may soon be augmented by others.

Mere information is, of course, a means rather than an end. In step with the extension of comprehension required in the programme of study for English (NCC 1989a, pp. 41–5), children will be expected to show critical understanding of what they read. Neatness of transcription, with an occasional misspelling that an indulgent teacher is expected to overlook because of 'Julie's splendid effort', will not be good enough in future. Evaluation will be needed, and can be introduced by this kind of stimulus:

> You have told us about the exploring you did on your holiday. How do we know that you told us *all* about it? How do we know that you didn't miss out the bits you didn't really want us to hear? . . . Then how do we know that this explorer's journal didn't miss out the bits that he didn't want the king to hear? . . . And if you think he didn't miss them out, why?

In this way reference skills can be linked to the next category:

Thinking skills related to methodological concepts

In addition to this kind of evaluative thinking, 'Exploring' gives plenty of opportunity for the exercise of thinking related to the methodological concepts of similarity/difference and continuity/change. There are contrasts between children's exploring and 'real' exploring; between present and past; between recent past and more distant past; between land, sea, air and space exploration. It is also possible to ask searching questions about causes and concomitance: Why did explorations happen when they did? Was it anything to do with technical improvements, with changing ideas, or with the growth of riches and of empires? Or did these things just happen at the same time? In turn, this can almost immediately lead into the formulation of hypotheses and generalizations about human behaviour, involving feeling as well as knowing; attitudes as well as skills. Examples might be:

- Why did some people believe that the world was flat?
- How and why do you think that that belief changed?
- Why did it take so long for people from Europe to reach the interior of Africa?
- Why did it take so long for anybody to reach the South Pole?

and, more tellingly and not to be evaded just because it is Y4:

- Why do we take more notice of some kinds of exploration than others?
- What was it like to be explored, and perhaps conquered and enslaved?

Such issues will be more fully considered in secondary education, but Y4 can and should begin to think about them.

Discussion, expressive and social skills

Clearly it is abortive to try to develop individual representational skills, reference skills and thinking skills without taking account of social interaction. It is scarcely necessary to spell out the ways in which discussion can be introduced as a means of sharing ideas and of mutual stimulation, in addition to its value as social development. Similarly the engagement of children with different forms of expression in language, drama and art, music and dance, now to be reinforced by the demands of the national curriculum in the English core and in the aesthetic foundation subjects, has obvious relevance and value for 'Exploring', though it must never be forgotten that they are also in the curricular universe in their own right, as humanities is.

Task procedures

One of the purposes of an enabling curriculum in primary humanities is to encourage children to become managers of their own learning. This involves the marshalling of skills in a strategy that they themselves have devised. This is not straightforward. For example, the eight-year-olds in our example may not at first know whether they want to know anything at all about exploring or, if they do, how to find out anything about it. A few will probably remain unmoved by the topic, prepared just to do enough to get by. More are likely to engage with it and to learn, step by step, what to find out and how. As they go, formulating together with the teacher and with other children an actual plan for 'exploring' the topic itself, both (as the summary indicates) under adult guidance and on their own, and as they become more alive to 'real' exploring, they are likely to see a little more about how it fits into place and time, how to use reference and thinking skills, and how to take more initiative in planning their own learning. It is through interactions of this mind, rather than in any set sequence, that skills are deployed and task procedures appropriate to humanities developed. At the Y4 age-level, it is unlikely that the capacity to direct their own learning will have developed very far, but there are always surprises, and all children should be encouraged to develop in this way as far as they can. The one assumption that should never be made is that, because they are 'only' 8, they are therefore too young to try.

Substantive concepts

'Exploring' provides marvellous opportunities for the enrichment of the stock of concepts that children are all the time building up. Key concepts such as Communication, Power and Values are all clearly important and likely to figure in the teacher's selection of material, though it is unlikely that the actual terminology would figure in the classroom interaction. Some 'open' concepts are more likely to be emphasized, vocabulary and all: Exploration itself, Discovery, Expedition,

Navigation (and its attendant technology), Globe, Space (in relation to space exploration). There will also be reinforcement of ideas and vocabulary in relation to such other open concepts as continent, ocean, latitude, longitude, Trade Wind, river basin, astronaut/cosmonaut (and why there are *two* words there). There might also be a few 'closed' concepts without much general application, such as caravanserai, North-West Passage, or moon buggy. In a topic such as this, it is particularly important to try to ensure that the words are not used parrotwise without the NOFAN sequences needed for the attainment of the concepts themselves.

Task attitudes

These are quite important in 'Exploring'. One of them, already referred to, is the need for critical evaluation of sources. This task attitude should actually be spelled out more precisely, for it involves not only the *capacity* to stand back and evaluate sources, but also the *readiness* to do so, spontaneously, as part of the task procedure. Maybe only a little progress can be made, among eight-year-olds, with this quite demanding aspect of growing up: the combination of intellectual independence with the formulation of personal values. As with task procedures, so with task attitudes; they are not too young to try, though they may need a lot of support.

General attitudes

Here, as always, it is very difficult to specify what attitudes a topic will engender; whether, if at all, they will be changed; and if they are changed, in what direction. A teacher is likely to have her own chosen set of values that she would like to see developing, but in practice the situation is often much more complex.

Among the many attitudes that might become salient through 'Exploring', two may be mentioned. The first is admiration and respect for the sheer *courage* that explorers have to display, not just physical courage, but often also the social, emotional and intellectual courage needed to defy convention and suspicion. Children's own experience may help them with this attitude. They may themselves have felt a tingle of fear in a sandpit or on the crags or the seashore and be able thus to identify a little with the feelings of explorers. They may also know what it is to feel the need for social, and even intellectual, courage in their own lives at home and school, especially when defending a minority interest, or activity, or point of view. The other attitude that is often linked with this one but stands in contrast to it is criticism of the *inhumanity* that explorers have often (but not always) displayed towards the 'natives' whom they 'discovered'. This was often the outcome of mutual perceptions of threat and suspicion of the unknown, with consequences that often depended on who had the greater military and economic power: the balance was usually tilted in favour of the explorers. Here again, children's own experience of exploring as trespassers or as violators of other gangs' territories can involve some genuine empathetic understanding, though the temptation to run riot with empathy must, as Knight (1989) reminds us, be resisted. Meanwhile it is also valuable to emphasize that courage and inhumanity frequently went together in the same people; not an easy lesson to learn.

Many other attitudes are, or could be, involved in this topic, but these will be sufficient to emphasize the complexity of the issue and, needless to say, of its assessment.

Knowledge

It is important that the aspects of a topic chosen for a scheme of work should not only foster the process strands through the Attainment Targets, but should also be significant in their own right. Some kind of choice must be made, and made with children's understanding and agreement, a procedure which has the additional value of emphasizing how much there is to choose from and how necessary it is to do a little, well, while remembering how it fits into the potential whole as shown by the atlas and time-line. By establishing from the outset that the work to be undertaken should be strenuous and rewarding, but practicable within the time available, it is possible to avoid the sad situation when some children, the ones most in need of satisfaction derived from success, are left floundering in a welter of scrappy unfinished tasks and eventually disengage from the topic itself.

It is also imperative that what is learned should be accurate. This may seem both obvious and impossible; obvious, because nobody would want children to learn what is false, and impossible, because experts disagree about what is true. The second contention is not in fact very weighty, for there is a great measure of agreement about the main stories of exploration, if not about all aspects of their interpretation. The first point may seem obvious but is not always honoured to the extent that it should be. For it is sometimes thought that, if statements or interpretations are vivid and appealing to children, it does not matter too much if they are generous with colour rather than with truth. But it does matter. To overlook the need for accuracy would be to fly in the face of one of the most important of process strands, that of evaluation of evidence. Fortunately, the flood of available published material that will follow the national curriculum programmes of study should ensure that accuracy is attainable.

Insistence on selection and accuracy may still not ensure the desired outcome in knowledge. It remains difficult to forge the link between the particular information and reflection involved in studying, say, Vasco da Gama, and that backcloth of history and geography which is being gradually built up. Indeed, one of the pitfalls of a defined national curriculum is that children – and parents and teachers – may think that, because a topic figures in a programme of study, then when they move past that landmark, in this case on the road from Y4 to Y5, they have therefore 'done' 'Exploring'. There is no easy way to avoid that impression. It is still better to travel hopefully with Vasco da Gama than to arrive with a lifeless set of worksheets that purport to 'cover' 'Exploring'.

Organization and conduct of the topic

Figure 10.1 suggests, in flow-chart form, how the actual programme can be put together. The first stage, purposefully related to children's own experience of exploring, involves discussion skills and also personal mapping (and recognition of how far each child is prepared to allow that personal mapping to be monitored), combined with some writing of prose or poem and even song. The next stage would be to discuss the major theme of exploring in human history and to relate it to place and time skills, leading to discussion and choice of one example of exploration. This step might in fact be differently handled in different situations. For example, a verbally capable class with well-developed work habits and high 'norms of production' (Chapter 7) might volunteer to try two examples, or to divide into groups each looking at an example of its own, while a heterogeneous class presenting a teacher with behaviour difficulties might well gain more from adhering to a simple, structured concentration on one explorer.

The later phase of the study would involve a move towards some kind of satisfying dramatic conclusion, whether through a display or through some other medium such as a mock TV presentation. This is intended to provide an incentive as well as a means of rounding off the learning of particular aspects. Any such finale would however be incomplete if it were not related in some way to the place and time continuum that is being built up. The sample of 'Exploring' undertaken must be handled in such a way as to leave an impression of how much else there is to learn and know about it.

The final element in Figure 10.1 is that of assessment. It is shown as an integral part of the programme, especially where everyday appraisal and concurrent assessment are concerned, but with a more specific place towards the end of the scheme of work. The concluding section of this chapter looks more closely at how the different forms of assessment could be related to 'Exploring'.

Assessment procedures

A further diagram, Figure 10.2, is used to indicate the match between kinds of assessment and the main elements in the topic. The content of this diagram is nothing more than a general and rather subjective indication of how this match might be developed in an average situation. A tick shows where a form of assessment seems appropriate. Where the tick appears in brackets, the implication is that this form might be appropriate though that is less certain. A blank, however, implies that it is unlikely to be useful.

From this table one or two other points are noticeable. One is that the forms of assessment most suitable for formative and diagnostic purposes, namely everyday appraisal and concurrent assessment, are not the most efficient as summative tools. That is not surprising, but it underlines a point that the Task Group on Assessment and Testing (TGAT) *Report* itself emphasizes, namely that a variety of methods must be used. No one method will be adequate without supplementation. If, for example, it becomes evident in practice that Standard Assessment Tasks (SATs) appear to provide adequate information for summative purposes, there may be a temptation to disregard any kind of teacher-based assessment, thus ignoring the superiority that 'close-up' methods are bound to have for formative and diagnostic purposes. From this, incidentally, it would be only a short step to claim that formative and diagnostic procedures are unimportant anyhow and that summative, comparative data are all that really matter. Long before that stage, the TGAT message should be reiterated loudly.

The second feature to emerge from Figure 10.2 may suggest one way in which

Figure 10.2 Assessment foci as evidence for curricular progress: a tentative summary devised for EXPLORING

Aspects of curriculum		Evidence of progress derived from:						
		Everyday appraisal			Concurrent assessment			Testing
		Observation	Interrogation	Discussion	Worksheets/topic books (including maps, timelines)	Artwork	Artefacts	
Process / Skills	Representational	✓	(✓)	(✓)	✓	✓		✓
	Investigational	✓	✓	✓	✓	✓	(✓)	✓
	Thinking		✓	✓	✓	(✓)	✓	✓
	Manipulative	✓				✓	✓	
	Social	✓		✓	(✓)	(✓)	(✓)	
	Expressive	✓		(✓)	✓	✓	(✓)	
	Task procedures	✓	✓	✓	✓	(✓)		✓
Structures / Concepts	Categorical		✓	✓	✓			✓
	Methodological	(✓)	✓	✓	✓	(✓)		✓
	Substantive (general)	(✓)	(✓)	(✓)	(✓)			(✓)
	Substantive (open specific)	(✓)	✓	✓	✓	(✓)	(✓)	✓
	Substantive (closed specific)		✓	✓	✓	(✓)	(✓)	✓
Attitudes	Task	✓	✓	✓	(✓)	(✓)	(✓)	(✓)
	Other	✓	✓	✓	(✓)	✓		
Knowledge and understanding	Local		✓	✓	✓	(✓)		(✓)
	Particular exploration(s)		✓	✓	✓	✓	✓	✓
	'Backcloth'		✓	✓	✓			✓

single-method assessment can be resisted. For the second and third columns of the 'Everyday appraisal' section serve as a reminder that, as was indicated in Chapter 8, much more potential for genuine assessment arises from questioning and discussion (themselves process strands) than from mere observation. In addition, the column on topic books appears to tap the whole range of process strands and content, so this suggests itself as a principal means of assessment generally. Of course, all of this assumes that assessment is to be of the kind appropriate to an enabling curriculum, and that the TGAT assumptions about the purposes of assessment will be sustained. That is the issue now at stake. I personally have no doubt that assessment itself should be 'broadly based and balanced' if it is to be of educational, and not merely of political and administrative, value. It is on that assumption that suggestions will be made about actual assessment procedures that could be applied to 'Exploring'.

The nature of those procedures depends on the approaches to assessment discussed in Chapter 4. Figure 10.1 reminds us that it is for a set of clients, of which the children themselves come first. So it must be of a kind that will enable positive feedback to be given. Second, it must allow diagnostic and formative processes as well as summative assessment to take place. The emphasis must also be on self-referencing, which means that any data collected should be used primarily for comparison with the child's immediate baseline and not with other children. It must also allow for a variety of methods, as has just been indicated. Finally, its 'range' must allow for transfer and generalization, using thinking skills, rather than for simple recall. In what follows, these considerations will be borne in mind. They would form the basis for a teacher's running records.

In actual practice, the first step would necessarily be some form of baselining. This could emerge partly from previous records (see Chapter 11) but also from the quality of the initial discussion about children's own explorations and their capacity to record what they do. This, together with knowledge of their general literacy, other skills and personal qualities, would make it possible for a teacher to conjecture, broadly, what each child is likely to gain from taking part in the topic work. These baseline data can then be used formatively in further discussions with the children about the work-plan itself, as a result of which the plan itself would be adjusted, and with it the teacher's emerging goals for individuals, which are also liable to amendment owing to such intervening variables as absence, involvement in school drama, or the emergence of an unanticipated interest. In this way the whole process develops by negotiation, as indicated in Chapter 7, and not by some neat prepackaged design. None the less, as the work proceeds, the target for each child becomes firmer and the extent of his or her progress easier to determine. It is necessary to consider how.

Among instances of *everyday appraisal*, emphasis could be laid on the nature of the discussion skills and social skills employed in organizing the scheme of work itself, and on the readiness with which the children are able and willing to communicate about their own personal explorations, bearing in mind that boys may generally prove more wide-ranging than girls in their movements and consequent personal mapping (Matthews 1986). Later, their use of relevant information skills and thinking skills could be monitored, and observations made also on emotional reactions and on particular empathetic insights into the distinctive nature of 'Exploring' on the world stage. To use the terminology outlined in Chapter 8, some of these skills are overt and others more implicit. The former could usually be covered by focused observation; the latter might call for interrogation of at least some small groups of those children who had not participated conspicuously in the general activity, and for focused discussion with them. For it is the higher thinking skills, the more demanding ones, that often call for exposure in these ways.

There is, however, more scope for using *concurrent assessment*. In 'Exploring', topic books could be particularly rich as sources of material. At the outset personal maps, as mentioned in Chapter 3, could themselves provide fascinating information about individual interests, capacities, personalities and social perspectives, as much through what they conceal as through what they reveal (Moore 1986). Later in the topic it would be possible to use some of the following as assessed material: observations on and interpretations of actual and perhaps conflicting extracts from explorers' logs and diaries (but not attempts at making up imaginary and inaccurate ones); Mercator maps with routes of one or more explorers, with a sentence of comment; list of gear required for an Arctic expedition; artwork of a moon landing or a planetary probe. All these examples would provide evidence of process-strand development as well as of knowledge-content, and opportunities, when returning work to children, for making formative oral comments such as:

> There's a book about this in the Library; you know the section where you can find it. It will tell you more about how those ships were rigged. I shall ask you next week how they did it.

Simple worksheets, maps and time-lines can provide more focused material for assessment. Figure 10.1 indicates where they might figure. A worksheet on Magellan's last voyage might, for example, include a map (Mercator again) on which the route would be marked, with symbols for particular perils, as far as the place and date where he was killed, and then the return route followed by the residue of the expedition. Children could be asked also to indicate the direction in which the expedition was sailing at particular points during the circumnavigation; to name and explain three foods that the sailors ate, and one disease to which they were liable, and so forth, care having been taken to ensure that the requisite information is available from the sources provided. A taped discussion about the expedition, and about how far it had been accurately chronicled, might perhaps figure among the assessment procedures. A less exclusively verbal exercise would be to ask for a drawing or painting of the *Victoria* and for a comparison of its dimensions and perhaps its draught with those of a modern yacht or cabin cruiser. The place of worksheets with eight-year-olds would be in most cases a rather subordinate one, however seductive they may be to teachers. As for the 'things-to-do' section sometimes found in older texts, they are so predetermined that, with the best will in the world, they are unlikely to fit a teacher's actual work on exploring and are likely to be used only as a last resort.

There would probably be still less place for teacher-made testing. However, as Figure 10.1 shows, this could be incorporated in the final stage of the work, especially if school policy were to require this, as is not impossible in the new framework. Such tests would need to concentrate on the essence of the topic, yet bearing in mind the importance of thinking skills through questions such as:

- Where, on your map, is the last part of the world to be explored?
- What was special about Marco Polo's journeys?
- Which of these has been used most often in exploring?
    horses   ships   sledges   rockets   jeeps   huskies
- Write down three things that you would have to take with you if you wanted to explore in the Sahara Desert.

It looks rather formal for eight-year-olds, and it should not be done if avoidable. It may not be avoidable. If it does have to be fitted in, then it could perhaps be combined with a worksheet and given to individuals to do, quietly on their own, at the end of a busy afternoon. It would at least have some summative value, indicating how far the common experience of the topic had been incorporated into the children's understanding – or, at least, how far they can or will divulge how far this has taken place. This information could be related to attainment targets which, as discussed in Chapter 11, may be central to the involvement of teachers' assessments, additional to SATs, in the national programme. It might also provide useful evaluation from the teacher's point of view. It would in any case have some diagnostic and formative value, suggesting something of a baselining nature for the design of the next topic and indicating how individuals might respond, and especially what they had gained in capacity for self-assessment and self-direction.

If 'Exploring' had occupied centre stage for its duration, the curriculum for Y4 as a whole might next lay emphasis on a topic outside humanities. If so, the information arising from the summative assessment of 'Exploring' might have to be put partly into cold storage and not brought fully into play until the Y5 stage. In the scheme outlined in Appendix 2, the next humanities topic would then be 'Gran's World', where a different emphasis on process strands would be required.

Formative and diagnostic procedures are not always so straightforward as they may appear in a simple model. For other topics would not have the same 'shape' as 'Exploring'. Even within one topic, teachers and children would vary considerably in their procedures, as indicated in Chapter 7. Yet, in the national curriculum, there would be sufficient common ground between teachers and schools to ensure that all children could gain something from each topic in terms both of process strands and of knowledge, and that assessment could reveal something of what they had gained, something that could contribute to their developmental profile in terms of attainment targets and could be carried forward to annual reporting to parents and taken into account when the next reporting age is reached. Just how, and how much, each individual has gained by his or her engagement with the topic is another question that must lie partly outside the scope of any kind of assessment. However, I believe that 'Exploring' is the kind of theme that is likely to have much in the way of enabling development to give to most Y4 children, and that they can respond to this theme by making more informed and meaningful judgements about themselves, what they can do, what they ought to do, and what they want to do, as they see their own future opening up. I also believe that there are reasonably practicable ways of assessing most of what 'Exploring' has given to them, so that when they reach Y5, their next teacher will be able to discern, for each one of them, baselines for further learning.

11 Record-keeping and continuity

In Chapter 8 I emphasized the importance of running records kept by individual teachers in the course of everyday appraisal and concurrent assessment and suggested that there should be two further stages in record-keeping. The first of these was to be the maintenance of systematic records within a school, drawing on those running records and on the outcomes of teacher-made testing, and the second the contribution of whole schools to the national databank. In the present chapter suggestions will be made about these further stages, together with indications as to how records might be used in relation to continuity within and between schools. The use of the national databank is a different issue, about which further information and comment will become available a-plenty, though perhaps not with particular emphasis on primary humanities.

Suggestions from earlier studies

Before considering what schools could do with respect to maintaining systematic records in primary humanities, it might be helpful to start by looking at some of the ideas that have already been mooted. Some years ago Dean (1972) made a wise survey of the whole field of primary-school record-keeping which is still well worth using as a source of ideas. As regards specific recommendations for primary humanities, the pioneering study by Keith Cooper (1976), built on something like NOFAN sequences, remains almost the only example. It has proved stimulating to teachers, and I have drawn on it in the formulation of my own ideas. Its central suggestion about record-keeping is that records should be designed so as to monitor each child's progress from term to term and from year to year in the pursuit of the particular objectives proposed by *Place, Time and Society 8–13* (W.A.L. Blyth *et al.* 1976). Although these objectives were defined as emergent and provisional ones, the resulting framework might now appear slightly rigid, but it served a useful purpose and broke new ground in a comprehensible manner.

The subsequent survey by Clift *et al.* (1981) for the Schools Council was the most authoritative account of primary practice current at its time, but has little specific to say about humanities, either in its survey of current practice or in its own recommendations. Clift and his colleagues did find a high measure of professional interest and skill in record-keeping in the basic curriculum as it then was. Mathematics gave rise to the main difficulties, while some of the advice given about language and study skills remains very pertinent to humanities. They also detected a considerable interest in personal/social development, but a striking lack of precision in records kept for that purpose when compared with those for the basic skills. Physical and aesthetic development occupied a position intermediate between the basic skills and personal/social matters: in this Clift's survey mirrored quite closely the experience of the Assessment of Performance Unit at that time. The subsequent account by the Schools Council (1983, especially Chapter X and Appendices C and D), and the valuable general statement by Shipman (1983), indicated no significant changes in practice.

In more recent years there has been a considerable increase in the serious study of profiling and records of achievement, especially at the secondary level where it has been linked with assessment of the General Certificate of Secondary Education (GCSE) and of the Technical and Vocational Education Initiative (TVEI) and subsequent innovations. Two features of this activity are particularly interesting for their implications for primary humanities. One of these is that they represent a thread in official policy that is quite different from the prescriptive rhetoric that surrounds much of the new national framework. The other, perhaps linked with the first, is that there have been increasing calls for the downward extension of records of achievement into primary schools where, indeed, some exploratory work has already been carried out by Hall (1989), Munby *et al.* (1989) and others. However, the RANSC (Records of Achievement National Steering Committee) Report recently issued (DES/WO 1989d) asserts rather sweepingly (p. 23) that:

> We have no evidence – and we understand that there has been very little development work on the ground to date – on records of achievement in primary schools; and we have very little evidence on them in middle schools . . .

and proceeds to call for their introduction from 5 to 16 in the interest of continuity in the national curriculum. This would be a welcome development in view of the nature of the work already carried out at secondary level, because of the breadth of the records, their cumulative nature, their emphasis on the positive features of an individual's development, and their emphasis on self-assessment and ownership of the record, rather than on comparisons with others.

Other relevant initiatives also mentioned in Chapter 4 include those of Harlen (1977a; 1977b; 1983) who developed a system for recording development in primary science somewhat akin to Cooper's suggestions for humanities, but in a much more extended format. Using two series of five-stage developmental scales very similar, in a sense, to NOFAN sequences, one for ages 5–8 and another for 8–11, she worked out with teachers a detailed procedure which has formed a basis for further initiatives, though it presents teachers with a sizeable commitment, especially if they are working without group or administrative support. There are also valuable suggestions at the primary level for comparable approaches in individual humanities perspectives: history (Joan Blyth 1988) and geography (Mills 1988). Meanwhile an interesting parallel to one of Cooper's initial suggestions has been developed in infant language work by Waterland (1985). In this kind of record, development is shown by outward movement through concentric circles, with sectors that merge and overlap, thus allowing for something more flexible than the categories postulated by Harlen and others. However, none of these authors would claim that their proposals should be woodenly or inflexibly adopted; that is why they all represent constructive advances in the search for suitable procedures for systematic record-keeping.

Meanwhile Hicks (1986; 1987) has stressed the need, over the primary curriculum as a whole, for a wide-ranging profile covering many aspects of children's development from 5 to 11, and also the need to combine rigour of record-maintenance with practicability. In her second article, she indicated that most junior schools in a West Midlands study did 'emphasize the keeping of class records, *and in particular of topic work done* (Hicks 1987 p. 15: my italics)', and this is encouraging. Apart from this, there was in her study no evidence of particular value to record-keeping in primary humanities. However, there have been in this field a number of thorough and constructive unpublished schemes, and a few outstanding ones, from individual schools and Local Education Authorities, so that the national situation is altering quite rapidly. This is timely, because there will soon be a sharp demand for a more rigorous national system, and those who have already succeeded in devising effective local procedures will have the strongest argument for continuing to do what is demonstrably practicable. Even those will, however, need to conform broadly to the national requirements, which will be discussed next.

Official guidance on record keeping

With the establishment of the new national framework, indications have already been given of how teachers will be required to keep official records in future. One such indication appeared in the *Policy to Practice* document (DES 1989, para. 6.9), to the effect that: 'Teachers will . . . be expected to keep a record of pupils' progress in relation to each attainment target: this will provide a general basis for planning their work' and also for informal discussions with parents and with other teachers. This approach was further spelled out in Circular 6/89. That Circular, in addition to embodying the Mathematics and Science Orders, indicated (para. 52) that schools would be expected to 'build on their existing assessment and recording procedures' to monitor individuals' progress according not only to attainment targets but also according to programmes of study, and also to

> build up a bank of relevant information about a pupil's progress, including possibly samples of work, on which to draw in the context of any discussions about the level that a pupil is judged to have reached at the end of the key stage.

These suggestions do thus apparently allow some place for concurrent assessment but also tie teachers' observations to attainment targets, a tighter prescription than in the official reporting procedures where profile components, rather than attainment targets, will form the basis (DES 1989, para. 6.8). It could indeed prove quite a demanding task for teachers, since the three core subjects alone had already generated between thirty and forty attainment targets, before the foundation subjects, including history and geography, staked their claims. In that case it may be legitimate to speculate that profile components rather than attainment targets may become the basis for teachers' records also. Meanwhile it is necessary to proceed according to such official advice as has already been given.

For that reason I shall not in this chapter discuss any alternative system of record-keeping. Wray (1985; 1988) made some interesting suggestions, and I had taken these and other ideas such as Morrison and Taylor's (1988) into account when attempting to devise a simple procedure for teachers to use. However, in view of this official advice, I shall confine myself to suggesting how policy at school level might be conducted in accordance with what is to be required, while preserving and extending 'existing assessment and recording practices' appropriate to an enabling approach.

Systematic recording in schools

The main purpose of keeping systematic records in schools, quite apart from the national requirements, is to ensure that there will be a shared statement of each child's curricular experience, of what he or she has gained from it, and of any particular qualities, interests, or difficulties that have appeared. This shared statement must be intelligible to the staff generally and, if the suggestions about linking these records with moderation are to be followed up, also to teachers and others outside the particular school. Governors too, entrusted with new responsibilities, may wish to interpret the nature of records, even if there is some doubt about the appropriateness of their considering the actual records of individual children. So, although these systematic records will be partly constructed on the basis of the running records described in Chapter 9, they should not show the personal style and subjectivity that are of the essence of good running records. In the latter there is a valid place for comments such as 'One more try to get Ann to use her own words' or 'Mustn't repeat the local joke about X Street: Arshed lives there, was badly teased, so wouldn't help clear up'. They would hardly be in place in systematic records.

However, it is not sufficient to confine systematic records to an edited and entirely retrospective statement. They do also have to convey something of the process of education, from baselining to summative recording of completion. Some teachers might prefer to 'write up' their systematic record only after a topic or episode of work is completed; others might find it easier to compile the systematic record alongside their personal running record. Several suggestions have been made about what sort of systematic record might be appropriate within the new national framework, notably in the proposals made by the Association for Science Education, the Association of Teachers of Mathematics, the Mathematics Association and the National Association of Teachers of English (ASE 1989) for a joint approach to the core subjects in the primary curriculum. In

Class	Y5 (Mrs Jones)
Date(s)	April–May 1990
Topic	WORKPLACES
Outline	General ideas: study of local bakery (Breadline plc): cake-making mini-enterprise

Process strands emphasized in topic

Skills	Specific concepts	Attitudes	'New' knowledge emphasized
Map, interviewing, reporting → thinking → manipulative, social and expressive	Work, location, production, → organization, hierarchy, division of labour	To work, industry, employment and their opposites	Particular local workplaces, their location and organization: experience in mini-enterprise

Baselining of competences identified as initially important

Children	Knowledge — General and skills	Concepts — Work	Concepts — Location	Concepts — Production	Knowledge — Local workplaces	Knowledge — Particular jobs	'Expanding' of individual potential	Task procedures and attitudes — Progress shown (self-referenced)	Comments (summative, diagnostic and formative)
Andrea	1	1	1	1	2	2	Try to develop general ideas	✓	Prefers working alone
Brendan	1	1	1	1	1	1		✓	Very keen on the cake-making
Carol	1	2	1	1	1	2	Emphasize writer economic aspects	✓	Parents both work for the council
Darren	1	1	1	1	0	1	Emphasize local knowledge	✓	Recently moved into district
Elspeth	2	1	2	1	3	2	Challenge with critical thinking questions	✓	
Farouk	1	1	1	1	1	1		+	Showed unexpected initiative in planning own and group work
Gemma	2	1	1	1	1	2	Try to develop general ideas	✓	
Harry	1	1	1	1	1	1		−	Disappointing. Stress at home?
(etc.) →									(etc.)

Figure 11.1 A suggestion for systematic summary record-keeping applicable to primary humanities

drawing up the following suggestions, I have taken these and other proposals into account. I have done so with some vigilance because, with its authoritative backing, this might become a kind of prototype for systematic primary-school record-keeping, in which case it would be particularly necessary to watch its implications for and its impact on humanities.

I suggest that the systematic recording of what a class has done in a particular topic should first embody a statement about the class and topic, together with an indication of the process strands and knowledge/understanding that the teacher considers centrally involved. The top panel of Figure 11.1 gives some idea of how this could be tried with the topic 'Workplaces' discussed in Chapter 8. This general statement would enable anyone subsequently consulting the record to know what, broadly, the members of the class had done during the stipulated time.

Turning next to individual recording, I suggest that this should involve three stages:

Baselining   Some systematic record of the baselining process should be kept. In fact, much of it will already be accounted for through the required monitoring of core-subject attainment targets (or profile components) that would allow an estimate of each child's study skills, mathematical competence, and aspects of science and technology apposite to the subject. As suggested in Chapter 8, this would be an instance of making good use of the data that the national curriculum will demand. As Attainment Targets multiply, monitoring will regularly cover such matters of central significance to humanities as competence in representational skills and familiarity with background knowledge. So it would be necessary to record only the specific baselining designed for the topic itself, perhaps together with any other relevant general matter not included within the core and foundations framework: this could apply to the social-science perspective in humanities, unless some procedure is laid down whereby regular recording of something like attainment targets in the cross-curricular themes is required.

This specific baselining, as systematically recorded, would be brief and focused. In the case of 'Workplaces', it might be confined to what, after careful consideration, the teacher identified as the three basic key elements to be considered in the topic:

- the concept of work
- the factories (or other workplaces) in the vicinity
- how workplaces are organized.

From the running records of the initial baselining process, a simple summary could be made, as indicated in the left-hand part of Figure 11.1. Here the recording device is simple and straightforward, if unusual. The number 1 under each heading denotes that the child in question has the necessary minimum understanding, as discussed in Chapter 8. Higher figures (2, 3, 4) indicate the extent to which some individuals exceed that necessary minimum: a 4 would imply a rare grasp of the centrally important ideas, or being at the 'naturally' level in most of the relevant NOFAN sequences. Notice that 1 is not necessarily the average initial performance, though it may well be the modal or most usual level. Above 1 the distribution is skewed away towards 4. Below it there is a rare o, representing lack of the necessary minimum, which may entail particular help (for example, in the case of a child who has been absent, or who does not have English as first language). In this way, sufficient baseline data can be transcribed into the systematic school records.

Extending The next brief step would be to decide on the planning of the topic work itself. For the majority of the children, this would probably be on relatively similar and predictable lines. The outcome would be summarized in the list of skills, concepts and knowledge/understanding specified in the top panel. For some, however, it would be necessary to negotiate with them the part that they are to play. The essence of this opening out of possibilities is indicated by the use of the term 'extending' rather than 'targeting' or anything similar. The next column in Figure 11.1 shows how 'extending' might be applied in the case of those children.

Progress When the topic is complete, the systematic record can be completed by transcribing from the running records and perhaps from test results some indication of whether each child has reached, exceeded, or fallen short of the target set. For this purpose a different, but equally simple, notation is suggested, but it is important that it should be understood. This time a tick implies that the particular goal determined through the 'extending' process has been reasonably attained. In Figure 11.1, Elspeth is given a higher goal, in view of her baseline data, and reaches it, while Brendan has a more modest one and again reaches it. If the teacher believes that a child's estimated progress has been substantially surpassed, then a + can be used: in a really dramatic instance, a + + would be possible. A minus (−) or double minus (=) would have the opposite connotation. In Figure 11.1, a plus applies to Farouk and a minus to Harry. Those symbols do not mean that either boy has a high or low performance relative to the rest of the class (a norm-referenced assumption) but that this is how their performance appears in relation to expectation of their individual powers. The basis of this way of looking at 'Progress' is thus a self-referent one.

It could be made more positively so if the children themselves were to play some part in its compilation. That would certainly be in accordance with the aim of self-assessment, and in some schools it is done. That would still leave open the question of what parts of the systematic record should be known by children, or parents or others. My own view is that as much should be open as circumstances permit.

Comments Clearly some kind of written explanatory comment is also needed if systematic records are to be complete. The final column in Figure 11.1 shows the kind of comment that might arise. It would cover both tentative explanations of outcomes and suggestions for action.

The whole systematic record, compiled in this way, would then be filed appropriately. It would provide a thumbnail sketch of a class, and of its individual members, as they move through a school, and of the development and performance of its individual members in its formal and informal life. Within that record, humanities would have adequate representation.

Translation into the national system

A school's systematic records, completed in this way, are likely to be both too extensive and too specific to fit unchanged into whatever framework is eventually approved by the School Examinations and Assessment Council. However, just as running records can be used in the compilation of systematic records, so these in turn can be the basis for national requirements.

For example, they could provide data for recording progress in the core-subject attainment targets; here they would in fact be repaying, hopefully with accrued interest, the information taken from core-subject records at the baselining stage. Subsequently a similar procedure may apply in history and geography and perhaps more widely.

The relationship between this kind of translation into attainment targets (or profile components) and the administration of Standard Assessment Tasks (SATs) and the implications of that relationship for local or wider moderation schemes remain uncertain and must be carefully watched, if the value of teacher assessment is not to be lost. The Task Group on Assessment and Testing *Report* proposed a happy blend between the two, but the possibility still exists that SATs, especially well-designed and apparently cross-curricular ones, may come to be regarded as the key element in assessment and the school's systematic records taken seriously only when they endorse the SAT results and the Levels which they suggest. This should be resisted, both generally and because humanities could fare unfortunately where SATs are concerned. A worst-case scenario would be one in which discrepancies between teachers' assessments and SATs were assumed to be a measure of teachers' competence in teaching or assessment or both, rather than as a genuine means of catering for parts of learning that SATs cannot reach.

If profiling and records of achievement are substantially introduced at the primary level, a desirable development if resources can be found, then a different sort of translation from systematic records would also become necessary, one which would afford a more central position to children's own self-assessment. This could also provide a more secure niche for information not limited to attainment targets or profile components in the core and foundation subjects, information which is none the less essential to the recording of development as envisaged in an enabling curriculum.

On the other hand, it must be faced that even the minimal recording suggested in this chapter may be seen by teachers as a back-breaking spectre. It is most unfortunate that, just when it becomes possible to introduce a necessary and overdue component of record-keeping into primary humanities, this should coincide with a seemingly endless series of additions to the primary teacher's role, almost guaranteeing opposition to any further suggestion irrespective of its merits. It is difficult enough in any event to steer between the Scylla of overcomplexity in assessment, towards which many enthusiastic groups of teachers and even advisers have tended, and the Charybdis of mere vacuous generalization which adds nothing to genuine knowledge of children's progress. I have tried for years to grapple with this dilemma, and my awareness that these suggestions fall short of resolving it is tempered by a realization that nobody else has done much better.

Indeed, it remains to be seen whether what is officially called for in the new national framework will prove practicably possible, and what will happen if it doesn't. Meanwhile I hope I have pointed towards a means of navigating between that Scylla and that Charybdis. I also hope that somebody will find the passage more readily than I have done. It will still remain necessary to give teachers the time and encouragement and reward needed if they are to sail through it.

Of course, some teachers are always more ready than others to undertake such voyages. To change the metaphor rather abruptly from sea to land, these are the ones that I have described as 'hikers' rather than 'strollers' on the paths of assessment (W.A.L. Blyth 1987), though they too need some incentives. Some may even be 'fell-walkers', for whose benefit Chapter 12 has been written. But the system of national assessment and record-keeping will function only if all the strollers, as well as the hikers and fell-walkers, can manage to play their part. In Chapter 7 I indicated some of the issues which might influence their capacities and judgements even in the most favourable of circumstances, and these issues will apply, perhaps even to SATs, however blandly the results of assessment are presented.

There may be one way of alleviating the burden of record-keeping for all teachers, and that is by timing it sensibly and humanely. By building up systematic records from running records periodically over a year, the end-of-year scramble can be minimized, and incidentally the records themselves can be made available in time for further planning within the school, or for transmission to the next school. For the same reason, translation from school to national recording should be a manageable process, but only if it is taken seriously by management and carefully timed and organized: no mean task in any primary school, but one in which information technology could play at least some part. No doubt official advice, and the expertise of writers on primary-school management will be beamed towards this problem, for it is a very important one.

So is another issue germane to the Chapter 7 considerations, namely the inadequacy of relying on one teacher's subjective views. This may appear to contradict what has been said about the importance of running records, but it need not. All that is required is to encourage the practice of interchange whereby a subject consultant, or a head or other member of management, takes some part in everyday appraisal and checks 'products' in concurrent assessment or in teacher-made testing. This must involve some sacrifice of autonomy, as discussed in Chapter 6, but is a small price to pay to buttress the case for the teaching profession as a whole to be trusted in its assessments. Moreover, it may be good for the children to experience interaction with different adults more often than has been the case in the past.

Clearly the compilation of records is a difficult and yet an essential task. Much will be said publicly, in future, and much controversy engendered about how national records will be used. But the rest of this chapter will be devoted to the use of systematic records within and between schools, a procedure that must remain largely within the competence and obligations of the schools themselves.

Using records: continuity within schools

Curriculum continuity is now a commonplace of educational discourse. Yet it is only recently that attention has really been focused on continuity from one year to the next within schools. Of course, for a long time past, some schools have developed whole-school policies, occasionally in a rather idiosyncratic way. What the national curriculum aims to do is to make this practice universal, and to ensure that it embodies, for all children, progression as well as continuity. In an enabling curriculum this implies progression in process strands and widening knowledge, so that, as children move from term to term, year to year and school to school, they should meet continuing appropriate challenges to their capacities. Too often, in the past, children have encountered a series of topics embodying changes in content but not in approach or, even worse, repetitions of the same topic with the same approach. Yet if there is to be genuine extension of process strands, combined with appropriate knowledge content, it is important that each teacher should know what a class and its individual members (who may change substantially within and between years) have already achieved. So one teacher's records become, at least in part, another teacher's baselines. Systematic school records should facilitate this process. Meanwhile, the issues raised in Chapter 7 suggest that the quality of interaction between one teacher and her class can never be a complete guide to how that class, and its individual members, will react to another teacher. However, the very fact that some record data are available can itself help to give the successor teacher some measure of confidence and understanding in developing the new relationship.

This class-to-class continuity is, of course, necessarily modified where a teacher 'goes up' with her class, and still more so where there is a policy of vertical or family grouping, or where the school is so small that this takes place willy-nilly.

Until official policy is finally decided by the School Examinations and Assessment Council and the Secretaries of State, it is not entirely certain what use can be made of internal records in complying with the national requirements, or thence in the annual reporting to be made to parents or in formal statements about attainments at 7 and 11. Nor is it certain what kinds of moderation, within or between schools, will be encouraged. The one aspect of record-keeping that can be anticipated with some confidence is that its reliability and its public esteem will depend on the willingness of schools to allow some modification of their autonomy, just as class teachers will need to concede something of their autonomy to colleagues. Confidence in records cannot be obtained through imposition from above, nor through complete subjectivity from below, but through a collaborative strategy build up from class to class and school to school, as suggested in Chapter 6.

All the suggestions made in the foregoing pages are based on the assumption that records should be essentially self-referenced, or at least criterion-referenced, and that they should trace learning in some form of NOFAN sequence. The 'grade' which this book advocates is essentially independent of what others achieve, but very much dependent on improving one's own capability, including capability for self-assessment, and doing so as far and as fast as possible. Even criterion-referencing is used only in order to mark out publicly identifiable evidence of progress.

It is only reasonable that this identifiable evidence should be sought. Parents are entitled to ask for more than a teacher's bland assurance that Tommy is doing well, or that he and his friend are so interested in their topic work that it is difficult to get them to go out to play. His parents also need to be convinced that he is in most ways generally abreast of his age-group and in some ways making his particular mark. What they are not entitled to emphasize is his place in the class order, coupled with a pointed enquiry as to why he is not in the top three. To help in the process of mutual understanding, parents should not only be given annual reports, or even allowed access to records. They should also be entitled to have those records explained and, as far as possible, to be invited to discuss with the teachers and, as appropriate, also with the children, what the school proposes to say, and then to countersign the record itself. Meanwhile adverse comments, especially about behaviour and attitudes, should not be written into systematic, or national, records; this is regularly emphasized by those concerned with records of achievement which must by definition be positive in quality. There are other and better ways of conveying disapproval of particular behaviours than by indulging in the equivalent of an endorsement on a driving licence.

There still remains the possibility that norm-referenced grading, yielding a quantifiable score, might become legally required from teachers' assessment as well as from SATs. That would, of course, contradict the whole tenor of the recommendations made in this chapter and, if that were to happen, it could not be reconciled with the system of everyday appraisal, concurrent assessment and teacher-made testing that has been outlined here. It would have to be based on external testing and be seen to be based on that kind of testing, while the procedure suggested here should continue and to some extent counterbalance, or even challenge, it. That, too, would need to be explained to parents. The effect of that counterbalance would, I realize, depend on how far a school staff or a Local Education Authority would be united in supporting it. I hope they would be.

Using records: continuity between schools

Records will certainly have an important part to play in the monitoring of individual children's development between, as well as within, schools. For change of school is change of class writ large. In addition to moving to a teacher, or teachers, involving perhaps differences in personal style, children may well now be moving to an institution with a different professional 'ideology' (King 1978; 1988: Galton and Willcocks 1983). Such moves are different according to the levels involved.

From pre-school to infant or first school

Even at this first threshold, which is becoming increasingly important now that the entry age to schools is widely extended below the statutory limits of compulsory education, records can play a significant part in the first 'baselining' process, helping teachers to know something about the experiences and powers of individuals. A few studies have already been made at this first transfer age; a useful review is provided by C.A. Blyth and Wallace (1988). Not surprisingly, there is no direct reference to humanities, but some awareness of 'where?', 'when?', 'who?', 'how?' and 'why?' may indeed be indicated, and incorporated into infant teachers' planning of individual topic work.

From infant to junior (and first to middle)

Now that seven is to be a major threshold in the national framework, this second transition will become formally more important than hitherto. In view of the contrast between infant and junior schools, it is strange that so few studies have been made at this level, but one by Woods (1987) indicates something of pupil perspectives at this stage, while it is clearly becoming more important as a management issue, both when the transition takes place between schools on separate sites and when it involves moving from one 'department' to another within a junior-and-infant or a combined school. If humanities is represented to some extent in the general records maintained in the infant or first school, there will again be something positive on which the next baselining can be established, and also some kind of guarantee that there will not be too much in the way of vain repetition in topic work, a possibility that could still remain even when the national curriculum is fully in force.

From junior to secondary (and middle to upper)

This is where the majority of studies of transition and continuity have been focused, because it is the major rite of passage in school education, and the stage at which the interface between one professional ideology and another is most marked.

A number of studies of transition between schools, including comparatively recent ones such as those by Galton and Willcocks (1983), Stillman and Maychell (1984), Measor and Woods (1984), Derricott (1985), Gorwood (1986) and Delamont and Galton (1986) have emphasized the curricular and social consequences of movement from junior to secondary schools and have sometimes revealed a disquieting lack of effective communication between staffs in the different schools. In the field of humanities, Williams and Howley (1989) have shown how this can apply specifically in geography, while an account by Lackenby and French (1989) indicates how problems of primary–secondary transfer may be approached in the case of history. These and other studies have shown that most children do not suffer much from this lack, but this provides no grounds for complacency. For it suggests either that teaching doesn't matter much anyhow or, that if the liaison had been better, children might have achieved much more. Since the spate of studies in the mid-80s, there has been notable improvement, at least at the level of LEA organization. Yet it is still occasionally possible to come across glaring instances of lack of communication, such as that exemplified by a head of mathematics in a comprehensive school who complained how little he knew about his new intake, only to be informed that a set of records had been brought specially from a junior school and placed in his cupboard, though apparently nobody had actually thought to tell him that this had been done. If that can happen in the case of one of the core subjects, arguably the one in which records are most meticulously maintained, it becomes necessary, to say the least, to exercise considerable vigilance in order to ensure that records in humanities are effectively transmitted.

At this third transition stage, records do in fact become much more important. In future, the process strands will already have been identified in each child's development, in the form of attainment targets or profile components, and should be clearly noted in whatever information is passed on, together with some indication of what topics have been covered.

The actual ways in which the records could be used in practice is another issue. For example, would there be ample opportunity for records to be considered so that they could be taken into account formatively in the planning of work? For it is so easy to ignore such matters in the welter of starting the new school year with newcomers. Yet it is here that they can be used with particularly positive effect. First, they can help to break down the earnest anonymity of the new 'intake', so that teachers can build on it purposively before the bloom of vigilant innocence wears off. Second, it can help to avoid this kind of jaded interchange: 'Please, we did that at the other school!' 'How many did that at their other school? . . . Oh, well then, I suppose we'd all better do it again now!'

In my own explorations in schools, I was able to take part in one quite valuable piece of liaison between what are now Y6 and Y7, helping to negotiate assessment in the primary school in such a way as to be most useful to the secondary humanities teachers, and also following the children themselves from one school to the other. In the process I was able both to monitor their individual progress and also to discuss with them their experience of being assessed. With my knowledge of those children in the primary school, I was even able to predict their initial progress in the new school with some measure of success: for once, my activities almost verged on research. Where such procedures are introduced, transfer can be much smoother, though never automatic.

Of course, there is a particular challenge for secondary teachers to plan in such a way as to incorporate uneven baselines, but at the same time the experience of some can be brought constructively to bear on the common enterprise. A useful extension of this building upon earlier experience applies in particular to local studies, where the different schools' immediate local knowledge can be pooled in such a way as to extend everybody's understanding but also to help to establish positive reputations and to cement new social relationships, especially in that challenging and often neglected interim before separate subject studies crystallize out.

Alongside this general pooling of experience for which records are essential, there comes the equally demanding task of identifying individual children's emerging capacities as revealed in their documents, and the planning of work formatively for individuals and groups. To maintain the momentum from primary into secondary school, or from middle into upper school, it can be valuable to supplement the records themselves with actual examples of children's work which, at the very least, reveal to a teacher what this hitherto unknown Marvin or Rebecca was once capable of doing, and to remind Rebecca and Marvin, in their turn, that their former achievements are known and open to new challenges, rather than being conveniently overlooked so that both children can coast along, concealed by the general upheaval of transfer. The significance of this carrying forward of 'products' from earlier years has already been mentioned in Chapter 6.

Of course, even these suggestions are liable to many other potentially disturbing complications. A new teacher in a secondary school has many other things to do than to ponder over the records of new pupils, especially since there are so many classes of so many different ages to get to know, some of them with urgent examination demands. Yet it quite often, and quite justifiably, happens that new children are matched with a new teacher who thus becomes the member of staff most likely to need to see their records. Moreover, in the humanities area, where the convention is (and is likely to remain so in the national curriculum) for a relatively small part of the week to be devoted to subjects such as history, geography and religious education, the number of new faces and records to be met by a humanities teacher is likely to be proportionately still greater than in, say, English. Add to this the likelihood that some of the children will have come from other localities, regions and even continents, and the effectiveness of local record-keeping and of local curricular continuity will probably be still further eroded. Yet this is only like everything else in schooling, and such record-transmission and mechanisms for promoting curricular continuity should not be avoided simply because they may not work perfectly. Nothing ever works perfectly. No time is ever spent exactly as the teacher making curricular plans intends. Curriculum planning, assessment and record-keeping are still worth doing.

With the transfer of children and their records to secondary or upper school and the completion of the assessment procedures to be required at the age of 11, the informal as well as the formal demands of assessment in primary humanities reach completion. One whole age-cohort has, as it were, graduated or passed out. To reach that point will, in future, require more in the way of official assessment than has been the case in the lifetime of primary teachers. Yet no age-cohort exists in isolation. The team of teachers in a primary school is, inevitably, already engaged in monitoring the next cohort, and the next, and the one after that. In that process teachers will be necessarily, through experience, continuously improving their capacity to assess children, as was mentioned in Chapter 7. Some of them will be in transition from strollers to hikers. Some may indeed feel a need to develop from hikers to fell-walkers. This they may be inclined to do from sheer professional inclination or interest, or from – which may be much the same – a desire to deepen their understanding of education for their own sake and for that of other people. For them I have included Chapter 12.

12 Postscript for 'fell-walkers'

I have elsewhere (W.A.L. Blyth 1987: see also Chapter 11 above) suggested that teachers setting about the assessment of children can be compared to walkers reaching a national park who find that three kinds of excursion are recommended. The first is a gentle one for beginners, or for those not in trim; they are the strollers who are like teachers just starting to undertake assessment. The foregoing chapters, combined with shared experience and instruction, could help them take the first steps. The second category suggested is a more strenuous hike; and this resembles the energetic prospect held out to those with some experience of both teaching and assessment. Such hikers might include humanities consultants who have in addition acquired some experience in assessment in the core subjects. Most primary schools will have their complement of strollers, reinforced by sufficient hikers to enable destinations to be reached. Yet if the teaching profession is itself to 'make the grade for primary humanities', it must also produce a cluster of pioneers who feel able to embark on a more sustained, original and ambitious enterprise, aiming at the summits. These are the fell-walkers of assessment, and this concluding chapter is for them.

It is not intended as a comprehensive introduction to further study or research, but only as an indication of what remains to be done and how fell-walkers might start to climb away from the haunts of hikers and strollers in pursuit of their goals. For they can extend their professional capabilities in three ways.

Developing and assessing a more coherent humanities curriculum within the national framework

It seems likely that the proposals for the foundation subjects of history and geography will allow some autonomy in curriculum and assessment on the part of individual schools. As indicated in Chapter 6, schools and localities will probably make plans for the exercise of that autonomy, plans that will be of great help to strollers and hikers. However, some teachers may wish to design something more complete, and to suggest to colleagues how their ideas might be translated in practice.

For example, a school curricular framework could be implemented by a teacher of fell-walker calibre in a particularly thorough way, more amply resourced and linked with closer study of the development of individual children. Such a teacher would want to take the agreed school programme and adapt it for himself or herself and maybe enlist the help of colleagues who would in turn welcome the additional support that would result. A vigorous fell-walker head teacher might consider going further and devising a thoroughgoing scheme for humanities, or indeed for the whole curriculum, which would cover the statutory requirements but would also give a distinctive stamp to the experience of children attending that school. A programme of this nature would entail a characteristic kind of everyday appraisal, concurrent assessment and perhaps of teacher-made testing too, devised in concert with colleagues and built up over a period of time. The encouragement given to schools to develop their own individuality in order to attract custom in a free-market situation might well lead to enterprises of this kind. Such ventures would, of course, depend on a particularly favourable set of relationships with parents, colleagues and children alike. Where such relationships do exist, this kind of curriculum planning might indeed be one means of resolving the contradiction between uniform curricular requirements and the rhetoric of choice which the Education Reform Act itself embodies. The problem would be that there are not enough fell-walker head teachers to enable every primary school to compete in that curricular marathon.

That is not the only kind of fell-walking that can benefit primary humanities. Most of the others depend rather more on guide-books and charts already produced by other fell-walkers. Some involve tackling new crags and adding to the sum total of charts and guidebooks available for others.

Learning more about what others have found out

The references already given in earlier chapters, and listed in the bibliography, will provide a substantial starting-point, a foothill, as it were, from which to start the ascent. So an important first step would be to study the general books mentioned particularly in Chapter 4, especially those by Shipman, Harlen and Conner that refer particularly to the primary years, and to supplement these with cognate studies of upper middle and lower secondary schools such as the survey by Clough and Davis (1984). These are now suggested not just as underpinning references, but as a bedrock for study. To these must be added, as essential reading, the Task Group on Assessment and Testing (TGAT) *Report* and the publications from the National Curriculum Council discussed in Chapter 5, and the torrent of official publications relating to the implementation of national assessment policy that have emerged, and will continue to emerge, as the national framework takes shape. Together, these will form an indispensable database for any systematic understanding of what is taking place.

Some of the basic books on assessment and some of the extensive range of journal articles referred to in those books constitute or at least embody substantial contributions to research. Most of these depend for their validity on sophisticated research and statistical techniques which entitle them to claim provisional conclusions where this book can only make suggestions. They build the highways across the peaks, where previous chapters have only offered glimpses from a passing aircraft. However, most of their highways have bypassed the part of the fells where primary humanities is located. I emphasize this in order to indicate how much remains to be done by way of systematic studies; more will be said about this in the following section. Meanwhile, it could well happen that would-be fell-walkers, following up relevant cognate studies, may need to learn something about research methods in order to be able to understand the general accounts already mentioned, let alone to plan their own. For this purpose it might be useful to look at one of the many recently published introductory texts on research methods, bearing in mind that these are usually produced for the benefit of people who want to do research, rather than just to understand other people's research.

Even when their studies are understood, it is still quite a usual experience to find that works on assessment generally do not quite 'fit' primary humanities. Most of the specific references to areas of the primary curriculum are to the core subjects, in which the sheer volume of study in respect of both teaching and assessment is quite immense. Yet when an attempt is made to transfer their findings to humanities, it often becomes apparent that they refer to skills and concepts that are different in nature, and this is as would be expected if the three models presented in Chapter 2 are valid. A useful means of handling data of this kind would be to annotate each study with a comment about how far it is relevant to humanities, and what differences in approach would be necessary in order to carry out a meaningful, comparable study in our field. For such studies will become increasingly necessary.

This is an exercise that may be worth carrying out collectively rather than individually. It could well figure, in suitable circumstances, as a part of the staff development exercises discussed in Chapter 6 and now given some official direction by the National Curriculum Council (Moon 1989; NCC 1989b). Perhaps two or more experienced teachers, wishing to embark on fell-walker studies, could work together in a collective enterprise within a school or a local cluster and could thus throw more light on the discussions in which their colleagues were taking part at a less ambitious level.

A further extension of such collaborative activity could be particularly applicable if, as is to be hoped, a substantial moderation procedure comes to be introduced. For it could then become necessary to find somebody capable of handling data at more than a descriptive level. Local Education Authority advisers may not themselves have sufficient time or opportunity to carry out the necessary analysis and so may be very glad to turn for help to fell-walkers among the teachers concerned, even to the extent of negotiating some form of secondment for them. Such procedures as the adjustment of a threshold criterion might draw usefully on simple measurement techniques that a fell-walker had acquired. For example, the means of recognizing a minimum competence in map interpretation, sufficient to signify a particular Level in an Attainment Target, might be a case in which specific expertise in test construction might be called upon. Substantial guidance would be required for this purpose, and it is unlikely that the manuals and in-service training to be provided will constitute an adequate substitute for understanding based on actual insight and experience. From the standpoint of primary humanities, it is important that there should be somebody capable of carrying out this kind of operation locally, without dependence on rule-of-thumb application of centrally issued instructions. It would be most regrettable if this kind of expertise were to be guaranteed for the core subjects only.

Hitherto the role of the fell-walker has been presented as primarily that of a skilful follower of paths discovered by champions of the peaks and presented in a packaged, if sophisticated, form. But those champions are always busy with new treks. So anyone aiming to join their still more select number should not only read the basic literature but should also monitor what is being published each year. The rate of output is such that substantial new studies in assessment, with clear relevance to what takes place in primary humanities, are likely to appear between the completion of this book and its publication. Therefore one of the first things for a really ambitious fell-walker to do would be to follow advertisements and reviews in order to locate such studies. The situation is similar to the publication of a railway timetable which always seems to need an updating supplement by the time at which it actually appears. If that is true of books, then it is much more markedly the case where journal articles are concerned. These too have to be monitored, since a fell-walker may need to know of them before they are processed into still more books.

Some of the relevant sources are fairly obvious. Relevant research material may appear in *Educational Research, Research in Education*, and the *British Educational Research Journal*, in addition to which there are other national and regional journals that occasionally carry relevant material. Some of these journals figure in the bibliography, and it would be tedious to list them all here. Another kind of journal that may carry useful material is the *genre* concerned with teaching as such. *Teaching History* and *Teaching Geography* are both clearly relevant, as is the welcome new journal *Primary Geographer* and the *Newsletter* of the newly formed Primary History Association. It is predictable that these will be preoccupied with the reports of the Working Groups in their subjects, as will the Historical and Geographical Associations, while the Economics Association and the Association of Teachers of Social Science (ATSS) will also be keeping an eye on the place achieved by their disciplines in the national framework of core and foundation subjects and cross-curricular themes. A watching brief will also be kept by the three major journals on curriculum, namely *Curriculum*, the *Curriculum Journal* published by what is now the Curriculum Association (formerly Association for the Study of Curriculum) and the *Journal of Curriculum Studies*, and also the other main journals concerned with primary education, namely *Education 3–13, Child Education* and *Junior Education*. A number of other national and regional journals may at any time carry similar material, and at least their contents pages should be regularly monitored. As for international and overseas journals, they are far too numerous to be listed, but a few American titles such as *History and Social Science Teacher* and *Elementary School Journal*, may be worth watching.

It is, of course, quite possible, in so diffuse a field involving so many aspects of educational and humanities studies, to miss some quite important article that happens to be published somewhere else, in the United Kingdom or overseas. Therefore really experienced fell-walkers should always expect to supplement direct monitoring by a systematic search through an information-retrieval system such as ERIC, using a computer terminal. Such fell-walkers would, however, be likely to be exploring on their own account, and thus to qualify for inclusion in the élite of their company, whose needs occupy the remaining part of this chapter.

Learning more as a teacher-researcher

There is really no division between teaching and research. Every teacher is necessarily engaged in experimentation. Some teachers, those who aspire to be champion fell-walkers, undertake more systematic research. At one time this meant carrying out experimental designs, distinct from teaching and often involving working with children outside a teacher's normal sphere of activity. With the advent of action research, which the teacher-research model really implies (Stenhouse 1975), the unity of teaching and research can be restored. In recent years there has been a proliferation of action research of various kinds in primary schools (e.g. Armstrong 1981; Rowland 1984; Pollard 1985) and of guides to such approaches in the classroom (e.g. Hammersley and Atkinson 1983; Rudduck and Hopkins 1985; Hopkins 1985).

Nor is there a real distinction between teaching, research and assessment. They are interactive systems, each contributing to the other two. Yet, for a fell-walker, research into assessment implies the introduction of more rigour in investigation than is customary for most teachers in their everyday work. Within the general teaching–research–assessment process, certain elements would be consciously singled out for closer and more systematic attention.

The choice of field for this closer study depends in part on the general state of knowledge, and in part on the particular situation in which a teacher is working. In order to help a would-be fell-walker to focus on a particular topic, whether as part of a team venture or as a personal theme for a higher degree or other specific qualification, it may be useful to look again at the current situation as described in earlier chapters, and in particular to draw attention to some of the issues in respect of which I have had to point out the deficiencies of current knowledge and understanding. Of these, there is no lack. Some of them are easier for a lone fell-walker to investigate; others require something more like a team roped together. The more manageable ones will be considered first.

Analysis of everyday appraisal

The most obvious starting point for this venture into the fells is the tightening up of procedures for everyday appraisal. In Chapters 8 and 11 it became evident that the potential sensitivity of this form of assessment is offset by its subjectivity. Even the 'cover' provided by moderation procedures can go only some way towards mitigating this subjectivity. Yet there is a big gap between everyday appraisal and the elaborate triangulation and other ethnographic methods required in 'real' research of a case-study nature. Such methods, in their turn, even when rigorously enacted, still attract the mistrust of the stricter adherents to experimental methodologies. However, any teacher who wants to go a little above the hiker level in improving everyday appraisal has a reasonably promising course of action open. An agreement could be made with one or two colleagues to exchange classrooms in order to make systematic mutual checks on children's responses. If a school is able to secure further help, for example through the services of a consultant, or of a final-year BEd student embarking on a small-scale investigation, or both, then the advantages of a disengaged pair of eyes and ears become available. (The BEd student would probably have the further advantage to management of being paid in facilities and not in money.)

Such an arrangement would, of course, involve focused observation, much more so than in the simpler kinds of everyday appraisal. This observation would be focused in turn on specific process strands, with an observation schedule designed in such a way as to relate it rigorously to NOFAN sequences or, preferably, to a more theoretically adequate cognitive model. The analysis of the outcomes would not be based on the assumption that there was one right answer, any more than the children's own thinking should depend on that assumption at their own level. Rather, note would be taken of where the different observers agreed more, or disagreed more, thus allowing both for differences in variability from one strand to another (for example, more in thinking skills than in tool skills) and also for differences between teachers in assessment style. The outcome of a small-scale study of this kind and the light that it could throw on the processes of everyday appraisal would at least be available within one school; then perhaps in a cluster of schools; and, if the study were really well designed and cautiously interpreted, perhaps more widely still.

Analysis of concurrent assessment

The rather more tangible nature of concurrent assessment makes it relatively easier to investigate than everyday appraisal. Observational techniques are not essential to the investigation. Because the material is tangible, the same 'products' can be examined by several people and their verdicts compared. A lone fell-walker could well be in a position to invite colleagues to join in a collective operation of this kind, exchanging time and skill for mutual benefit. The distinctive role of the fell-walker would be that of responsibility for the design of the mini-study and for stipulating the initial suggestions about what to look for in the analysis, although it is of the essence of such investigations that further promising material may come to light in the course of the study. So, at the start, it would be necessary to decide what process strands and knowledge were intended to be involved, and in what ways progress could be expected to show in a written account, a worksheet, a piece of artwork or an artefact. In practice, the fell-walker might also come to be looked upon as something of an expert, even a local guru, in which case it would become necessary to disclaim that status as far as possible, not simply out of modesty or a desire to avoid the abrupt shift in reputation that would follow if things went wrong, but also because it is procedurally important to minimize the effect of differences in competence and experience.

For such purposes it should again be possible to model the intersubjective process on the approach used by the Assessment of Performance Unit (APU) in its language-testing programme in which there is an agreed schedule concerning five levels of performance (APU 1982). Similar procedures have been devised by others. This model of assessment can be adapted to other media and has the advantage of being holistic rather than atomistic, appraising the piece of work in its entirely rather than looking for the inclusion of particular details. It is also in accordance with the NOFAN model and (very importantly) it can be harmonized with the notion of Levels in Attainment Targets as adumbrated by the TGAT *Report* itself; for this approach is likely to figure in whatever substantive proposals for assessment are eventually made by the School Examinations and Assessment Council.

From a small-scale investigation of this kind, it might be possible to draw up a schedule for the analysis of 'products' and then to try it out in a neighbouring school or others in a cluster, or, with the assistance of the advisory service, more widely. Primary teachers in general would be more ready to use an approach devised by one of their own number than one imposed from outside – provided, of course, that this was one of their number who had earned their confidence. Fortunately it is no longer true that fell-walkers are regarded with suspicion simply because they are fell-walkers; but the possibility remains as a warning to the over-confident, the over-ambitious, or those who do not notice how much of their routine work is in fact falling on long-suffering others.

Analysis of teacher-made tests

Tests devised by teachers are still more open to intersubjective checks, for now there is more uniformity both about what children do and about when they do it. If a mix of questions is used, some of which allow of exact answers (e.g. in time-testing) while others encourage more lateral thinking, then different means will be needed for checking the answers. The more factual ones are open to simple percentage agreement, or where necessary to the application of appropriate correlational methods. For the others, the effect of differential competence in assessment would come into play if a mark or grade were to be assigned to every question, but would be considerably reduced (as indicated in Chapter 9) if a global, holistic approach on the lines of the APU language testing were to be used here also.

It might also be possible to go further and to draw up a bank of tests that could be used in a school or group of schools, thus evolving something between the tests that a teacher develops for a class, and the national testing programme itself. If this is attempted, then there is a case for introducing such tests in an intermediate position in time also, between the critical ages of 7 and 11. Any such procedure would need to be supported with a panoply of statistical and measurement techniques, so that more weight could be attached to the outcome than could be possible for a teacher using tests with one class. However, the more weighty and formal such a procedure were to become, the more it would resemble the national testing programme itself, or standardized Local-Education-Authority skills testings, and would thus run counter to TGAT's intentions by overtesting.

There is also another difficulty in test-bank compilation of this kind. For, if questions are to range from the more straightforward to the more challenging, they are likely to show greater homogeneity of 'marking' in the former than in the latter. So, if the conventional procedures of test construction were to be applied, these would probably lead to the elimination of the more challenging questions in favour of the others, thus depriving the tests of one of their major values. So the advantages of designing this kind of local tests are at best doubtful. What they gain in being home-grown and relatively user-friendly, they may lose through being too inflexible and too much like external tests. Nevertheless, there are places and circumstances in which they could be worth using, even as a means of convincing parents and governors that it is not necessary to look to national agencies for expertise in testing. For the rest, fell-walkers are probably well advised to concentrate on tightening up the procedures for everyday appraisal and concurrent assessment.

Diagnostic assessment

Another possibility, related to the preceding one, would be to break new ground in the diagnosis of particular kinds of blockage or miscue in process strands in primary humanities. This would involve being well versed in individual cognitive psychology. The outcome could be of great value as a contribution to the professional knowledge to be placed at the disposal of strollers and hikers as they carry out their everyday appraisal and concurrent assessment and testing.

Case-studies of innovations in assessment procedures

Another route that a fell-walker might like to tread is likely to become very important. It is a way of monitoring the effectiveness of the new national procedures themselves, and it is based on the case-study approach. The case-study has now become established as a respectable research procedure, so much so that it has now generated its own traditions, procedures, and critics. Wisely used, it remains a particularly revealing way of tracing how new developments actually become established within schools and localities, especially those which are imposed from outside in the confidently bureaucratic manner from which the new national framework is not immune, and also in locating any deficiencies or problems that may arise.

Of course, this kind of study is fraught with interpersonal issues too. It could, for example, be undertaken in a school only with the support of the head teacher and of the majority of the staff members. This consideration applies even more to case-studies than to the analysis of concurrent assessment already mentioned. It really is necessary that a case-study of this kind should be welcomed as a means of helping to ensure the success of an innovation, rather than as a means of hindering it, or as an argument for not even trying it. If a similar study were undertaken on a locality scale, or even (for a particular age-group or aspect of primary humanities) over an entire LEA, then the personal issues would become considerably more complex, though not beyond the powers of a head or an adviser. In one sense, indeed, studies of this kind are unlikely to be evenly distributed over schools and LEAs simply because they would be easier to mount where success is expected than where deficiencies are likely to come to light. That difficulty can be circumvented by a strategy based not on sampling along a success–failure distribution, but rather on following the 'good practice' approach. Here the aim is to find out what works well, rather than what does not, and to make general recommendations on that basis in the faith that good practice acutely analysed can be transferred elsewhere, *mutatis mutandis*, and will eventually drive out bad. A cautious critic could find many logical and even ethical objections to that approach, but it may be the only practicable one. What is more, the effective assessment of primary humanities within the national curriculum may ultimately depend on the sort of knowledge that such investigations can yield, and upon the good sense with which the ensuing information can be applied in different situations.

Longitudinal studies of children's development

All the suggestions hitherto made for fell-walkers have been related to the actual processes of assessment and to their institutional modification. Another field of investigation, concerned with the actual ways in which children learn, is also centrally relevant to assessment in primary humanities. The whole set of pro-cedures recommended in earlier chapters has been based on the models of learning, development and curriculum outlined in Chapter 2. I am conscious that those models are provisional and partly unsubstantiated. Research of a more fundamental kind is needed to verify, or supersede, those models and to produce a more adequate and convincing framework for assessment of primary humanities. Barrett (1985) indicates one possible line of approach. Research of the kind would constitute a major task, partly because the necessary procedures could not be completed until the children studied have themselves become adolescents or perhaps adults. Something on the scale of the studies carried out by the National Children's Bureau is really needed. So this is well beyond the range of the lone fell-walker, but not beyond what can be managed by a team of researchers working with a major research grant. This is what primary humanities has lacked, and I hope that the lack will be made up by a fund-granting foundation responding to a well-formulated research proposal from an institution able and willing to concentrate on, or at least not to omit, humanities in the planning of its activities. It might be practicable to design something comprehensive that would yield results not only for humanities but for many other purposes too.

Of course, it would be difficult to tap the data that are required. Metacognitive understanding, that is, understanding of one's own learning, is clearly desirable and it figures among the aims of an enabling curriculum, as indicated in Chapter 4. None the less, there are inherent difficulties for an adult, let alone a young child, in understanding how one has learned any particular aspect of a skill, or any particular piece of knowledge, or how one has acquired the capacity to deploy task procedures. Occasionally a child or adult may realize exactly how this advance has come about. For the most part, it might almost be argued that effective learning takes place in the way it does because the learner is not aware of how he or she is learning: so much of it depends on previous learning internalized at what I have termed the 'naturally' level. Some day computer-assisted learning might transform much of the basis of cognitive activity, but at present the nature of children's learning remains such that any major research expedition by fell-walkers would need to work out how this metacognitive barrier could be transcended.

These difficulties would apply to any attempt to unravel learning of skills, task procedures and particular knowledge content in humanities. Concepts and attitudes, which were deliberately omitted from the list in the previous paragraph, would be still more difficult to investigate. Yet these two process strands have been identified throughout as essential parts of what an enabling curriculum would try to foster in children's educational development. If we are obliged to say that we do not really know what they are, or how they can be acquired and modified, then we cut a sorry figure beside those who claim to demonstrate, citing research evidence, exactly what concepts and attitudes are needed in the core subjects, and on the other hand beside those who believe that all we need to assess, or even to teach, in primary humanities is factual information. We may be able to manage for a little longer, in this situation, by appealing to common sense and shared professional understanding, which is in large measure what has been done in the preceding chapters; but sooner or later it will be imperative to supplement those interim bases for assessment with something more demonstrable about concept formation which must be assessed, and preferably also about attitude change which, though not officially assessed, remains fundamentally important. This will call for even more fell-walker expertise than in the relatively more accessible case of skills, task procedures and knowledge.

A closer look at self-assessment

A further, and perhaps still more difficult, extension from such longitudinal studies would be an investigation of development in children's capacity for self-assessment, whose importance as an educational aim has been emphasized throughout the previous chapters. For this purpose it might be necessary to look at the whole curriculum, provided that humanities were well represented within it. It would involve close rapport with a sample of children, and their teachers and parents, over a period of time but, if it resulted in positive understanding, such an endeavour would be well worth the effort, for it has to be admitted that the rhetoric about self-assessment, in which I have shared in the earlier part of the book, badly needs empirical support.

Remembering all the children

When considering the implications of the preceding paragraph, it is also important to confront an issue that has hitherto been sidestepped, as happens in many such books and perhaps in the national curriculum itself. Because my main aim has been to discuss assessment of primary humanities as it applies to the majority of children and those who teach them, little has been said about the problems of assessment among those whose place in society is such that the call to engage in self-assessment and self-direction and to 'aim high', according to what the school defines as high, must ring hollow. Already, in their primary years, many of these have come to believe themselves effectively debarred from the choices that self-direction enables the majority to make. Even if assessment is self-referenced and humanities sensitively approached, their motivation is bound to be affected. Indeed, the better the humanities programme is, the more likely it is to etch their own situation more starkly. For some strong motivation may come from sources other than school; for others there may not even be an alternative source. Sooner or later, some concerned and robust fell-walker will need to look into assessment and self-direction among these losers in society and to bring the whole question forcefully to our attention. For, if self-direction and strenuous progression in learning are to be upheld as an aim for all children, we have to remember that these are some of the all. Moreover, there are strollers and hikers who have to teach and assess them, and in some cases many of them, right now, without the benefit of the specific expert advice that they need. There is some urgency for that concerned and robust fell-walker, or a few of them, to step forward.

The same is true of that other aspect of the whole subject that I explicitly excluded from my brief, namely the assessment of humanities among young children with (other kinds of) special needs. There is here a whole set of problems that could well be approached by fell-walkers with professional experience in special education. This issue has a different kind of urgency, but it too must be faced. Of course, as has been emphasized in recent years, it overlaps with the previous issue. Physical deficiency, learning difficulties and social exclusion so often reinforce and even define each other.

Manageable fell-walker research

Most of these kinds of research would need in practice to be broken down into manageable tasks, for example, by age-levels or process strands or both, with each fell-walker concentrating on one, thus supplementing the relatively few pioneer studies mentioned in earlier chapters. Although these individual studies would be less well co-ordinated, they might be easier to start. Even so, each fell-walker would need to carry gear drawn from two kinds of expertise: from the psychology of learning and from educational studies generally, but also from the humanities disciplines themselves. A further truncation of the individual tasks could be achieved if only one of the perspectives were considered in a particular study: historical understanding here, geographical understanding there, and economic or social understanding in a third instance, as has usually been the case in such studies as have already been carried out. Even as this range of research possibilities is spelled out, it is evident what a long way humanities still has to go if it is to begin to catch up with the core subjects and to establish a claim to be taken seriously, in its own terms, at foundation level. Yet, unless something more substantial and convincing can be established about children's learning of process strands and knowledge, it will not be possible to initiate the further and equally substantial research required in order to make significant improvements in assessment.

Fell-walkers and teacher education

Without substantial research it will also be impossible to develop, effectively, the work of one other group of fell-walkers not hitherto mentioned. I refer to those responsible for the initial and further professional education of new strollers, hikers and indeed future fell-walkers in the processes and practice of teaching and assessing primary humanities. For that aspect of professional education is going to be required. Already official recommendations for such purposes are being issued. Much depends on how they are carried out. The fell-walkers involved can in fact operate in a dual capacity, that of guides and that of explorers. They have to be guides. It is to be hoped that many of them will have the opportunity of becoming explorers too.

Fell-walkers and the inevitability of change in the national framework

As fell-walkers achieve little successes here and there, they are likely to be overtaken by a cumulative pressure to amend the national framework itself. For this is a new and untried system. It should be, and probably is being, monitored closely at local and national level as well as within schools. Indeed, the National Curriculum Council and the School Examinations and Assessment Council are themselves required to undertake a review of this kind. But their view is necessarily one from the bridge. That should not deter lone fell-walkers, or groups of them, from undertaking supplementary investigations of their own which could well throw different light on what is happening. If, building on the case-studies already mentioned, they can undertake these initiatives with the approval of Local Education Authorities and under the aegis of an institution of higher education on whose expertise they can draw, their efforts are likely to be more fully rewarded not only by means of additional qualifications, but through assistance of a consultancy nature in the work itself. In one sense, the status of the teaching profession and its claim to be innovative as well as responsive in the new situation will depend upon its fell-walkers and those who advise and support them. If anything should happen to weaken the LEAs and institutions of higher education themselves, then the fell-walkers would carry a still greater burden of responsibility. Just as the national assessment procedures will depend on the strollers and hikers for their successful operation, so they will depend on the fell-walkers for their successful improvement. Whatever the 1988 Education Reform Act may have achieved, it is not the end of the story.

For that reason, the process of *Making the grade for primary humanities* must continue. To summarize, this involves the two main aims spelled out in Chapter 1. First, teachers as a profession have to assert their claim to be able to monitor, sensitively, the development of every child in the perspectives of humanities and in the process strands and some aspects of knowledge associated with those perspectives. Second, in doing so, they have to Make the Grade for Humanities in the primary curriculum as a whole. I am conscious that this book has done no more than sketch some ways in which these two essential tasks can be approached. I am confident that others will be able to carry those tasks forward with conspicuous success, in the years that lie ahead.

Appendix 1
Glossary of terms

APPRAISAL A general form of assessment based on regular and systematic observation.

ASSESSMENT A procedure for monitoring children's progress.

ASSESSMENT NORM An average performance in a class or school or, more generally, one against which the performances of individuals are measured.

BASELINING A means of estimating relevant aspects of individual children's skills, knowledge and understanding at the outset of a piece of work.

CLOSED CONCEPT One related to a particular area of knowledge, e.g. *trireme*.

COGNATE TRANSFER Capacity to apply skills, concepts, etc., in a context slightly different from the one in which they were originally learned.

CONCOMITANCE A 'methodological' concept, meaning the tendency for things to happen together, without implying that either causes the other.

CONCURRENT ASSESSMENT Assessment in particular of 'products' emerging from children's work in humanities, e.g. topic books, worksheets, artwork, maps or computer printouts. It is 'take-away assessment'.

CRITERION REFERENCING Assessment by comparison with a relatively objective standard, and not with other children's performance.

DESCRIPTIVE NORM An unusual term, denoting what most children of a particular age-group or culture group can do, without implying that this, and no more, is what they all ought to be able to do.

DIAGNOSTIC ASSESSMENT A procedure for discovering the strengths and relative weaknesses of individual children in respect of particular aspects of humanities. It is involved in BASELINING (see above) and should be used in formative planning.

ENABLING CURRICULUM A curriculum based on teachers' 'planned intervention'. It takes account of children's development and their experience, but extends both by means of the relatively stable ways of understanding and endeavour that have taken shape over the ages.

EXTENDING The process following BASELINING, in which each individual's contribution to a scheme of work is negotiated in such a way as to make relevant, strenuous, but not excessive demands, in accordance with emerging capacities and interests.

FOCUSING OF ASSESSMENT Distinction between everyday appraisal, concurrent assessment and testing.

FOCUSED DISCUSSION A procedure, with a class or a group, intended to shape everyday appraisal towards a limited number of concepts, etc., considered to be central to a scheme of work.

FORMATIVE USES OF ASSESSMENT Following up BASELINING and DIAGNOSTIC ASSESSMENT with specific programmes intended to develop the powers of individual children.

GENERAL BASELINING Use of school records particularly in the core subjects, together with the 'feel' of a class, as a part of decision-making about the approach to a particular piece of work.

GENERAL TRANSFER: GENERALIZATION Going rather beyond COGNATE TRANSFER (see above) in an attempt to establish general principles.

HIGHER THINKING SKILLS Thinking that involves reasoning, interpretation, and a capacity to 'tolerate ambiguity', that is, to grasp that there may be no single explanation of a problem, but only the likelihood that one explanation is more viable than another, though perhaps both have some effect on the outcome.

IMPLICIT SKILLS Those which are necessary in a piece of work, but also have more general application.

INTERROGATION A special kind of questioning that, rather like focused discussion, is aimed at finding out how well individual children have grasped particular skills or concepts or knowledge.

MANIPULATIVE SKILLS Sometimes referred to as physical skills: for example, the capacity to use tools or equipment.

METHODOLOGICAL KEY CONCEPTS Concepts involved in the analysis of data (see Chapter 4).

MODERATION Procedures for ensuring comparability between assessments made by different teachers or schools.

NOFAN SEQUENCE A sequence of learning extending from 'Never' through 'Occasionally' and 'Frequently' to 'Always', and then to 'Naturally'.

NORM-REFERENCING Assessment by comparison with others rather than by comparison with a relatively objective measure (as in CRITERION REFERENCING).

NORM OF PRODUCTION A general term denoting the quantity and quality of work that a particular class is likely to produce, in the light of its cultural situation and previous history.

OPEN CONCEPT One capable of transfer beyond the immediate context and of 'spiral' development, e.g. *trade*.

OVERT SKILLS Those that are directly fostered through a piece of work – in contrast to implicit skills.

PERSONAL MAP A map revealing a child's (or an adult's) own view of a place or a region or the world. It can apply to psychological structures as well as to geographical maps.

PERSPECTIVE A term used in this book to denote a particular way of looking at issues or problems, one derived from a distinctive academic discipline, e.g. historical, geographical, social-scientific.

PROCESS STRANDS A term used here to cover skills, concepts, task procedures and attitudes that develop during the course of school education. It implies both the learning of process and the process of learning.

PRODUCT Something that children do or make that can be taken away and looked at. See under CONCURRENT ASSESSMENT (above).

PROFILE A record of a child's schooling based on a variety of activities and achievements.

RANGE OF ASSESSMENT A classification of modes of assessment that includes recall, cognate transfer and general transfer.

RECALL ASSESSMENT A procedure that requires a child simply to reproduce or 'play back' what has been learned, without showing any capacity to adapt it to new situations or circumstances.

RECORD OF ACHIEVEMENT A cumulative profile built up by individuals over the course of schooling and subsequently 'owned' by the young person.

REFERENCE SKILLS Skills required in order to locate information. These include retrieval skills.

RUNNING RECORDS Records kept by teachers, in ways that they find useful, in the course of teaching.

SELF-REFERENCING Assessment by comparison with an individual's previous achievements, rather than with an objective criterion or with the performance of others.

SOCIAL SKILLS Skills involved in co-operative learning and collective behaviour.

SPECIFIC BASELINING Probing of individuals' prior understanding of the particular skills, concepts, etc., involved in a specific scheme of work.

SPECIFIC CONCEPTS Concepts important to a subject perspective or to a topic: OPEN if they are shared with other subjects or topics, otherwise CLOSED.

STUDY SKILLS Almost identical with TASK PROCEDURES (see below).

SUBSTANTIVE KEY CONCEPTS Major categories for selecting and organizing the knowledge-content of schemes of work.

SUMMATIVE ASSESSMENT Assessment intended to demonstrate what children have gained from a scheme of work.

TASK ATTITUDES Attitudes showing readiness to undertake tasks, on the lines already learned, in order to solve problems.

TASK PROCEDURES Ways of setting about solving problems or seeking explanations by applying skills and concepts already learned: almost the same as STUDY SKILLS.

TGAT Task Group on Assessment and Testing, set up by the Secretary of State for Education and Science.

TOLERATION OF AMBIGUITY See under HIGHER THINKING SKILLS. It refers to readiness to accept situations in which there is no one right answer, only a best probability.

Appendix 2

Outline of a scheme of work for primary humanities designed for an enabling curriculum according to the principles and characteristics of *Place, Time and Society* (W.A.L. Blyth *et al.* 1976)

Infant years (Key Stage 1)

'Pre-disciplinary' experiences of a kind that are recognizably concerned with the past, with the physical, natural and human environment, and with social and economic relations. These experiences should be derived through topics such as: 'Family', 'Shops', 'Where We Live', 'Pets', etc., and also from imaginative and expressive work based on story, poetry and song, and from investigation of 'old things' and pictures of people engaged in different kinds of activity in different places.

Junior years (Key Stage 2)

A more structured approach would be followed, but alongside this there would be some space, probably diminishing in extent each year, in which humanities elements in events of current importance and interests introduced by the children could be extended.

7–8

'Folktales' A selection from different cultures past and present, according to the children's own background and the teacher's choice; analysis of this selection; composing a ballad.

'Reporters' Making a class newspaper based on aspects of the school itself and the locality, with emphasis on evidence, accuracy, arrangement and communication.

8–9

'Roots and Origins' Careful consideration of the class's own roots (involving social skills and empathy); other kinds of roots; the concepts of origins; early local settlement; other kinds of origins that affect the children; locating roots and origins in time.

'Exploring'   Children's own explorations, under adult guidance and otherwise; eminent explorers past and recent; detail about at least one major exploration and its consequences; relations in place and time.

9–10

'Gran's World'   Building up, initially from children's family resources, a period-picture of life after 1945 locally and elsewhere; scrutiny of evidence; then/now comparisons; a 'legacy' for some future class to examine when today is their Gran's World.

'Workplaces'   The concept of 'Work' (and lack of work); local workplaces; liaison with one of these in order to study it; perhaps development of a mini-enterprise in the class; elementary economic concepts and social relations linked with personal/social education; brief comment on workplaces elsewhere and on different ways of organizing workplaces.

10–11

In this final junior year three topics could quite possibly be introduced, as follows:

'Knowing Our Place'   More systematic local study, based on a variety of data; group study of various aspects and representation in a variety of ways, including 'history maps', time lines and contemporary maps; consideration of local issues and of future planning from different points of view.

'Here and There'   School twinning used to exchange information and experience with a nearby but contrasted environment, preferably through actual exchanges of visits but in any case by correspondence, etc.; development of skills in comparative study.

'Other People's Lands'   Sharing knowledge about living in and visiting other countries, preferably drawing on the children's own holiday and other experiences; choice of two contrasted political units both of manageable size; planning and experiencing imaginary journeys, involving comparisons, thus rounding off this sequence of topics in primary humanities by bringing together a number of acquired skills and concepts with potential for further development.

Of course, this scheme would require appropriate modification in schools with 5–8, 8–12, or 5–12 age-ranges, or with the other three-tier pattern 5–9, 9–13, 5–13. In the national curriculum the overlap into Key Stage 3 will almost certainly involve something more systematic in history and geography. However, this should cause no great difficulty, for *Place, Time and Society* was initially devised for the middle years of schooling then defined as 8–13, and it was quite customary in the 1970s to find a systematic introduction to subject study expected in the years beyond 11. If a humanities course from 5 to 11 is carried out on the lines and on the principles suggested here, subsequent subject study should be facilitated rather than impeded, though with a continuing recognition that humanities comprises more than the historical and geographical perspectives alone. This scheme is designed to develop, progressively, the skills, concepts and task procedures that belong to all the humanities perspectives, and also to build up the foreground and background knowledge associated with them.

Appendix 3
Taking account of the history
interim report

The Interim Report from the History Working Group was published, somewhat belatedly, while this book was already in production, but the publisher kindly agreed to the inclusion of this further Appendix. It is not intended as a review of the Report; only a comment on its implications for the suggestions made in the book itself, relating to the primary years.

The Working Group acknowledges a position for history in the primary curriculum that is neither over-assertive nor apologetic and it recognizes the importance of British history without over-emphasizing it. This standpoint does not conflict with mine.

The *process strands* are represented, as is now legally necessary, by Attainment Targets (ATs) grouped into Profile Components. These depart somewhat from the Historical Association's suggestions outlined in Chapter 5, and they represent one of many possible ways of classifying and expressing ideas that are necessarily interwoven. The list is simple:

PROFILE COMPONENT 1: HISTORICAL UNDERSTANDING
Attainment Target 1: Historical understanding displaying a sense of time and place.
Attainment Target 2: Understanding points of view and interpretations of history.

PROFILE COMPONENT 2: HISTORICAL INVESTIGATION AND ANALYSIS
Attainment Target 3: Acquisition and enquiry
Attainment Target 4: Analysis and evaluation of a wide range of sources.
Attainment Target 5: Organization and expression.

Within these five ATs, *skills*, the focus of so much controversy in history teaching, are well represented. Particular, and welcome, attention is paid to higher thinking skills, and to the grouping of skills in ATs 2, 3 and 4 into what I have termed *task procedures*. *Concepts* are deemed important but receive relatively less specific mention, though AT1 is clearly presented as being 'concerned with increasing conceptual development'. *Attitudes* are mostly implicit, but specific emphasis is laid on the task attitude of achieving balance between points of view. In general, it appears practicable to trace and record children's development in process strands according to these five ATs, in ways that are compatible with what has been suggested in this book.

The Report also stresses, rightly, that none of these Attainment Targets can be pursued without simultaneous acquisition of *knowledge*, and recognizes that local knowledge is the key to much understanding, and that 'background' knowledge should be gradually built up, though the Report does tend to lose sight of the wayward and unpredictable ways in which young children learn.

The actual knowledge-content recommended, for them to learn, is embodied in the *Programmes of Study*, which are only outlined now, with samples of detail: they are to be more fully worked out in the Final Report. For *Key Stage 1* a welcome, flexible, yet demanding, set of proposals is put forward, one that is fully compatible with the aims of an enabling curriculum, provided that it really is remembered how much help and encouragement some children will need if they are to gain fully from it. For *Key Stage 2*, and later, History Study Units are suggested. Four of these, at 7–11, would be broad British history topics, from Roman times to our own day, and three others would be taken from European and (other) World history: (ancient) Egypt and Greece; 'Explorations and encounters *c.* 1450–1550'; and the American Frontier *c.* 1750–1910. All seven of these would be compulsory. In addition there would be a selection of two from (brief titles): Ships and Seafarers; Food and Farming; Buildings and Builders; Writing and Printing; Land Transport; Domestic Life. Three more 'school-designed themes', largely based on local history, would make up a tally of twelve Units over the four years. *Ships and Seafarers* is the one spelled out in detail. It is intended that the whole series should be approached in a broadly chronological order.

These HTUs are judiciously balanced from the historian's point of view, and it is gratifying to see 'Exploring' represented in one compulsory and one optional Unit. However, despite the Working Group's disclaimers, the load seems heavy. Presumably it is expected that Geography will propose an equivalent addition. Yet in Appendix 2 I suggest a total of nine for the whole of Humanities over the same years, and I cannot help thinking of some schools I know, in which these proposals might result in a headlong rush to complete the tally of Units, rather than in the growth in historical understanding required in the Attainment Targets.

Assessment, described by the Chairperson as 'a complex area', is deferred until the Final Report, though there are intimations of a sensitive approach. Descriptions are given of what might be expected, presumably from average children, in each AT at 7 and 11, and these seem well pitched for those who are abler and more mature. There are also indications of how the Programmes of Study might be modified for those who are not, though more detail will be required about how adjustments between Programmes, Levels and Key Ages could be effected in practice. There is, however, little recognition that this whole set of recommendations might be superseded if assessment at Key Stages 1 and 2 is confined to the core subjects, or indeed of the effect that this might have on the 'equivalent of three or four periods (sic) in a 40 period week' that the Working Group has postulated for history in the years 5–11.

This is, of course, only an Interim Report, though a generally commendable one. Firm policy is still several steps away; and geography still has to deliver. Meanwhile the present Secretary of State, in his introductory letter, has indicated that more emphasis should be placed on chronology and British history and that historical knowledge should be an Attainment Target in its own right. He has also suggested that assessment should be organized on a precisely accountable basis, with due regard for factual knowledge. That could be fallacious. Perhaps, when policy is finally decided, the Secretary of State will have followed the Chairperson in recognising that assessment is indeed, as I have attempted to show, 'a complex area'.

Bibliography

Alexander, R.J. (1984). *Primary Teaching*. London, Holt, Rinehart & Winston.

Antonouris, G. and Wilson, J. (1989). *Equal Opportunities in Schools: New Dimensions in Topic Work*. London, Cassell.

Armstrong, M. (1981). *Closely Observed Children*. London, Writers and Readers Co-operative and Chameleon Press.

Assessment of Performance Unit (APU) (1982). *Language Performance in Schools: Primary Survey Report No. 2*. London, HMSO.

Association for Science Education (ASE) (1989). *The National Curriculum – Making it Work for the Primary School*. Report jointly prepared with other Associations. Hatfield, ASE.

Bale, J. (1987). *Geography in the Primary School*. London, Routledge & Kegan Paul.

Barrett, G. (1985). 'Structure of knowledge and the learner: an examination of cognitive learning skills, learning situations and knowledge.' *Cambridge Journal of Education* 18, 2, 73–80.

Becker, H.S. *et al.* (1968). *Making the Grade: The Academic Side of College Life*. New York, John Wiley.

Bennett, N. (1976). *Teaching Styles and Pupil Progress*. London, Open Books.

Bennett, N., Desforges, C. *et al.* (1984). *The Quality of Pupil Learning Experiences*. London, Lawrence Erlbaum Associates.

Biott, C. (1984). *Getting on Without the Teacher: Primary School Pupils in Co-operative Groups*. Collaborative Research Paper 1, Centre for Educational Research and Development, Sunderland Polytechnic.

Biott, C. and Clough, M. (1985). 'Co-operative group work in primary classrooms.' *Education 3–13* 11, 2, 33–6.

Black, H.D. and Broadfoot, P. (1982). *Keeping Track of Teaching*. London, Routledge & Kegan Paul.

Black, H.D. and Dockrell, W.B. (1980). *Diagnostic Assessment in Geography: A Teacher's Handbook*. Edinburgh, Scottish Council for Research in Education.

Black, H.D. and Dockrell, W.B. (1984). *Criterion-referenced Assessment in the Classroom*. SCRE Publication 84, Edinburgh, Scottish Council for Research in Education.

Blanchard, J. (1988). 'Assessment: friend or adversary.' *Curriculum* 9, 1, 43–7.

Blenkin, G.M. and Kelly, A.V. (1987a). *The Primary Curriculum* (2nd edition). London, Harper & Row.

Blenkin, G.M. and Kelly, A.V. (1987b). *Early Childhood Education: A Developmental Approach*. London, Paul Chapman.

Blyth, C.A. and Wallace, F.M.S. (1988). 'An investigation into the difficulties of transferring written records from the nursery school to the primary school.' *Educational Research* 30, 3, 219–23.

Blyth, J.E. (1988) *History 5–9*. London, Hodder & Stoughton.

Blyth, J.E. (1989) *History in Primary Schools* (New edition). Milton Keynes, Open University Press.

Blyth, W.A.L. (1984). *Development, Experience and Curriculum in Primary Education*. London, Croom Helm.

Blyth, W.A.L. (1987). 'Towards assessment in primary humanities.' *Journal of Education Policy* 2, 4, 353–60.

Blyth, W.A.L. (1988a). 'Appraising and assessing young children's understanding of industry', in D. Smith (ed.). *Industry in the Primary School Curriculum*. Lewes, Falmer Press.

Blyth, W.A.L. (ed.) (1988b). *Informal Primary Education Today: Essays and Studies*. Lewes, Falmer Press.

Blyth, W.A.L. *et al.* (1976). *Place, Time and Society 8–13: Curriculum Planning in History, Geography and Social Science*. Glasgow and Bristol, Collins/ESL Bristol.

Boardman, D.J. (1983). *Graphicacy and Geography Teaching*. London, Croom Helm.

Bolton, N. (1977). *Concept Formation*. Oxford, Pergamon.

Brimer, A. (1969). *Bristol Achievement Tests*. Windsor, National Foundation for Educational Research/Nelson.

Broadfoot, P. (ed.) (1984). *Selection, Certification and Control: Social Issues in Educational Measurement*. Lewes, Falmer Press.

Brown, R. (1988). *The Future of the Past: History in the Curriculum 5–16: A Personal Overview*. Occasional Paper No. 1, Historical Association.

Bruner, J.S. (1966). *Towards a Theory of Instruction*. Cambridge, Mass., Belknap Press.

Bruner, J.S. *et al.* (1956). *A Study of Thinking*. New York, John Wiley.

Campbell, R.J. (1985). *Developing the Primary School Curriculum*. London, Holt, Rinehart & Winston.

Campbell, R.J. (1989). *Assessing the National Curriculum: from Practice to Policy. Junior Education Report of 1989 National Primary Conference*. Leamington Spa, Scholastic Publications.

Campbell, R.J. and Little, V. (eds.) (1989). *Humanities in the Primary School*. Lewes, Falmer Press.

Catling, S. (1979). 'Maps and cognitive maps: the young child's perception.' *Geography* 64, 288–96.

Catling, S. (1980) 'Map use and objectives for map learning.' *Teaching Geography* 5, 15–17.

Catling, S. (1988). 'Environmental perception and maps' in D. Mills (ed.). *Geographical Work in Primary and Middle Schools* (revised edition). Sheffield, Geographical Association.

Clift, P.S. *et al.* (1981). *Record Keeping in Primary Schools*. Schools Council Research Studies. Basingstoke, Macmillan Education.

Clough, E.E. and Davis, J. (1984). *Assessing Pupils: A Study of Policy and Practice*. Windsor, National Foundation for Educational Research/Nelson.

Conner, C. (forthcoming). *Assessment and Testing in Primary Schools*. Lewes, Falmer Press.

Cooper, H. (forthcoming). Thesis on young children's historical concept formation, to be submitted to the University of London.

Cooper, K.R. (1976). *Evaluation, Assessment and Record Keeping in History, Geography and Social Science*. Glasgow and Bristol, Collins/ESL Bristol. (See also (1977) 'Diagnostic teaching'. *Education 3–13* 5, 1, 12–16.)

Crowther, E.W. (1982). 'Understanding of the concept of change among children and young adolescents.' *Educational Review* 34, 3, 279–84.

Cunningham, P. (1988). *Curriculum Change in the Primary School Since 1945*. Lews, Falmer Press.

Dahl, R. (1985). *Charlie and the Chocolate Factory*. (New edition). London, Puffin Books.

Daugherty, R. (ed.) (1989). *Geography in the National Curriculum*. Sheffield, Geographical Association.

Day, C. *et al.* (1986). *Managing Primary Schools: A Professional Development Approach*. London, Harper & Row.

Dean, J. (1972). *Recording Children's Progress*. London, Macmillan.

Dearden, R.F. (1968). *The Philosophy of Primary Education*. London, Routledge & Kegan Paul.

Dearden, R.F. (1979). 'The assessment of learning.' *British Journal of Educational Studies* XXVII, 2, 111–24.

Delamont, S. (ed.) (1987). *The Primary School Teacher*. Lewes, Falmer Press.

Delamont, S. and Galton, M. (1986). *Inside the Secondary Classroom*. London, Routledge & Kegan Paul.

Derricott, R. (ed.) (1985). *Curriculum Continuity: Primary to Secondary*. Windsor, National Foundation for Educational Research/Nelson.

Derricott, R. and Blyth, A. (1979), 'Cognitive development: the social dimension' in A. Floyd (ed.) *Cognitive Development in the School Years*. London, Croom Helm, for the Open University.

DES (1989). *National Curriculum: from Policy to Practice*. London, Department of Education and Science.

DES/WO (1980). *A Framework for the School Curriculum*. London, Department of Education and Science and Welsh Office.

DES/WO (1987). *The National Curriculum: A Consultation Document*. London, Department of Education and Science and Welsh Office.

DES/WO (1988a). *Mathematics for Ages 5 to 16: Proposals* . . . London, Department of Education and Science and Welsh Office.

DES/WO (1988b). *Science for Ages 5 to 16: Proposals* . . . London, Department of Education and Science and Welsh Office.

DES/WO (1988c). *English for Ages 5 to 11: Proposals* . . . London, Department of Education and Science and Welsh Office.

DES/WO (1989a). *Science in the National Curriculum*. London, Department of Education and Science and Welsh Office. HMSO.

DES/WO (1989b). *Mathematics in the National Curriculum*. London, Department of Education and Science and Welsh Office. HMSO.

DES/WO (1989c). *English in the National Curriculum: Key Stage 1*. London, Department of Education and Science and Welsh Office.

DES/WO (1989d). *Records of Achievement: Report of the Records of Achievement National Steering Committee*. London, Department of Education and Science and Welsh Office.

Desforges, C. (1989a). 'Getting down to bases.' *Times Educational Supplement*, 28 April.

Desforges, C. (1989b). *Testing and Assessment*. London, Cassell.

Driscoll, K. (1986). *Humanities Curriculum Guidelines*. Lewes, Falmer Press.

Duncan, A. and Dunn, W. (1988). *What Primary Teachers Should Know about Assessment*. London, Hodder & Stoughton.

Edelstein, W. (1987). 'The rise and fall of the Social Science Curriculum Project in Iceland, 1974–84: reflections on reason and power in educational progress.' *Journal of Curriculum Studies* 19, 1, 1–23.

Education Act (1944). 7 & 8 Geo. VI, c. 31. London, HMSO.

Education Reform Act (1988). *Statutes*, chapter 40. London, HMSO.

Elliott, G. (1976). *Teaching for Concepts*. Glasgow and Bristol, Collins/ESL Bristol.

Entwistle, N.J. (ed.) (1985). *New Directions in Educational Psychology: I – Learning and Teaching*. Lewes, Falmer Press.

Fisher, S. and Hicks, D. (1985). *World Studies 8–13: A Teacher's Handbook*. Edinburgh, Oliver & Boyd.

France, N. and Fraser, N. (1975 and revisions). *Richmond Tests of Basic Skills*. Windsor, National Foundation for Educational Research/Nelson.

Frith, D.S. and Macintosh, H.G. (1985). *A Teacher's Guide to Assessment*. Cheltenham, Stanley Thornes.

Furnham, A. (1986). 'Children's understanding of the economic world.' *Australian Journal of Education* 30, 3, 219–40.

Furth, H.G. (1980). *The World of Grown-ups: Children's Conceptions of Society*. New York, Elsevier.

Gabarino, J. *et al.* (1978). 'The social maps of children approaching adolescence: studying the ecology of youth development.' *Journal of Youth and Adolescence* 7, 4, 417–28.

Gagné, R.M. (1965). *The Conditions of Learning*. London, Holt, Rinehart & Winston.

Galton, M., Simon, B. and Croll, P. (1980). *Inside the Primary Classroom*. London, Routledge & Kegan Paul.

Galton, M. and Willcocks, B. (eds.) (1983). *Moving from the Primary Classroom*. London, Routledge & Kegan Paul.

Gibson, Tony (1989). *Education for Neighbourhood Change* series; the most recent pack for schools is *All Around Us*. School of Education, University of Nottingham, Nottingham NG7 2RD.

Gipps, C. (1985). 'A critique of the APU', in P. Raggatt and G. Weiner (eds.) *Curriculum and Assessment*. Oxford, Pergamon/Open University.

Gipps, C. and Goldstein, H. (1983). *Monitoring Children: An Evaluation of the Assessment of Performance Unit*. London, Heinemann Educational.

Goodson, I.F. (1983). *School Subjects and Curriculum Change*. London, Croom Helm.

Gorwood, B.T. (1986). *School Transfer and Curriculum Continuity*. London, Croom Helm.

Gunning, S., Gunning, D. and Wilson, J. (1981). *Topic Work in Primary Schools*. London, Croom Helm.

Gunning, D., Marsh, C. and Wilson, J. (1984). *Concept Ladders in Primary School Work*. Trent Papers in Primary School Topic Work 84/2, Nottingham, Trent Polytechnic.

Hall, G. (1989). *Records of Achievement: Issues and Practice*. London, Kogan Page.

Hammersley, M. and Atkinson, P. (1983). *Ethnography: Principles in Practice*. London, Methuen.

Harlen, W. (1977a). *Raising Questions*. Match and Mismatch Project. Edinburgh, Oliver & Boyd.

Harlen, W. (1977b). *Finding Answers*. Match and Mismatch Project. Edinburgh, Oliver & Boyd.

Harlen, W. (1983). *Guides to Assessment in Education: Science*. Basingstoke, Macmillan Education.

Harlen, W. *et al.* (forthcoming). *Assessing Science in the Primary Classroom* series. London, Paul Chapman.

Harris, M. (1972). *Environmental Studies 5–13: Teacher's Guide*. London, Rupert Hart-Davis.

Hicks, J. (1986). 'Pupil profiling and the primary school: a review of the issues.' *Educational Review* 38, 1, 21–30.

Hicks, J. (1987). 'Record keeping in infant and junior schools.' *Evaluation and Research in Education*. 1, 1, 9–18.

Hirst, P.H. (1965). 'Liberal education and the nature of knowledge' in R.D. Archambault (ed.) *Philosophical Analysis and Education*. London, Routledge & Kegan Paul. (The views initially expounded in this chapter underwent some subsequent revision.)

HMI (1978) *Primary Education in England: A Survey by HM Inspectors of Schools*. London, Her Majesty's Inspectors of Schools. HMSO.

HMI (1982). *Education 5 to 9: An Illustrative Survey of 80 First Schools in England*. London, Her Majesty's Inspectors of Schools. HMSO.

HMI (1983). *9–13 Middle Schools: An Illustrative Survey*. London, Her Majesty's Inspectors of Schools. HMSO.

HMI (1985a). *Education 8 to 12 in Combined and Middle Schools*. London, Her Majesty's Inspectors of Schools. HMSO.

HMI (1985b). *History in the Primary and Secondary Years*. London, Her Majesty's Inspectors of Schools. HMSO.

HMI (1985c). *The Curriculum from 5 to 16*. Curriculum Matters 2. London, Her Majesty's Inspectors of Schools. HMSO.

HMI (1986). *Geography from 5 to 16*. Curriculum Matters 7. London, Her Majesty's Inspectors of Schools. HMSO.

HMI (1988). *History from 5 to 16*. Curriculum Matters 11. London, Her Majesty's Inspectors of Schools. HMSO.

HMI (1989). *Environmental Education from 5 to 16*. Curriculum Matters 13. London, Her Majesty's Inspectors of Schools. HMSO.

Hopkins, D. (1985). *A Teacher's Guide to Classroom Research*. Milton Keynes, Open University Press.

Jahoda, G. (1963a). 'The development of children's ideas about country and nationality: I – the conceptual framework.' *British Journal of Educational Psychology* XXXIII, 1, 47–60.

Jahoda, G. (1963b). 'The development of children's ideas about country and nationality: II – national systems and themes.' *British Journal of Educational Psychology* XXXIII, 2, 143–53.

Kerry, T. and Eggleston, J. (1988). *Topic Work in the Primary School*. London, Routledge.

Kimberley, K., Hextall, I., Torrance, H. and Moon, R. (1989). 'National assessment testing; the TGAT Report.' *British Journal of Sociology of Education*, 10, 2, 233–51.

King, R.A. (1978). *All Things Bright and Beautiful? A Sociological Study of Infants' Classrooms*. Chichester, John Wiley.

King, R.A. (1988). 'Informality, ideology and infants' schooling' in W.A.L. Blyth (ed.). *Informal Primary Education Today: Essays and Studies*. Lewes, Falmer Press.

Knight, P. (1989). 'Empathy: concept, confusion and consequences in the national curriculum.' *Oxford Review of Education* 15, 1, 41–53.

Lackenby, P. and French, M. (1989). 'History across the primary/secondary divide: a Sunderland case-study.' *Teaching History* 56, 8–13.

Lally, J. and West, J. (1981). *The Child's Awareness of the Past: Teachers' Guide*. Hereford and Worcester County History Advisory Committee.

Langford, P. (1987). *Concept Development in the Primary School*. London, Croom Helm.

Lawton, D., Campbell, R.J. and Burkitt, V. (1971). *Social Studies 8–13*. Schools Council Working Paper 39, London Evans-Methuen Educational.

Lloyd, K. *et al.* (1985). *Management and Leadership in Primary Schools: The System and the Institution*. London, Holt, Rinehart & Winston.

Lloyd-Jones, R., Bray, E. *et al.* (1986). *Assessment: From Principles to Action*. London, Macmillan.

Marsden, W.E. (1976). *Evaluating the Geography Curriculum*. Edinburgh, Oliver & Boyd.

Matthews, M.H. (1986). 'The influence of gender on the environmental cognition of young boys and girls.' *Journal of Genetic Psychology*, 47, 3, 295–302.

Measor, L. and Woods, P. (1984). *Changing Schools: Pupils' Perspectives on Transfer to a Comprehensive*. Milton Keynes, Open University Press.

Mills, D. (ed.) (1988). *Geographical Work in Primary and Middle Schools* (revised edition). Sheffield, Geographical Association.

Moon, R. (1989). 'Crash course.' *Times Educational Supplement*, 12 May. (See also NCC 1989b, below.)

Moore, R. (1986). *Childhood's Domain: Play and Place in Child Development*. London, Croom Helm.

Morrison, K.R.B. (1988). 'Planning for skills progression and assessment in primary schools.' *Curriculum* 9, 2, 74–83.

Morrison, K.R.B. and Taylor, C. (1988). *Assessing Skills Progression in Environmental Studies Curricula.* Occasional Paper 12, National Association for Environmental Education.
Munby, S. *et al.* (1989). *Assessing and Recording Achievement.* Oxford, Basil Blackwell.
Murphy, P. (1988). 'TGAT: a conflict of purpose.' *Curriculum* 9, 3, 152–8.
Murphy, R. and Torrance, H. (1988). *The Changing Face of Educational Assessment.* Milton Keynes, Open University Press.
NCC (1988a). *Consultation Report: Science.* York, National Curriculum Council.
NCC (1988b). *Consultation Report: Mathematics.* York, National Curriculum Council.
NCC (1989a). *Consultation Report: English 5–11.* York, National Curriculum Council.
NCC (1989b). *Developing INSET Activities.* York, National Curriculum Council.
NCC (1989c). *A Framework for the Primary Curriculum.* York, National Curriculum Council.
Nicholls, A. (1983). *Managing Educational Innovations.* London, Allen & Unwin.
Oakden, E.C. and Sturt, M. (1922). 'The development of the knowledge of time in children.' *British Journal of Psychology* XII, 309–36.
Pluckrose, H. (1989). *Seen Locally.* London, Routledge.
Pollard, A. (1987). *The Social World of the Primary School.* London, Holt, Rinehart & Winston.
Prisk, T. (1987). 'Letting them get on with it: a study of unsupervised group talk in an infant school' in A. Pollard (ed.). *Children and their Primary Schools.* Lewes, Falmer Press.
Proctor, N. (1987). 'History, geography and humanities: a geographer's interpretation.' *Teaching History* 48, 8–12.
Rance, P. (1968). *Teaching by Topics.* London, Ward Lock.
Ransome, A. (1970). *Swallows and Amazons.* Paper-back edition, London, Puffin Books.
Raven, J.C. *et al.* (1985). *Opening in the Primary Classroom.* SCRE Publication 87. Edinburgh, Scottish Council for Research in Education.
Roberts, M. (ed.) (1989). *History in the National Curriculum: A Submission to the History Working Group.* London, Historical Association.
Ross, A. (1987). 'The social subjects' in M. Clarkson (ed.) *Emerging Issues in Primary Education.* Lewes, Falmer Press.
Ross, A. (1988). *Bright Ideas: Environmental Studies.* Leamington Spa, Scholastic Publications.
Rowland, S. (1984). *The Enquiring Classroom: An Introduction to Children's Learning.* Lewes, Falmer Press.
Rudduck, J. and Hopkins, D. (1985). *Research as a Basis for Teaching: Readings from the Work of Lawrence Stenhouse,* London, Heinemann Educational.
Satterly, D. (1981). *Assessment in Schools.* Oxford, Basil Blackwell.
Schools Council (1981). *The Practical Curriculum.* Working Paper 70. London, Methuen Educational.
Schools Council (1983). *Primary Practice.* Working Paper 75. London, Methuen Educational.
Schug, M.C. and Birkey, C.J. (1985). 'The development of children's economic reasoning.' *Theory and Research in Social Education* XIII, 1, 31–42.
Shipman, M.D. (1983). *Assessment in Primary and Middle Schools.* London, Croom Helm.
Smith, D. (ed.) (1988) *Industry in the Primary School Curriculum: Principles and Practice.* Lewes, Falmer Press.
Smith, R.N. and Tomlinson, P. (1977). 'The development of children's construction of historical duration: a new approach and some findings.' *Educational Research* 19, 3, 163–70.
Stanley, W.B. and Mathews, R.C. (1985). 'Recent research on concept learning: implications for social education.' *Theory and Research in Social Education* XII, 4, 57–74.
Stenhouse, L.A. (1975). *An Introduction to Curriculum Research and Development.* London, Heinemann.
Stillman, A. and Maychell, K. (1984). *School to School: LEA and Teacher Involvement in Educational Continuity.* Windsor, National Foundation for Educational Research/Nelson.

Stones, E. (1979). *Psychopedagogy: Psychological Theory and the Practice of Teaching.* London, Methuen.

Taba, H. (1962). *Curriculum Development: Theory and Practice.* London, Harcourt Brace & World.

Tann, C.S. (ed.) (1988). *Developing Topic Work in the Primary School.* Lewes, Falmer Press.

TGAT (1988a) *Report.* Task Group on Assessment and Testing. London, Department of Education and Science/Welsh Office.

TGAT (1988b) *Three Supplementary Reports.* Task Group on Assessment and Testing. London, Department of Education and Science/Welsh Office.

Thomas, N. (1987). 'The national curriculum and levels of achievement.' *Education 3–13* 15, 3, 16–25.

Torrance, H. (1988). (ed.). *National Assessment and Testing: A Research Response.* London, British Educational Research Association.

Tough, J. (1979). *Talk for Teaching and Learning.* Schools Council Communication Skills Project 7–13. London, Ward Lock Educational, in association with Drake Educational Associates.

Troman, G. (1988). 'Getting it right: selection and setting in a 9–13 years middle school.' *British Journal of Sociology of Education* 9, 4, 403–22.

Waterland, L. (1985). *Read with Me: An Apprenticeship Approach to Reading.* Stroud, Thimble Press.

West, J. (1981). *Children's Awareness of the Past.* Thesis for degree of PhD, University of Keele.

West, J. (1982). 'Time charts.' *Education 3–13* 10, 1, 48–50.

West, J. (1986). *Time Line.* London, Nelson.

Whitehead, M. (1987). 'Narrative, stories and the world of literature' in G.M. Blenkin and A.V. Kelly (eds.) *Early Childhood Education: a Developmental Approach.* London, Paul Chapman.

Williams, M. and Howley, R. (1989). 'Curriculum discontinuity: a study of a secondary school and its feeder primary schools.' *British Educational Research Journal* 15, 1, 61–76.

Winkley, D. (1985). *Diplomats and Detectives: LEA Advisers at Work.* London, Boyce.

Woods, P. (1987). 'Becoming a junior: pupil development following transfer from infants.' In A. Pollard (ed.) *Children and their Primary Schools.* Lewes, Falmer Press.

Wray, D. (1985). *Teaching Information Skills through Project Work.* London, Hodder & Stoughton, in association with the United Kingdom Reading Association.

Wray, D. (1988). *Project Teaching.* Bright Ideas Management Books. Leamington Spa, Scholastic Publications.

Attention should also be drawn to two other new publications, both from Open University Press, Milton Keynes:

Hargreaves, A. (1989) *Curriculum and Assessment Reform.*

Simons, H. and Elliott, J. (1989) *Rethinking Appraisal and Assessment.*

Author index

Subject index

(For meanings of terms, see Appendix I, pp. 159–61)